X-MEN LEGACY

PRODIGAL

PRODIGAL

writer **SIMON SPURRIER**
pencilers **TAN ENG HUAT** (#1-3) & **JORGE MOLINA** (#4-6)
inkers **CRAIG YEUNG** (#1-3 & #5), **JORGE MOLINA** (#4),
NORMAN LEE (#5-6) & **WALDEN WONG** (#5-6)
colorists **JOSÉ VILLARRUBIA** (#1-3) & **RACHELLE ROSENBERG** (#4-6)
letterer **VC'S CORY PETIT**
cover artist **MIKE DEL MUNDO**
assistant editor **JENNIFER M. SMITH**
editor **DANIEL KETCHUM**
x-men group editor **NICK LOWE**

Collection Editor: Cory Levine • Assistant Editors: Alex Starbuck & Nelson Ribeiro
Editors, Special Projects: Jennifer Grünwald & Mark D. Beazley • Senior Editor, Special Projects: Jeff Youngquist
SVP of Print & Digital Publishing Sales: David Gabriel • Book Design: Jeff Powell & Cory Levine

Editor in Chief: Axel Alonso • Chief Creative Officer: Joe Quesada
Publisher: Dan Buckley • Executive Producer: Alan Fine

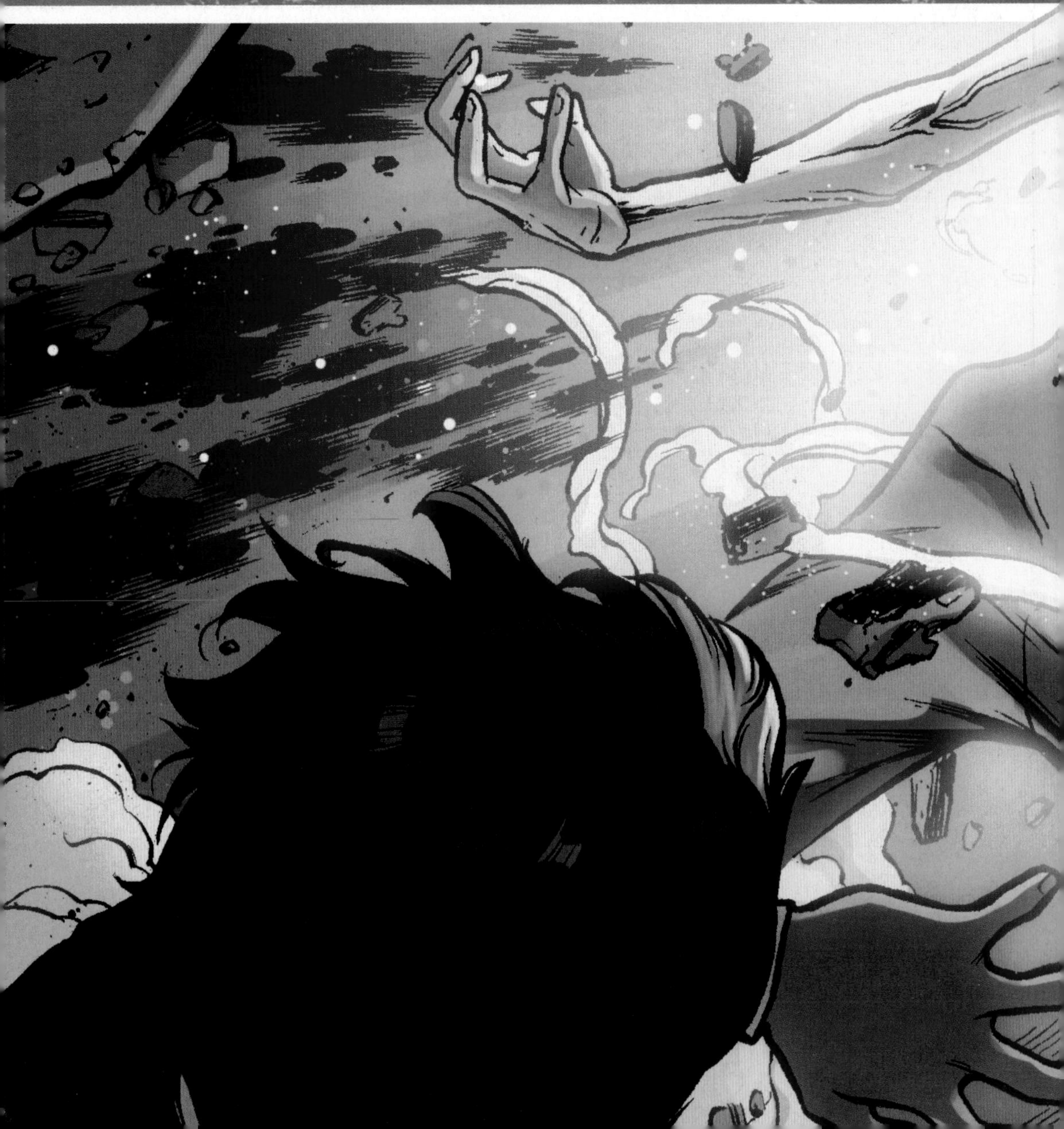

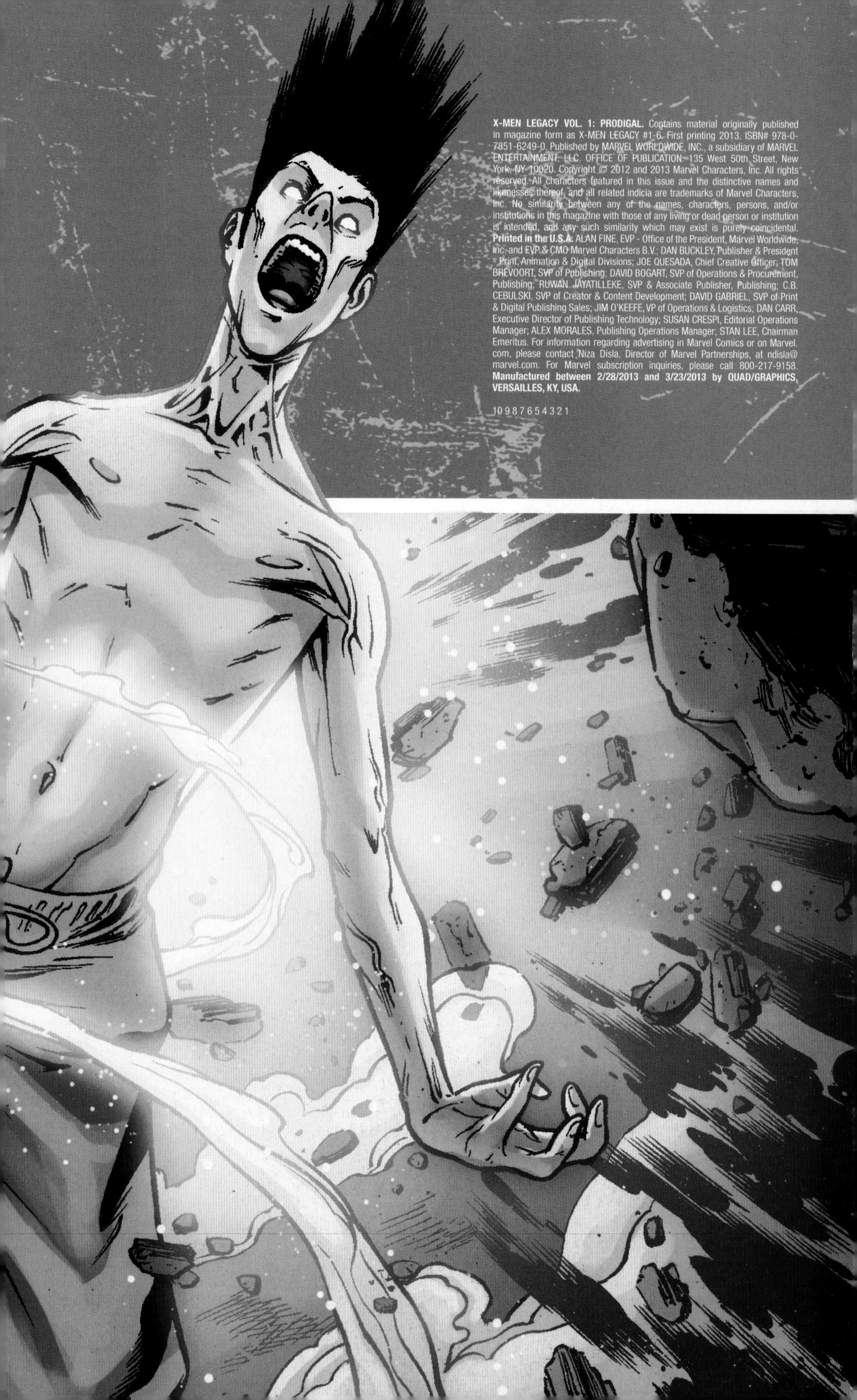

X-MEN LEGACY VOL. 1: PRODIGAL. Contains material originally published in magazine form as X-MEN LEGACY #1-6. First printing 2013. ISBN# 978-0-7851-6249-0. Published by MARVEL WORLDWIDE, INC., a subsidiary of MARVEL ENTERTAINMENT, LLC. OFFICE OF PUBLICATION: 135 West 50th Street, New York, NY 10020. **Printed in the U.S.A.** ALAN FINE, EVP - Office of the President, Marvel Worldwide, Inc. and EVP & CMO Marvel Characters B.V.; DAN BUCKLEY, Publisher & President - Print, Animation & Digital Divisions; JOE QUESADA, Chief Creative Officer; TOM BREVOORT, SVP of Publishing; DAVID BOGART, SVP of Operations & Procurement, Publishing; RUWAN JAYATILLEKE, SVP & Associate Publisher, Publishing; C.B. CEBULSKI, SVP of Creator & Content Development; DAVID GABRIEL, SVP of Print & Digital Publishing Sales; JIM O'KEEFE, VP of Operations & Logistics; DAN CARR, Executive Director of Publishing Technology; SUSAN CRESPI, Editorial Operations Manager; ALEX MORALES, Publishing Operations Manager; STAN LEE, Chairman Emeritus. For information regarding advertising in Marvel Comics or on Marvel.com, please contact Niza Disla, Director of Marvel Partnerships, at ndisla@marvel.com. For Marvel subscription inquiries, please call 800-217-9158. **Manufactured between 2/28/2013 and 3/23/2013 by QUAD/GRAPHICS, VERSAILLES, KY, USA.**

10 9 8 7 6 5 4 3 2 1

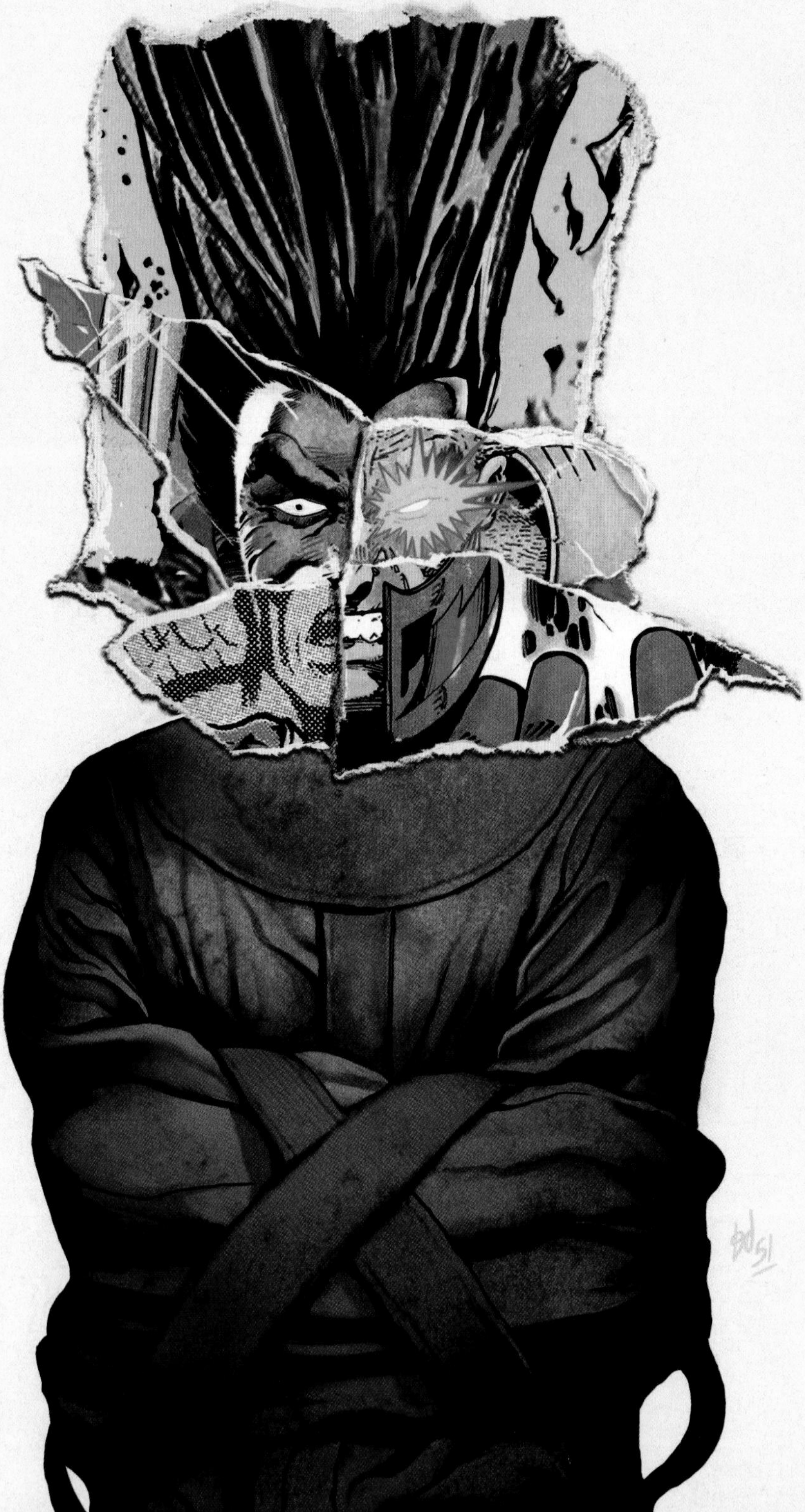

ONE

KILL YOU KILL YOU KILL YOU!

A PLACE OF *CAPTIVITY*. A PLACE WHERE THE *VILE* AND THE *VICIOUS* OF A DOZEN REALITIES *SUFFER* FOR THEIR *SINS*.

A PLACE WHERE *TYRRANIX* THE *ABOMINOID* SWIVELS A *MOUTHTUBE* THROUGH *COSINE VI-BARS* TO HISS--

HE'S DRAGGIN' OUT ONE OF THE *LEVITATORS*...

--AND WHERE *IONIC SCALPELS* DANCE LIKE *HATEFUL ANGELS* ON THE *PALMS* OF HIS *CELL-NEIGHBOR*.

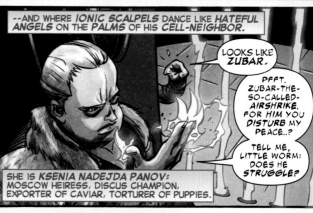

LOOKS LIKE *ZUBAR*.

PFFT. ZUBAR-THE-SO-CALLED-AIRSHRIKE. FOR HIM YOU *DISTURB* MY *PEACE*..?

TELL ME, LITTLE WORM: DOES HE *STRUGGLE*?

SHE IS *KSENIA NADEJDA PANOV*: MOSCOW HEIRESS, DISCUS CHAMPION, EXPORTER OF CAVIAR, TORTURER OF PUPPIES.

HE'S...HE'S *TRYIN'*. THE *HAZEGUARD'S* GOT HIM PRETTY *TIGHT*.

THEY'RE AT THE *CHAIR* NOW...HE'S STRAPPIN' ZUBAR *DOWN* AND... OH. I....

I CAN SEE THE *XTRACTOR*.

RRF.

...THE *NEEDLE*...

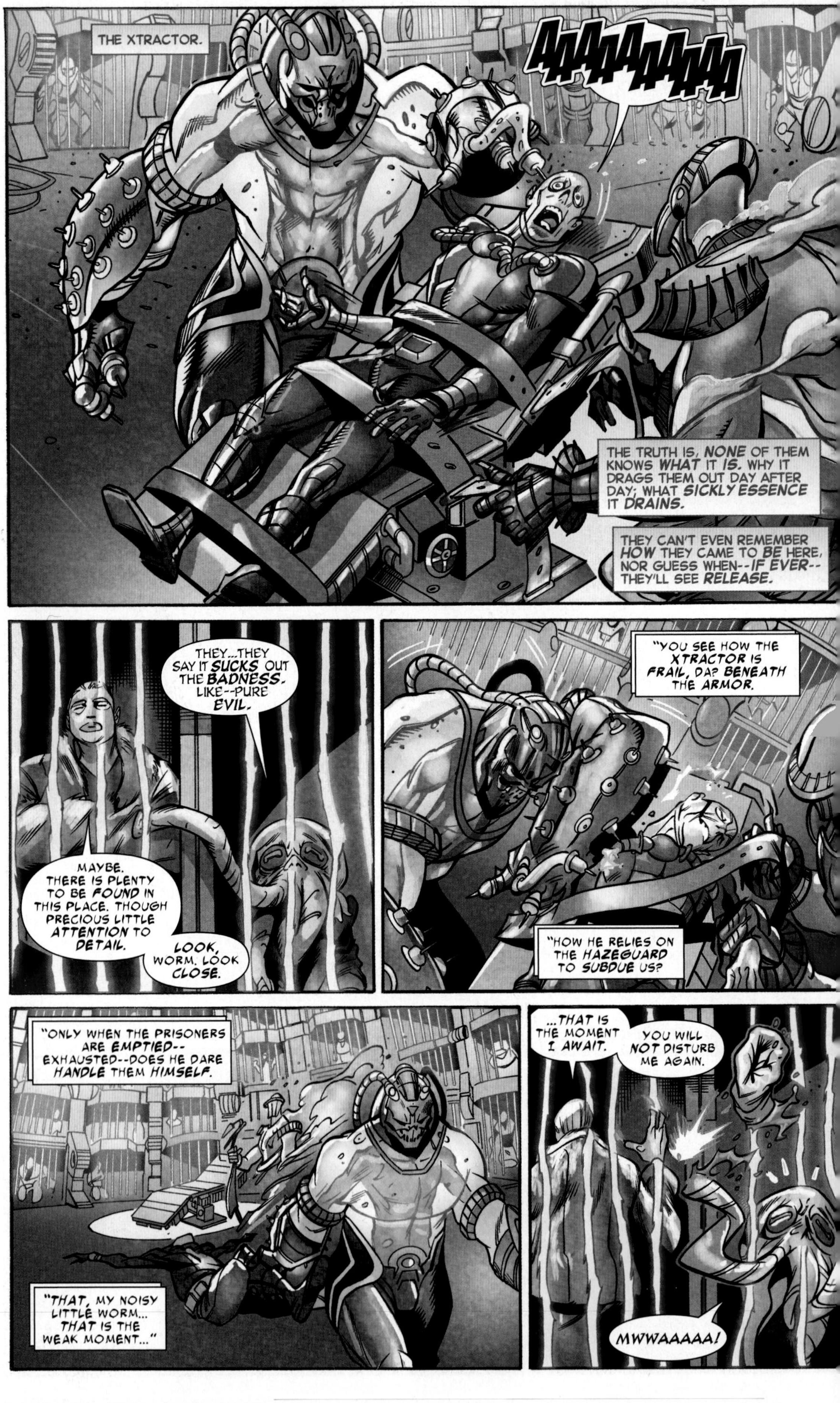
THE XTRACTOR.
AAAAAAAAAAA
THE TRUTH IS, NONE OF THEM KNOWS WHAT IT IS. WHY IT DRAGS THEM OUT DAY AFTER DAY; WHAT SICKLY ESSENCE IT DRAINS.
THEY CAN'T EVEN REMEMBER HOW THEY CAME TO BE HERE, NOR GUESS WHEN--IF EVER--THEY'LL SEE RELEASE.
THEY...THEY SAY IT SUCKS OUT THE BADNESS. LIKE--PURE EVIL.
MAYBE. THERE IS PLENTY TO BE FOUND IN THIS PLACE. THOUGH PRECIOUS LITTLE ATTENTION TO DETAIL.
LOOK, WORM. LOOK CLOSE.
"YOU SEE HOW THE XTRACTOR IS FRAIL, DA? BENEATH THE ARMOR.
"HOW HE RELIES ON THE HAZEGUARD TO SUBDUE US?
"ONLY WHEN THE PRISONERS ARE EMPTIED--EXHAUSTED--DOES HE DARE HANDLE THEM HIMSELF.
"THAT, MY NOISY LITTLE WORM... THAT IS THE WEAK MOMENT..."
...THAT IS THE MOMENT I AWAIT.
YOU WILL NOT DISTURB ME AGAIN.
MWWAAAAA!

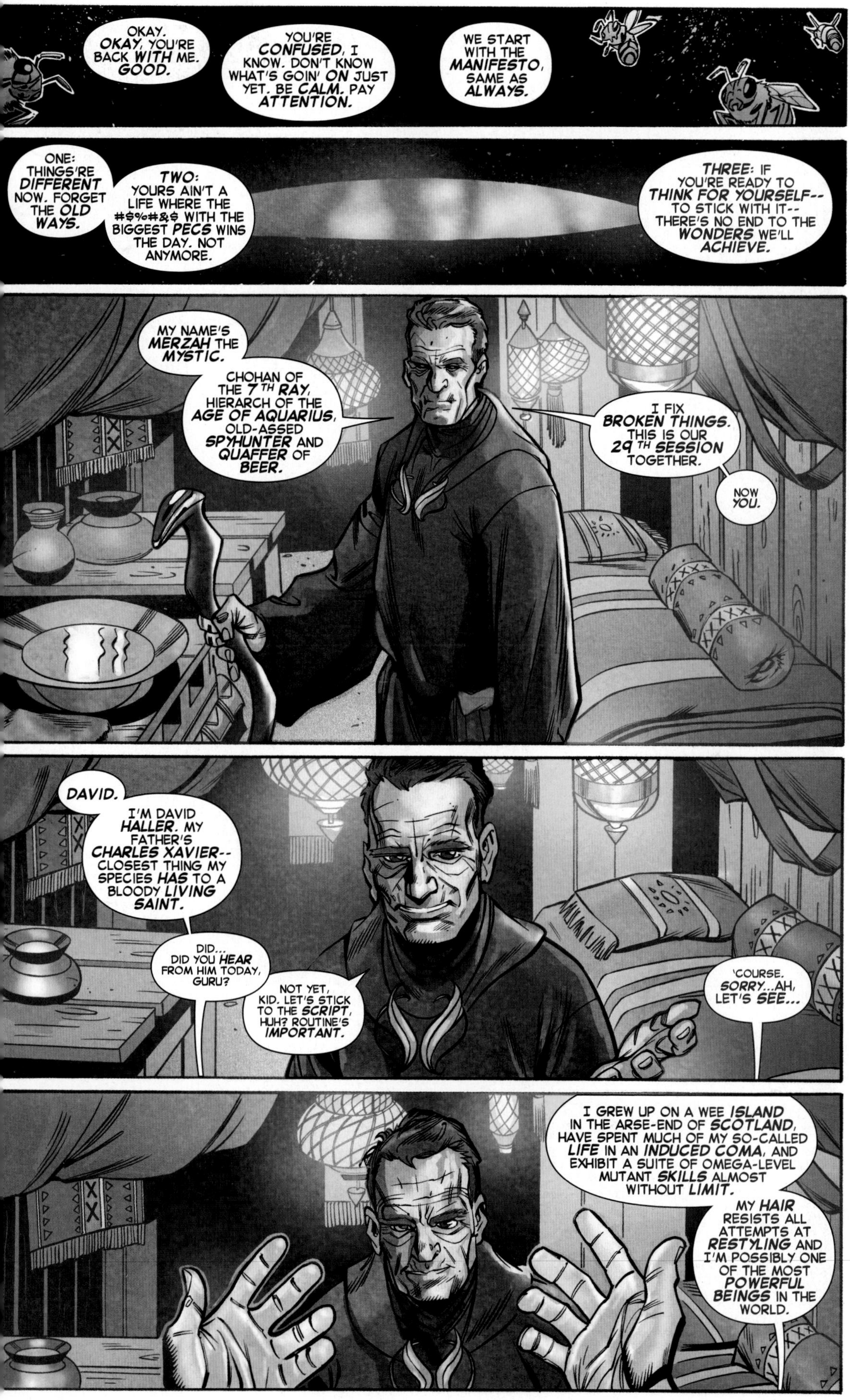
OKAY. OKAY, YOU'RE BACK WITH ME. GOOD.
YOU'RE CONFUSED, I KNOW. DON'T KNOW WHAT'S GOIN' ON JUST YET. BE CALM. PAY ATTENTION.
WE START WITH THE MANIFESTO, SAME AS ALWAYS.
ONE: THINGS'RE DIFFERENT NOW. FORGET THE OLD WAYS.
TWO: YOURS AIN'T A LIFE WHERE THE #$%#&$ WITH THE BIGGEST PECS WINS THE DAY. NOT ANYMORE.
THREE: IF YOU'RE READY TO THINK FOR YOURSELF-- TO STICK WITH IT-- THERE'S NO END TO THE WONDERS WE'LL ACHIEVE.
MY NAME'S MERZAH THE MYSTIC.
CHOHAN OF THE 7TH RAY, HIERARCH OF THE AGE OF AQUARIUS, OLD-ASSED SPYHUNTER AND QUAFFER OF BEER.
I FIX BROKEN THINGS. THIS IS OUR 29TH SESSION TOGETHER.
NOW YOU.
DAVID.
I'M DAVID HALLER. MY FATHER'S CHARLES XAVIER-- CLOSEST THING MY SPECIES HAS TO A BLOODY LIVING SAINT.
DID... DID YOU HEAR FROM HIM TODAY, GURU?
NOT YET, KID. LET'S STICK TO THE SCRIPT, HUH? ROUTINE'S IMPORTANT.
'COURSE. SORRY...AH, LET'S SEE...
I GREW UP ON A WEE ISLAND IN THE ARSE-END OF SCOTLAND, HAVE SPENT MUCH OF MY SO-CALLED LIFE IN AN INDUCED COMA, AND EXHIBIT A SUITE OF OMEGA-LEVEL MUTANT SKILLS ALMOST WITHOUT LIMIT.
MY HAIR RESISTS ALL ATTEMPTS AT RESTYLING AND I'M POSSIBLY ONE OF THE MOST POWERFUL BEINGS IN THE WORLD.

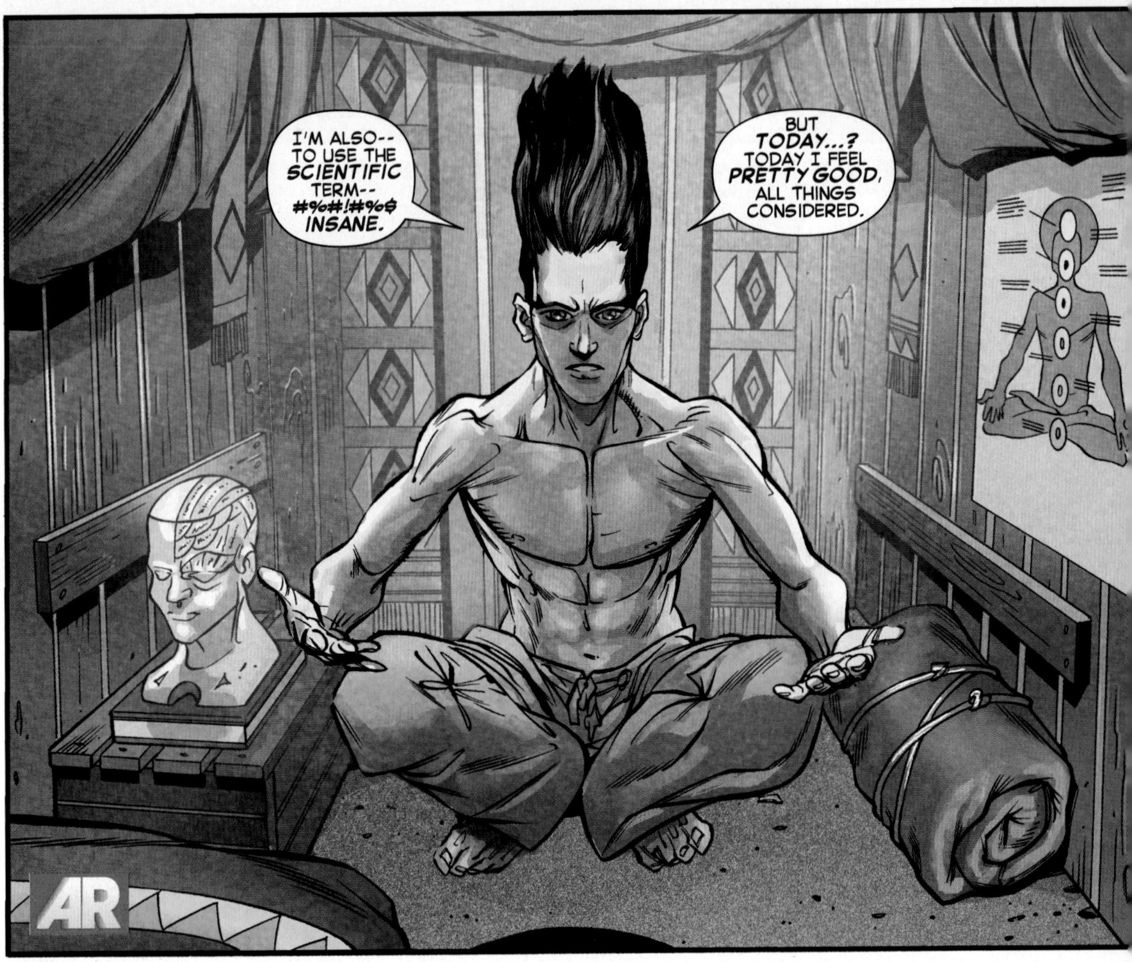
I'M ALSO-- TO USE THE SCIENTIFIC TERM-- #%#!#%$ INSANE.
BUT TODAY...? TODAY I FEEL PRETTY GOOD, ALL THINGS CONSIDERED.

PRODIGAL

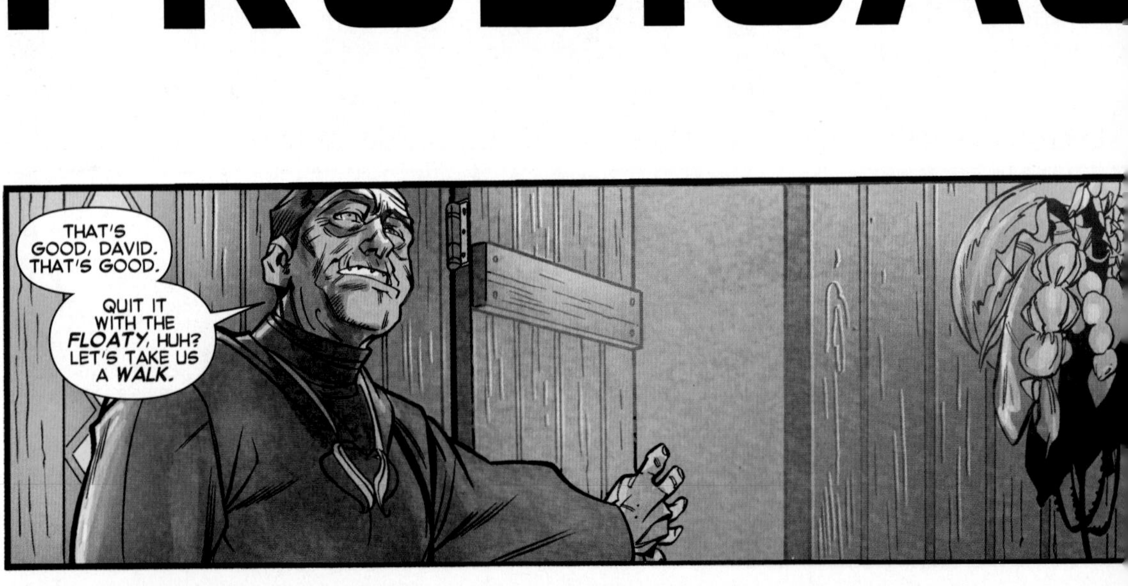
THAT'S GOOD, DAVID. THAT'S GOOD.
QUIT IT WITH THE FLOATY, HUH? LET'S TAKE US A WALK.

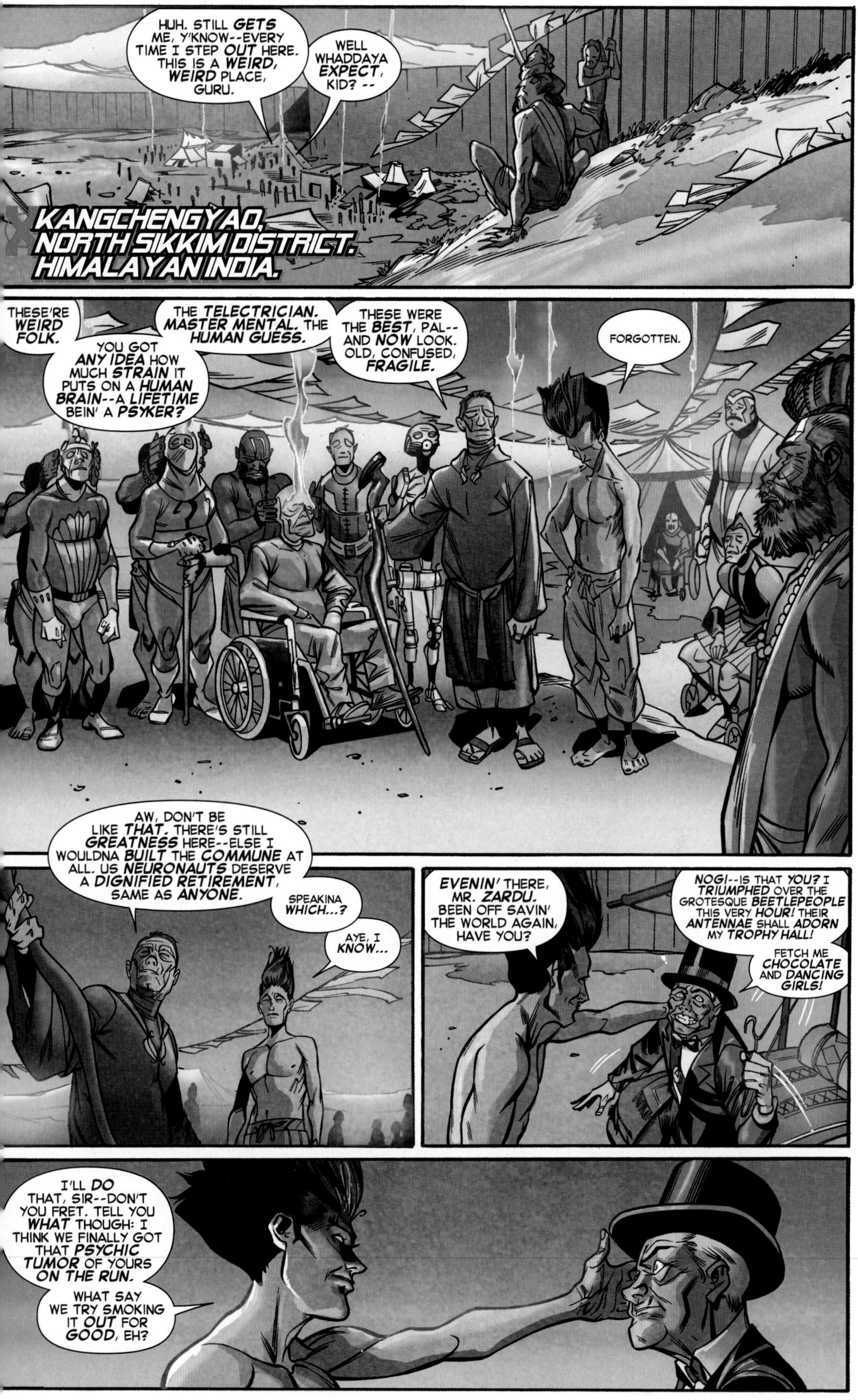
HUH. STILL GETS ME, Y'KNOW--EVERY TIME I STEP OUT HERE. THIS IS A WEIRD, WEIRD PLACE, GURU.
WELL WHADDAYA EXPECT, KID? --
KANGCHENGYAO, NORTH SIKKIM DISTRICT. HIMALAYAN INDIA.
THESE'RE WEIRD FOLK.
THE TELECTRICIAN. MASTER MENTAL. THE HUMAN GUESS.
YOU GOT ANY IDEA HOW MUCH STRAIN IT PUTS ON A HUMAN BRAIN--A LIFETIME BEIN' A PSYKER?
THESE WERE THE BEST, PAL--AND NOW LOOK. OLD, CONFUSED, FRAGILE.
FORGOTTEN.
AW, DON'T BE LIKE THAT. THERE'S STILL GREATNESS HERE--ELSE I WOULDNA BUILT THE COMMUNE AT ALL. US NEURONAUTS DESERVE A DIGNIFIED RETIREMENT, SAME AS ANYONE.
SPEAKINA WHICH...?
AYE, I KNOW...
EVENIN' THERE, MR. ZARDU. BEEN OFF SAVIN' THE WORLD AGAIN, HAVE YOU?
NOGI--IS THAT YOU? I TRIUMPHED OVER THE GROTESQUE BEETLEPEOPLE THIS VERY HOUR! THEIR ANTENNAE SHALL ADORN MY TROPHY HALL!
FETCH ME CHOCOLATE AND DANCING GIRLS!
I'LL DO THAT, SIR--DON'T YOU FRET. TELL YOU WHAT THOUGH: I THINK WE FINALLY GOT THAT PSYCHIC TUMOR OF YOURS ON THE RUN.
WHAT SAY WE TRY SMOKING IT OUT FOR GOOD, EH?

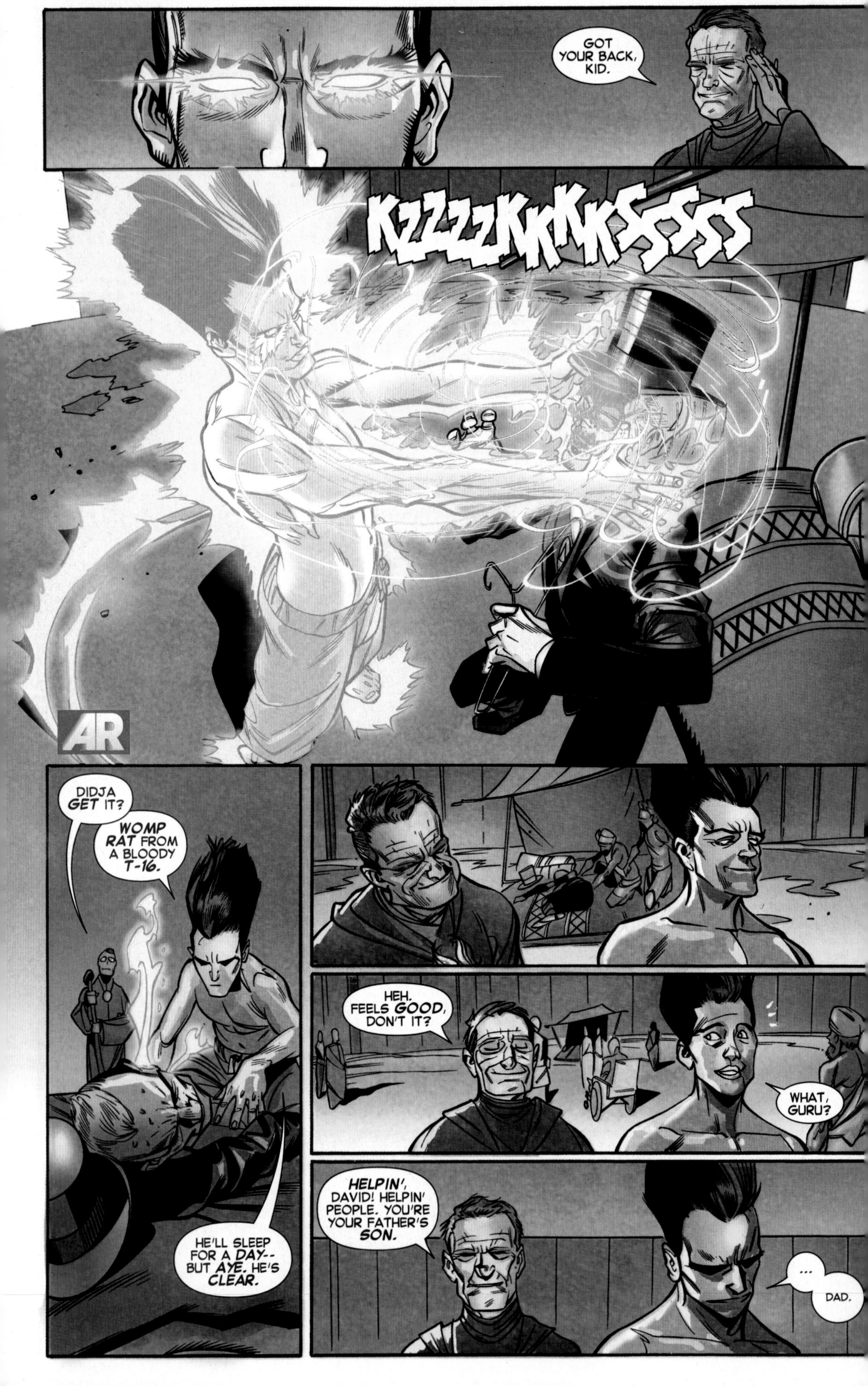

GOT YOUR BACK, KID.
KZZZZKKKKSSSSS
DIDJA GET IT?
WOMP RAT FROM A BLOODY T-16.
HE'LL SLEEP FOR A DAY-- BUT AYE. HE'S CLEAR.
HEH. FEELS GOOD, DON'T IT?
WHAT, GURU?
HELPIN', DAVID! HELPIN' PEOPLE. YOU'RE YOUR FATHER'S SON.
...
DAD.

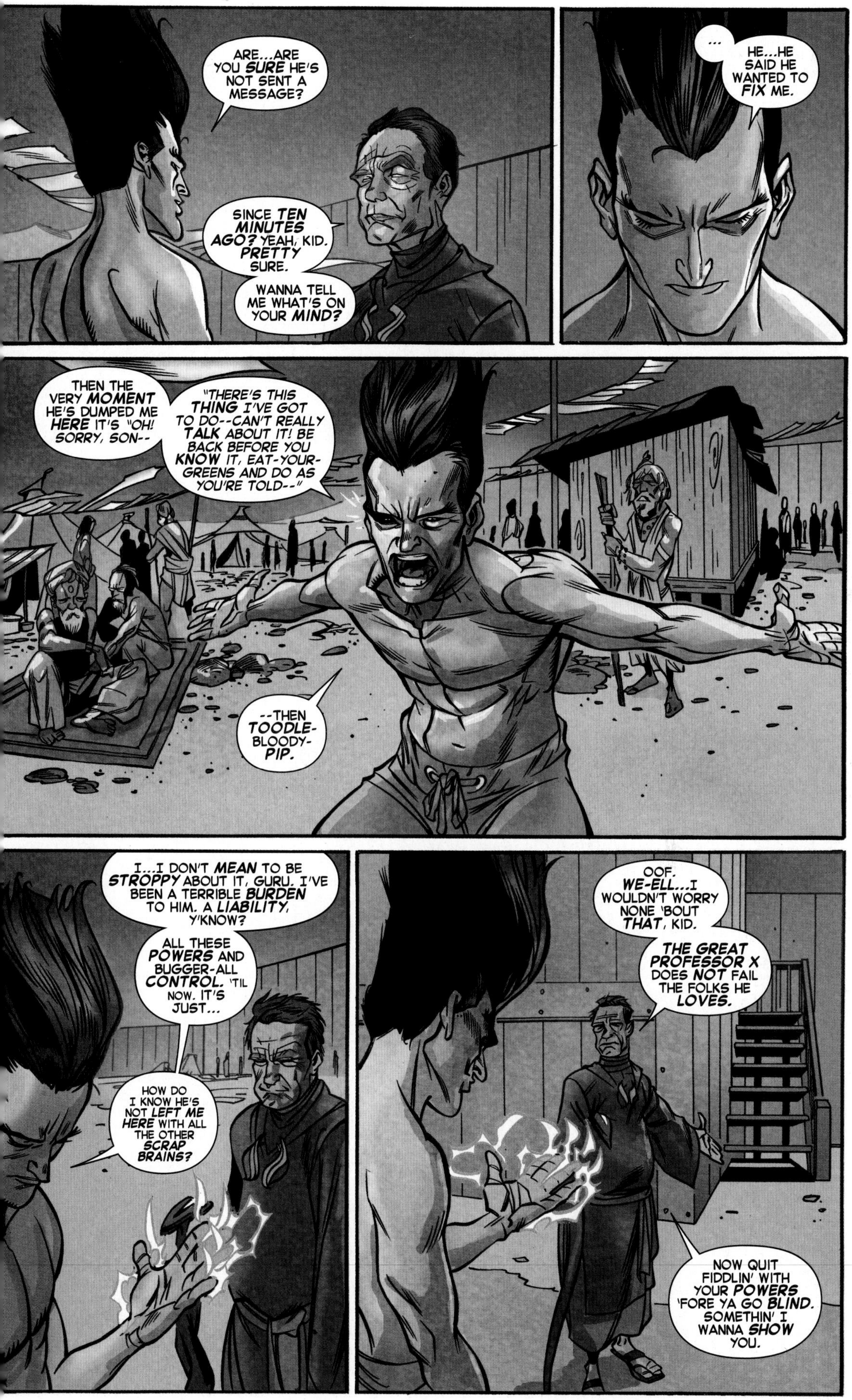

ARE...ARE YOU SURE HE'S NOT SENT A MESSAGE?
SINCE TEN MINUTES AGO? YEAH, KID. PRETTY SURE.
WANNA TELL ME WHAT'S ON YOUR MIND?
...
HE...HE SAID HE WANTED TO FIX ME.
THEN THE VERY MOMENT HE'S DUMPED ME HERE IT'S "OH! SORRY, SON--
"THERE'S THIS THING I'VE GOT TO DO--CAN'T REALLY TALK ABOUT IT! BE BACK BEFORE YOU KNOW IT, EAT-YOUR-GREENS AND DO AS YOU'RE TOLD--"
--THEN TOODLE-BLOODY-PIP.
I...I DON'T MEAN TO BE STROPPY ABOUT IT, GURU. I'VE BEEN A TERRIBLE BURDEN TO HIM. A LIABILITY, Y'KNOW?
ALL THESE POWERS AND BUGGER-ALL CONTROL. 'TIL NOW. IT'S JUST...
HOW DO I KNOW HE'S NOT LEFT ME HERE WITH ALL THE OTHER SCRAP BRAINS?
OOF. WE-ELL...I WOULDN'T WORRY NONE 'BOUT THAT, KID.
THE GREAT PROFESSOR X DOES NOT FAIL THE FOLKS HE LOVES.
NOW QUIT FIDDLIN' WITH YOUR POWERS 'FORE YA GO BLIND. SOMETHIN' I WANNA SHOW YOU.

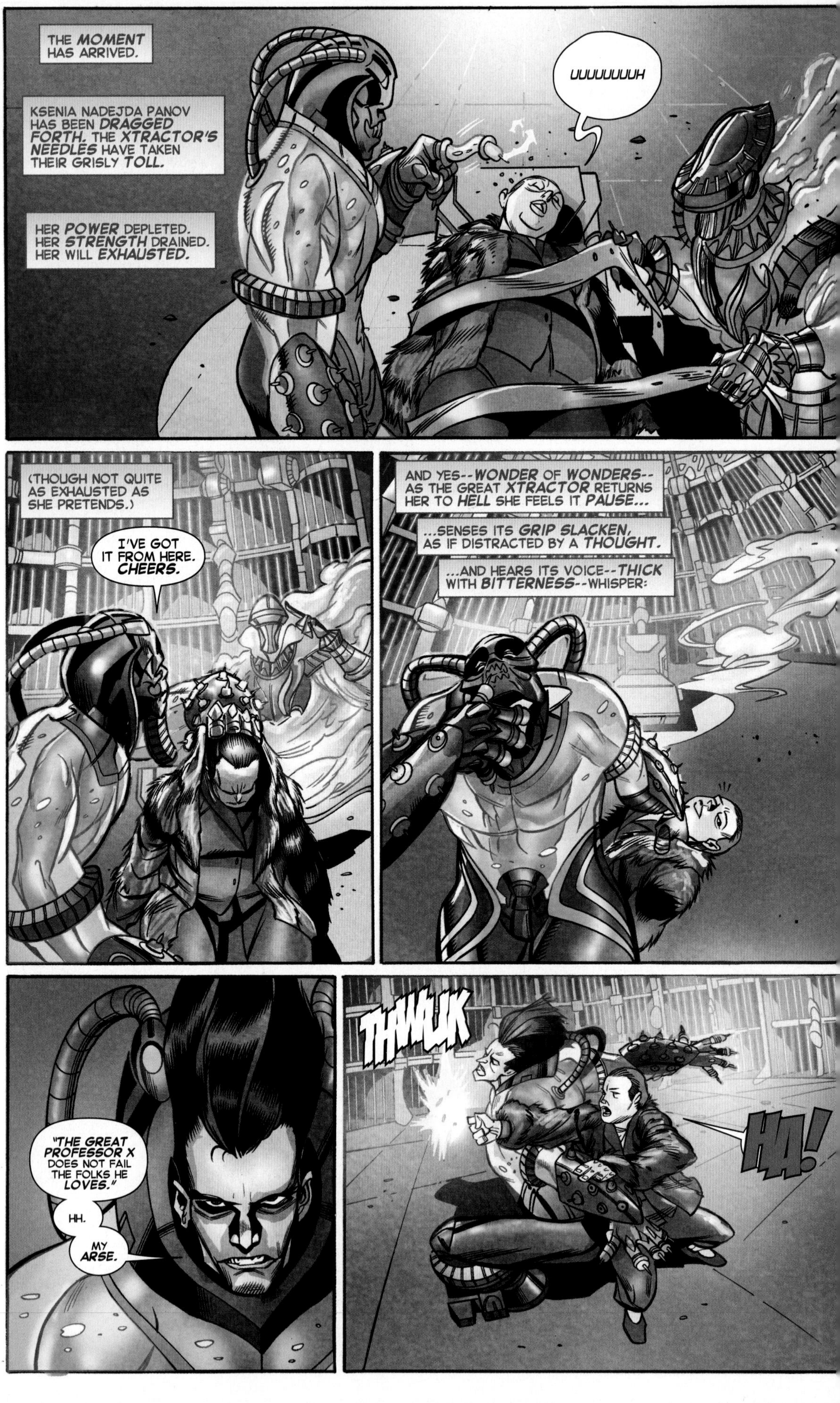
THE MOMENT HAS ARRIVED.
UUUUUUUUH
KSENIA NADEJDA PANOV HAS BEEN DRAGGED FORTH. THE XTRACTOR'S NEEDLES HAVE TAKEN THEIR GRISLY TOLL.
HER POWER DEPLETED. HER STRENGTH DRAINED. HER WILL EXHAUSTED.
(THOUGH NOT QUITE AS EXHAUSTED AS SHE PRETENDS.)
I'VE GOT IT FROM HERE. CHEERS.
AND YES--WONDER OF WONDERS--AS THE GREAT XTRACTOR RETURNS HER TO HELL SHE FEELS IT PAUSE...
...SENSES ITS GRIP SLACKEN, AS IF DISTRACTED BY A THOUGHT.
...AND HEARS ITS VOICE--THICK WITH BITTERNESS--WHISPER:
"THE GREAT PROFESSOR X DOES NOT FAIL THE FOLKS HE LOVES."
HH.
MY ARSE.
THWUK
HA!

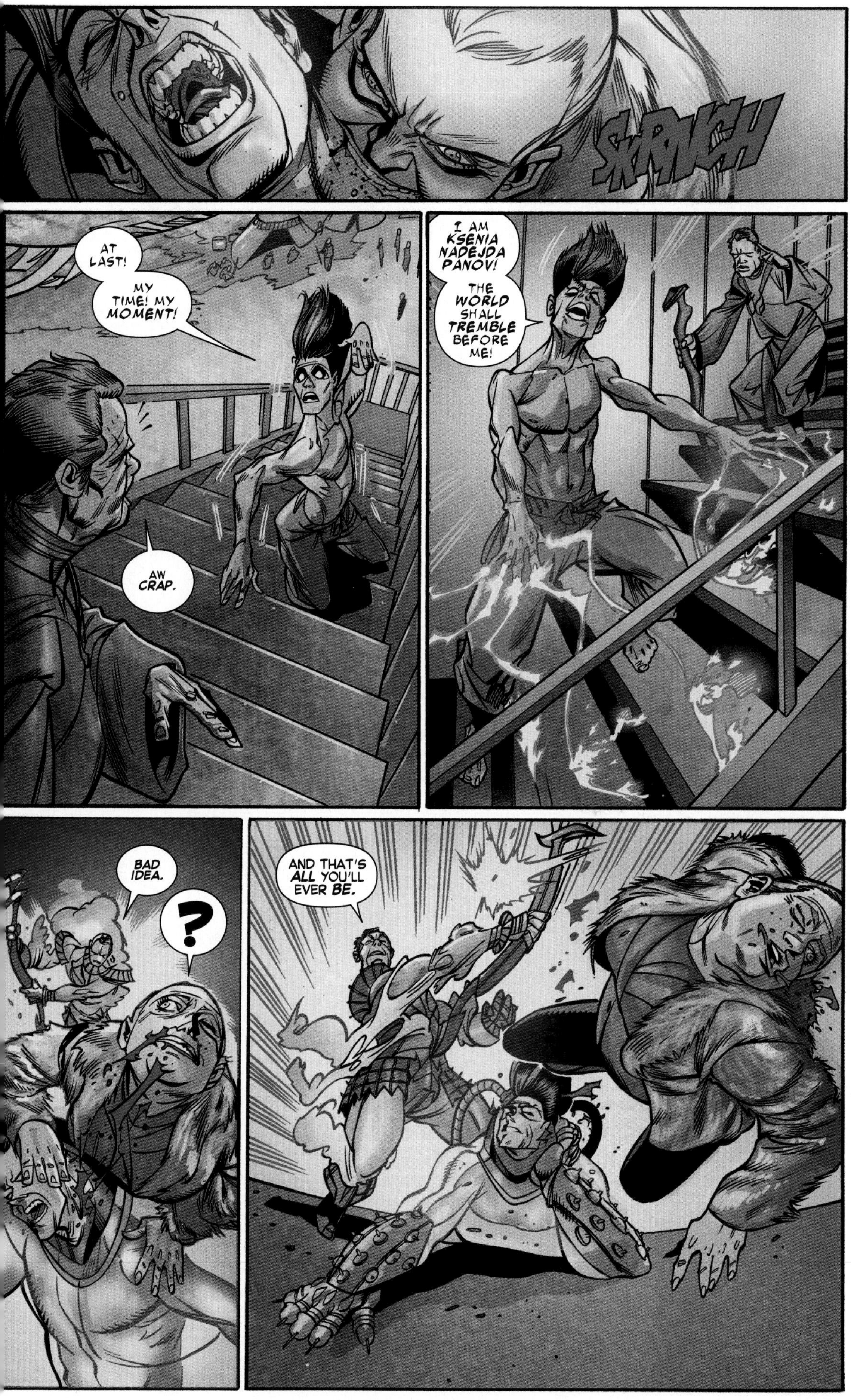
SKRNCH
AT LAST!
MY TIME! MY MOMENT!
AW CRAP.
I AM KSENIA NADEJDA PANOV!
THE WORLD SHALL TREMBLE BEFORE ME!
BAD IDEA.
?
AND THAT'S ALL YOU'LL EVER BE.

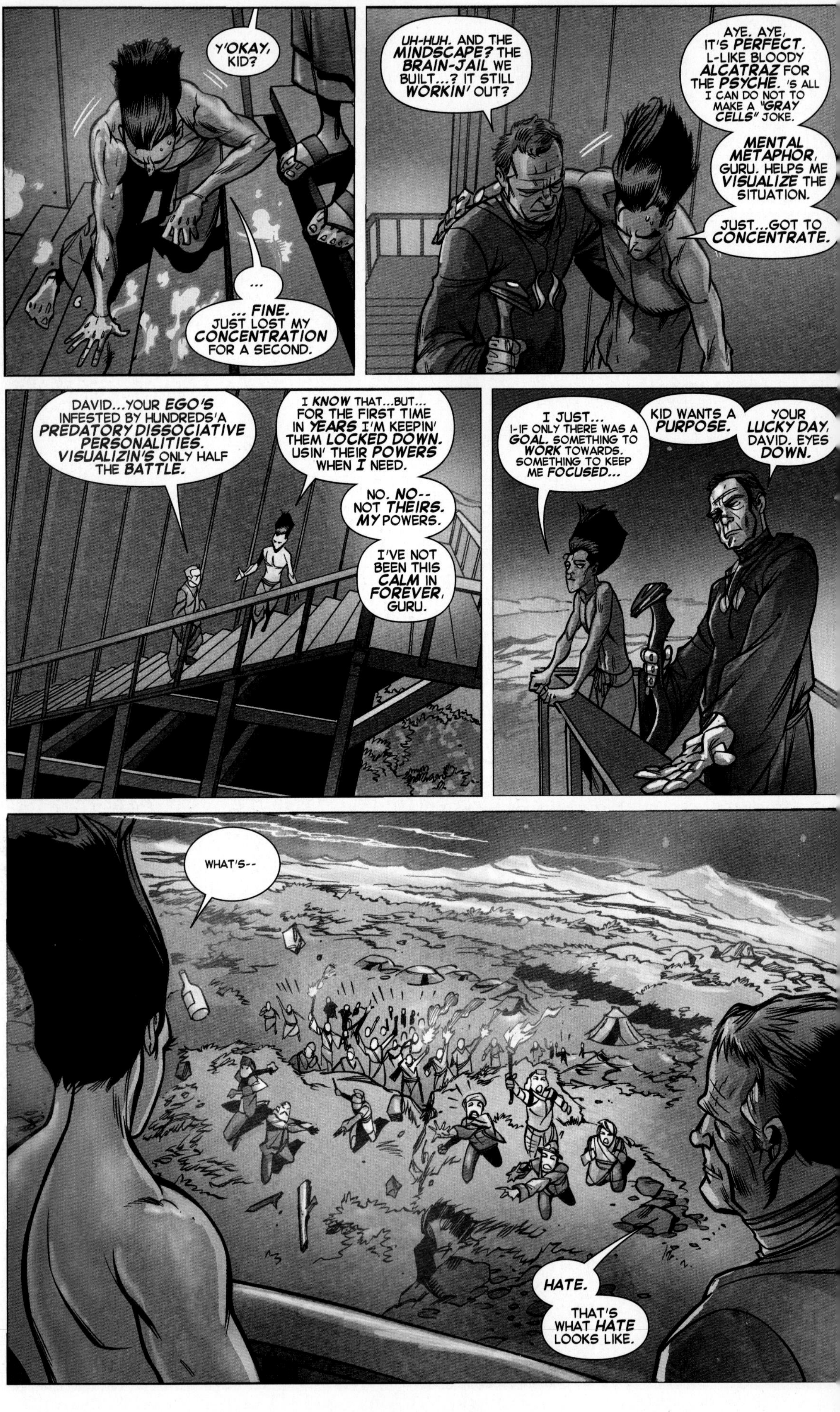

Y'OKAY, KID?
...
... FINE. JUST LOST MY CONCENTRATION FOR A SECOND.
UH-HUH. AND THE MINDSCAPE? THE BRAIN-JAIL WE BUILT...? IT STILL WORKIN' OUT?
AYE. AYE, IT'S PERFECT. L-LIKE BLOODY ALCATRAZ FOR THE PSYCHE. 'S ALL I CAN DO NOT TO MAKE A "GRAY CELLS" JOKE.
MENTAL METAPHOR, GURU. HELPS ME VISUALIZE THE SITUATION.
JUST...GOT TO CONCENTRATE.
DAVID...YOUR EGO'S INFESTED BY HUNDREDS'A PREDATORY DISSOCIATIVE PERSONALITIES. VISUALIZIN'S ONLY HALF THE BATTLE.
I KNOW THAT...BUT... FOR THE FIRST TIME IN YEARS I'M KEEPIN' THEM LOCKED DOWN. USIN' THEIR POWERS WHEN I NEED.
NO. NO-- NOT THEIRS. MY POWERS.
I'VE NOT BEEN THIS CALM IN FOREVER, GURU.
I JUST... I-IF ONLY THERE WAS A GOAL. SOMETHING TO WORK TOWARDS. SOMETHING TO KEEP ME FOCUSED...
KID WANTS A PURPOSE.
YOUR LUCKY DAY, DAVID. EYES DOWN.
WHAT'S--
HATE.
THAT'S WHAT HATE LOOKS LIKE.

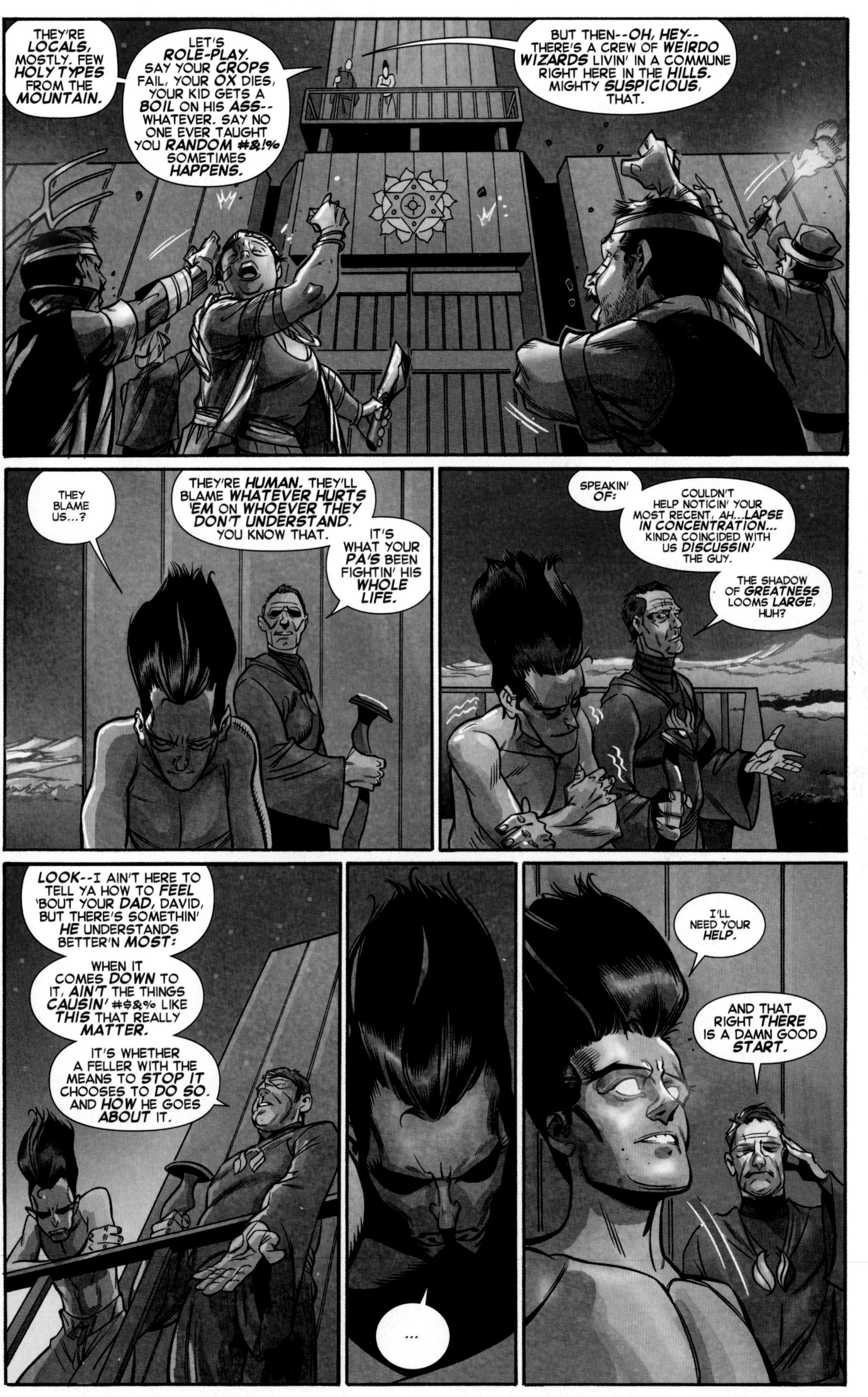
THEY'RE LOCALS, MOSTLY. FEW HOLY TYPES FROM THE MOUNTAIN.
LET'S ROLE-PLAY. SAY YOUR CROPS FAIL, YOUR OX DIES, YOUR KID GETS A BOIL ON HIS ASS--WHATEVER. SAY NO ONE EVER TAUGHT YOU RANDOM #&!% SOMETIMES HAPPENS.
BUT THEN--OH, HEY--THERE'S A CREW OF WEIRDO WIZARDS LIVIN' IN A COMMUNE RIGHT HERE IN THE HILLS. MIGHTY SUSPICIOUS, THAT.
THEY BLAME US...?
THEY'RE HUMAN. THEY'LL BLAME WHATEVER HURTS 'EM ON WHOEVER THEY DON'T UNDERSTAND. YOU KNOW THAT.
IT'S WHAT YOUR PA'S BEEN FIGHTIN' HIS WHOLE LIFE.
SPEAKIN' OF:
COULDN'T HELP NOTICIN' YOUR MOST RECENT, AH...LAPSE IN CONCENTRATION... KINDA COINCIDED WITH US DISCUSSIN' THE GUY.
THE SHADOW OF GREATNESS LOOMS LARGE, HUH?
LOOK--I AIN'T HERE TO TELL YA HOW TO FEEL 'BOUT YOUR DAD, DAVID, BUT THERE'S SOMETHIN' HE UNDERSTANDS BETTER'N MOST:
WHEN IT COMES DOWN TO IT, AIN'T THE THINGS CAUSIN' #$&% LIKE THIS THAT REALLY MATTER.
IT'S WHETHER A FELLER WITH THE MEANS TO STOP IT CHOOSES TO DO SO. AND HOW HE GOES ABOUT IT.
...
I'LL NEED YOUR HELP.
AND THAT RIGHT THERE IS A DAMN GOOD START.

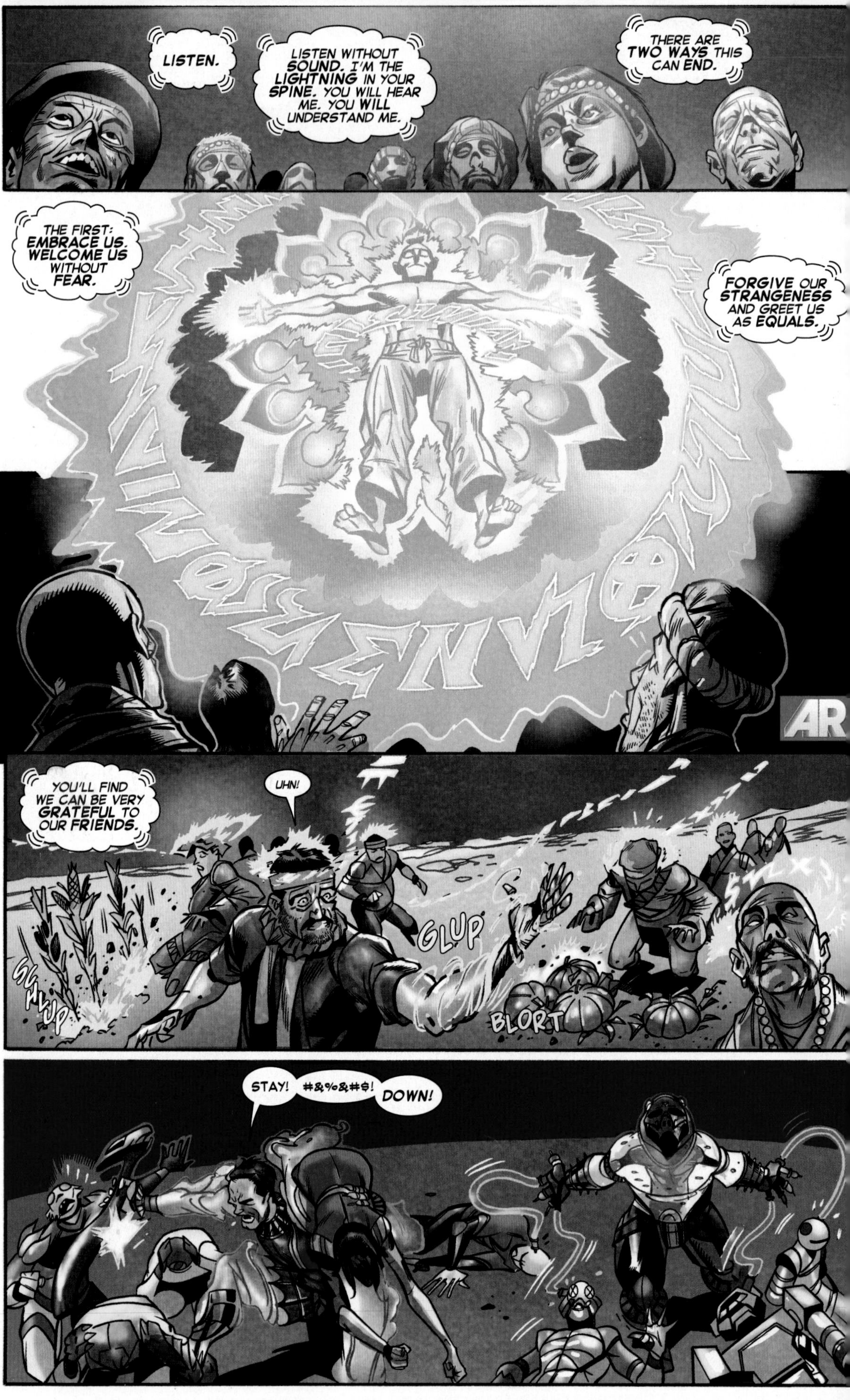
LISTEN.
LISTEN WITHOUT SOUND. I'M THE LIGHTNING IN YOUR SPINE. YOU WILL HEAR ME. YOU WILL UNDERSTAND ME.
THERE ARE TWO WAYS THIS CAN END.
THE FIRST: EMBRACE US. WELCOME US WITHOUT FEAR.
FORGIVE OUR STRANGENESS AND GREET US AS EQUALS.
YOU'LL FIND WE CAN BE VERY GRATEFUL TO OUR FRIENDS.
UHN!
GLUP
SCHLUP
BLORT
STAY!
#&%&#$!
DOWN!

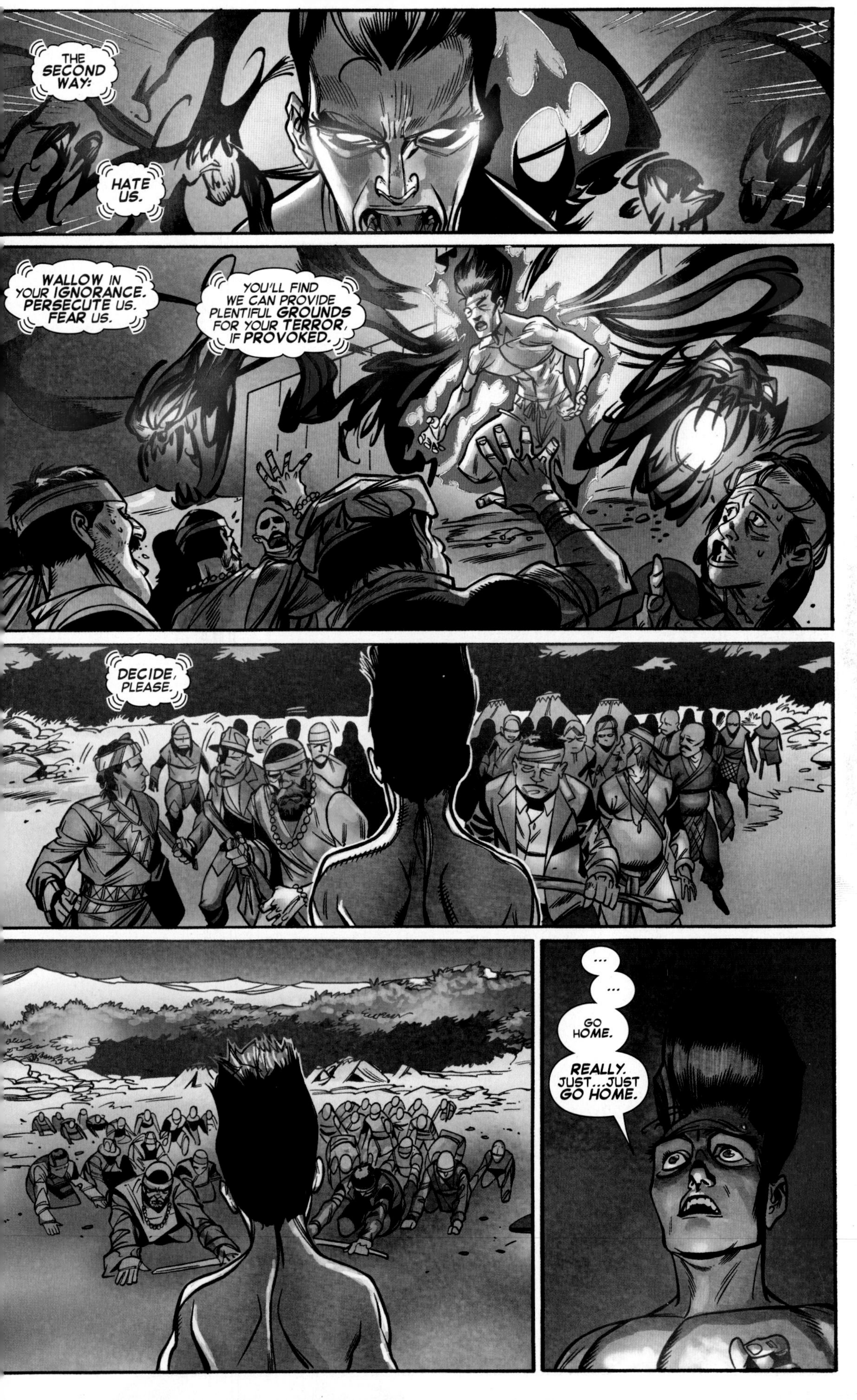
THE SECOND WAY:
HATE US.
WALLOW IN YOUR IGNORANCE. PERSECUTE US. FEAR US.
YOU'LL FIND WE CAN PROVIDE PLENTIFUL GROUNDS FOR YOUR TERROR, IF PROVOKED.
DECIDE, PLEASE.
...
...
GO HOME.
REALLY. JUST...JUST GO HOME.

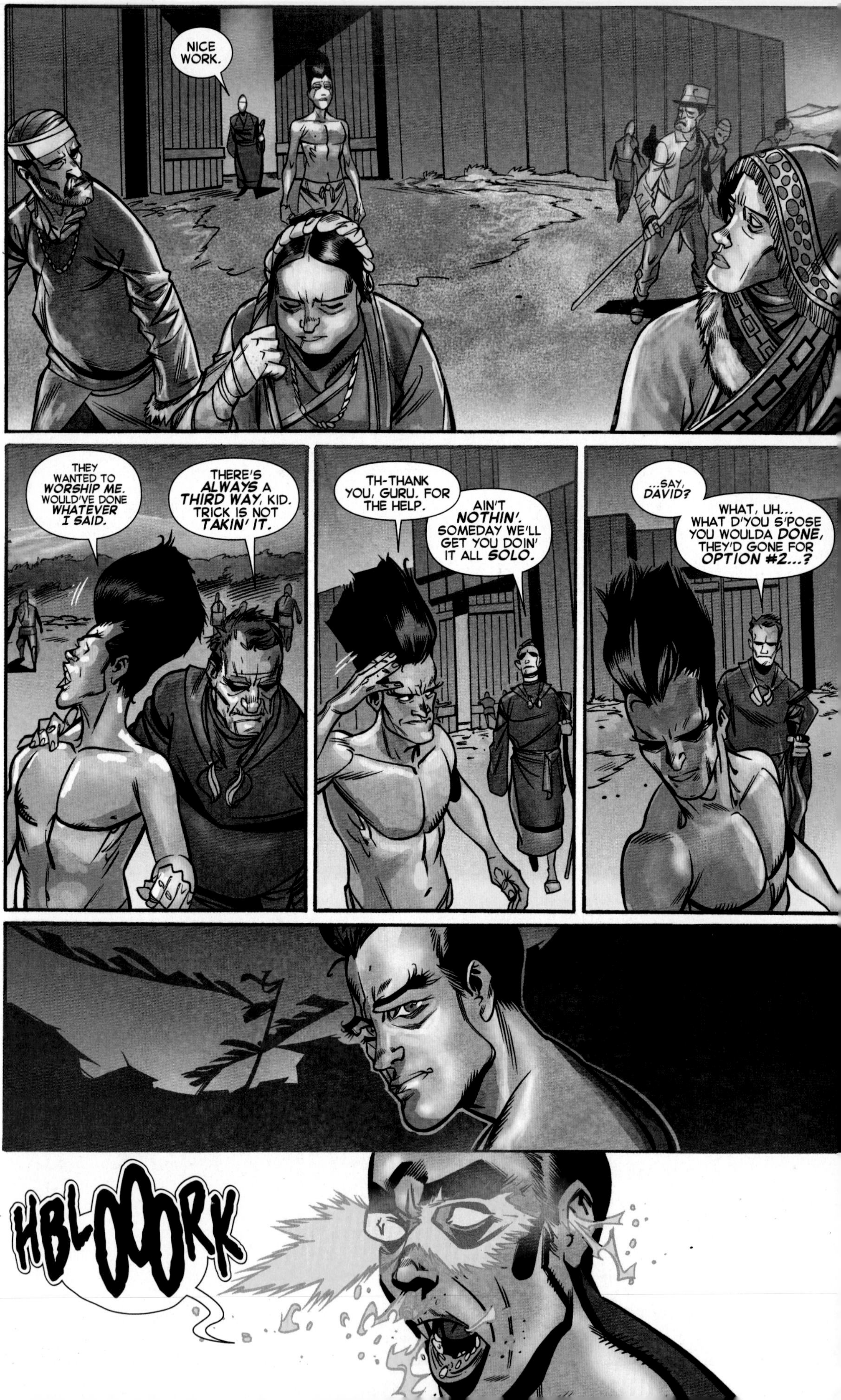
NICE WORK.
THEY WANTED TO WORSHIP ME. WOULD'VE DONE WHATEVER I SAID.
THERE'S ALWAYS A THIRD WAY, KID. TRICK IS NOT TAKIN' IT.
TH-THANK YOU, GURU. FOR THE HELP.
AIN'T NOTHIN'. SOMEDAY WE'LL GET YOU DOIN' IT ALL SOLO.
...SAY, DAVID?
WHAT, UH... WHAT D'YOU S'POSE YOU WOULDA DONE, THEY'D GONE FOR OPTION #2...?
HBLOOORK

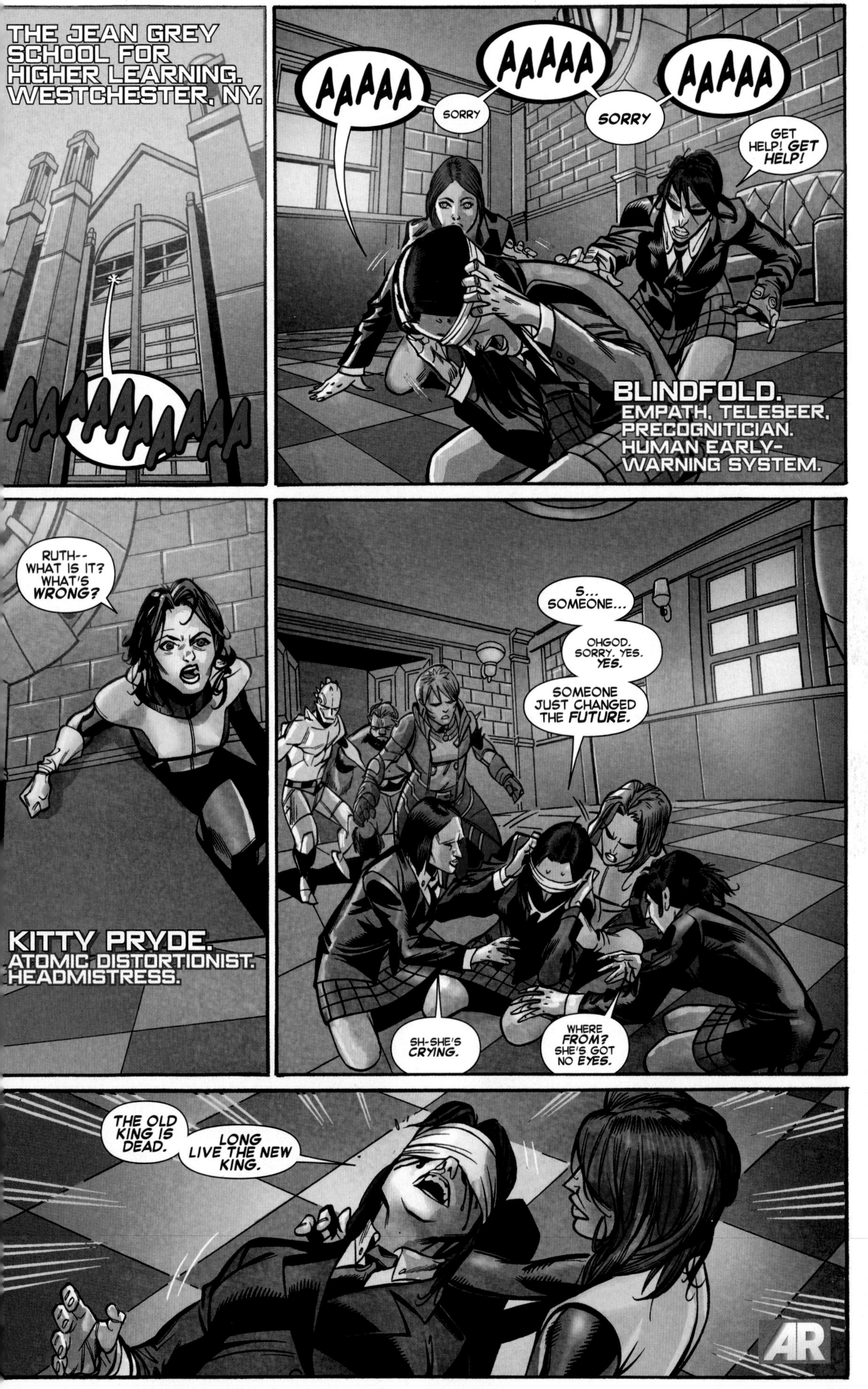
THE JEAN GREY SCHOOL FOR HIGHER LEARNING. WESTCHESTER, NY.
AAAAAAAAAAA
AAAAA
SORRY
AAAAA
SORRY
AAAAA
GET HELP! GET HELP!
BLINDFOLD.
EMPATH, TELESEER, PRECOGNITICIAN. HUMAN EARLY-WARNING SYSTEM.
RUTH-- WHAT IS IT? WHAT'S WRONG?
KITTY PRYDE.
ATOMIC DISTORTIONIST. HEADMISTRESS.
S... SOMEONE...
OHGOD. SORRY. YES. YES.
SOMEONE JUST CHANGED THE FUTURE.
SH-SHE'S CRYING.
WHERE FROM? SHE'S GOT NO EYES.
THE OLD KING IS DEAD.
LONG LIVE THE NEW KING.
AR

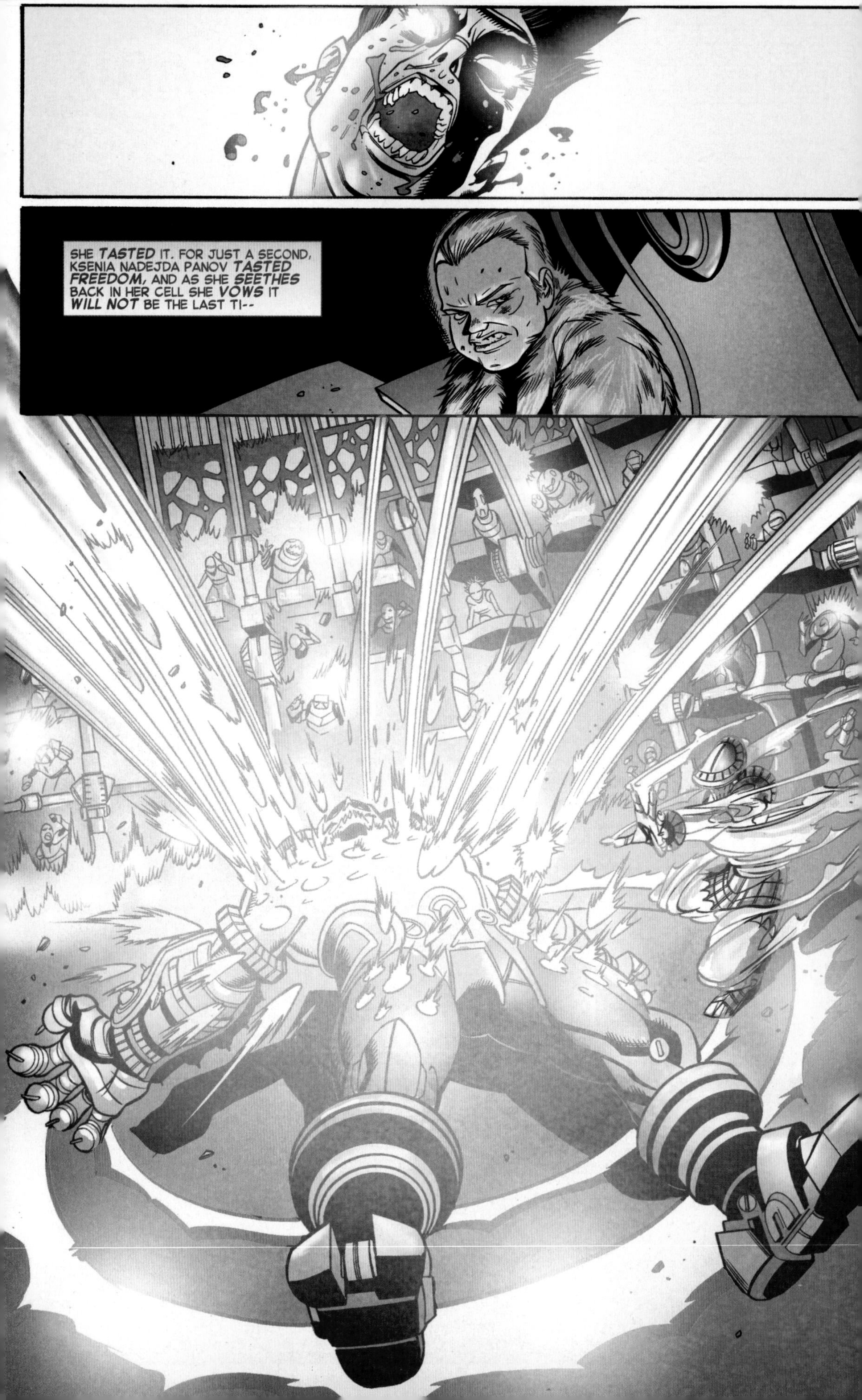
SHE TASTED IT. FOR JUST A SECOND, KSENIA NADEJDA PANOV TASTED FREEDOM, AND AS SHE SEETHES BACK IN HER CELL SHE VOWS IT WILL NOT BE THE LAST TI--

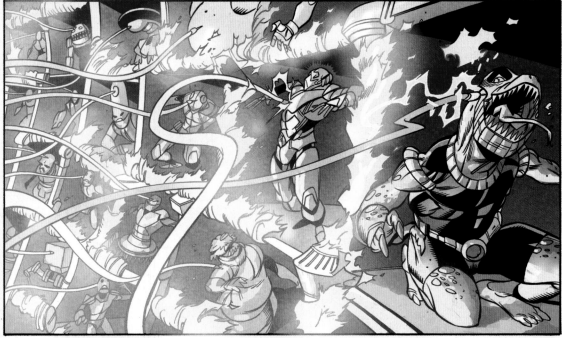

DAD?

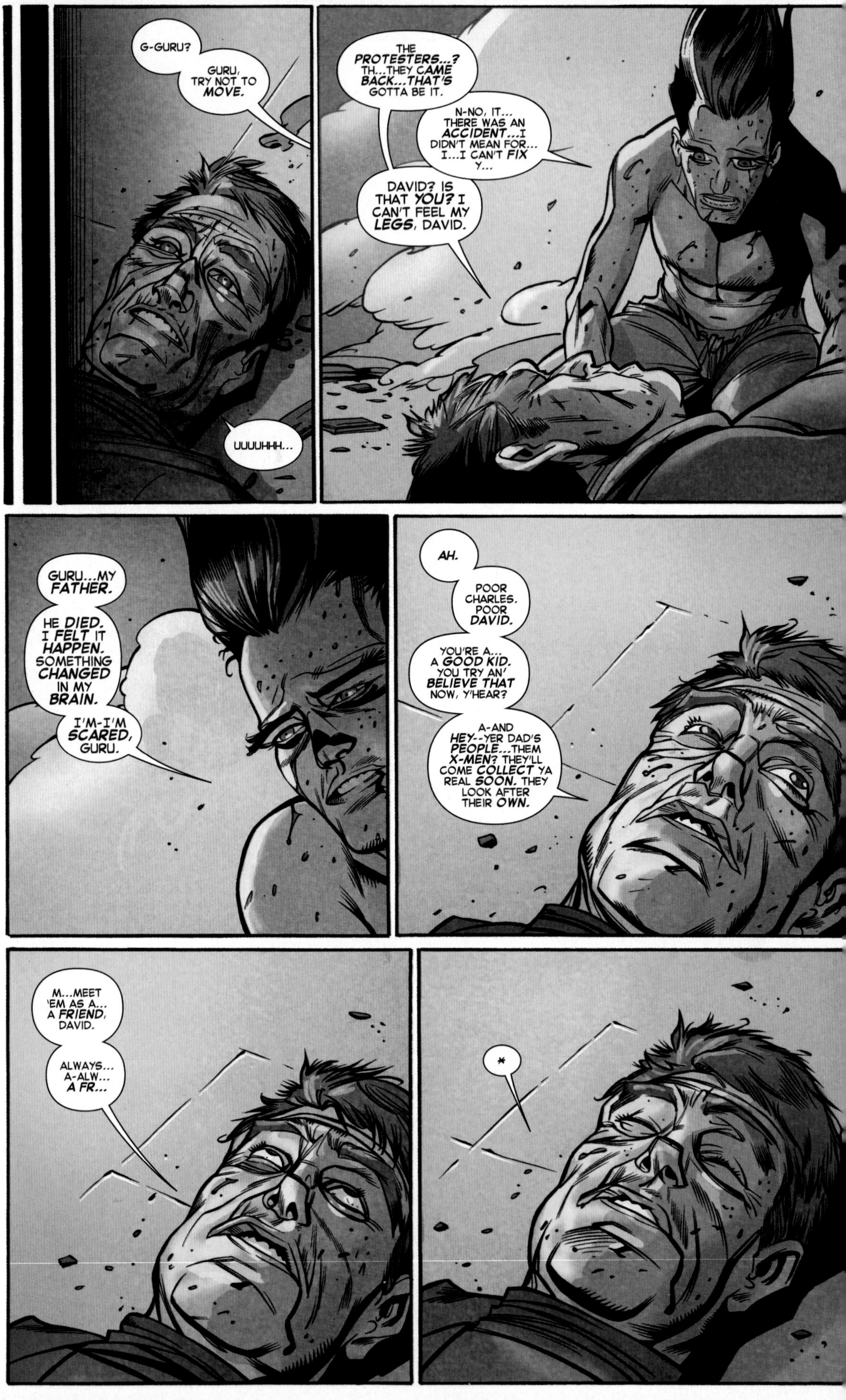
G-GURU?
GURU, TRY NOT TO MOVE.
UUUUHHH...
THE PROTESTERS...? TH...THEY CAME BACK...THAT'S GOTTA BE IT.
N-NO, IT... THERE WAS AN ACCIDENT...I DIDN'T MEAN FOR... I...I CAN'T FIX Y...
DAVID? IS THAT YOU? I CAN'T FEEL MY LEGS, DAVID.
GURU...MY FATHER.
HE DIED. I FELT IT HAPPEN. SOMETHING CHANGED IN MY BRAIN.
I'M-I'M SCARED, GURU.
AH.
POOR CHARLES. POOR DAVID.
YOU'RE A... A GOOD KID. YOU TRY AN' BELIEVE THAT NOW, Y'HEAR?
A-AND HEY--YER DAD'S PEOPLE...THEM X-MEN? THEY'LL COME COLLECT YA REAL SOON. THEY LOOK AFTER THEIR OWN.
M...MEET 'EM AS A... A FRIEND, DAVID.
ALWAYS... A-ALW... A FR...
*

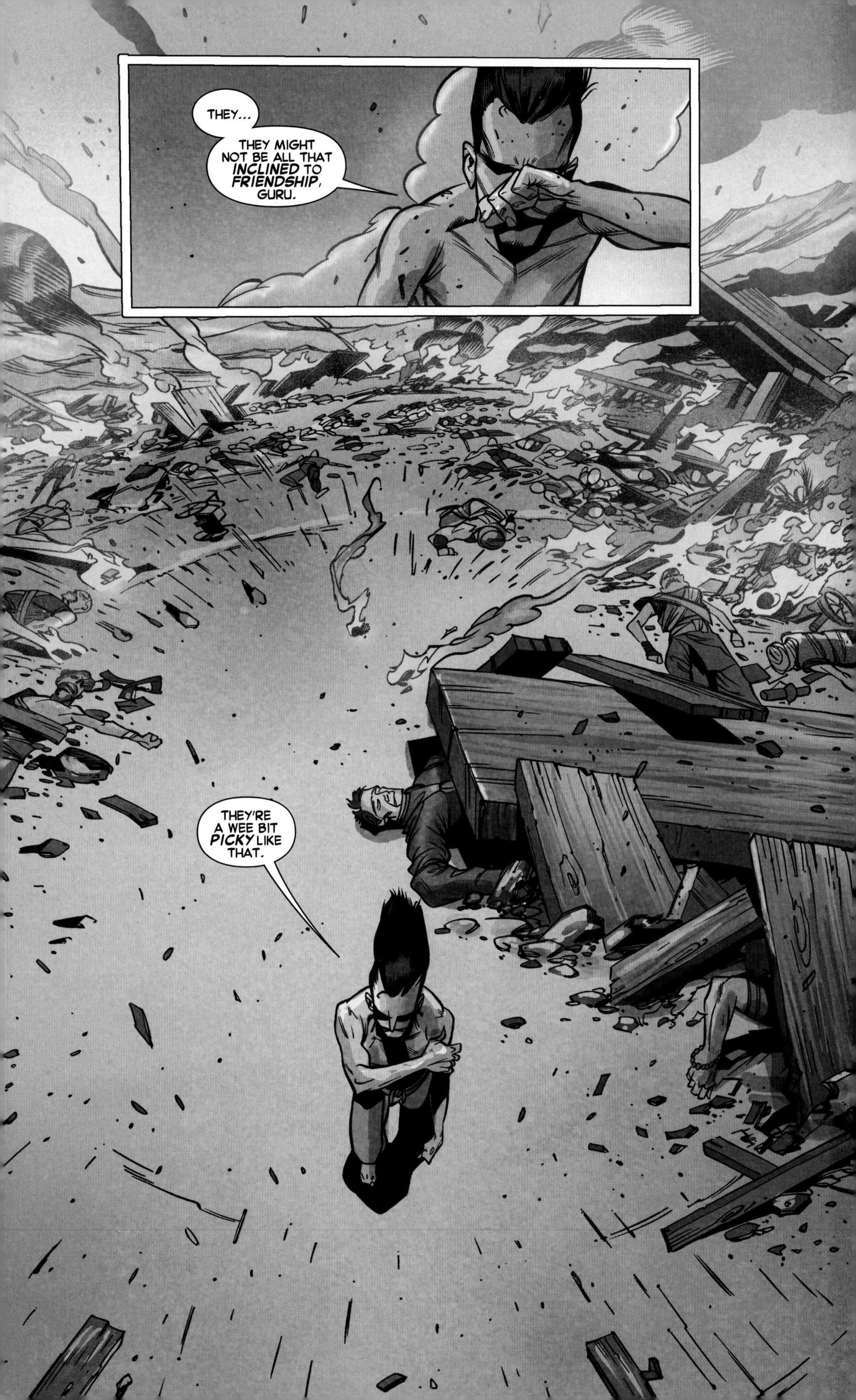
THEY...
THEY MIGHT NOT BE ALL THAT INCLINED TO FRIENDSHIP, GURU.
THEY'RE A WEE BIT PICKY LIKE THAT.

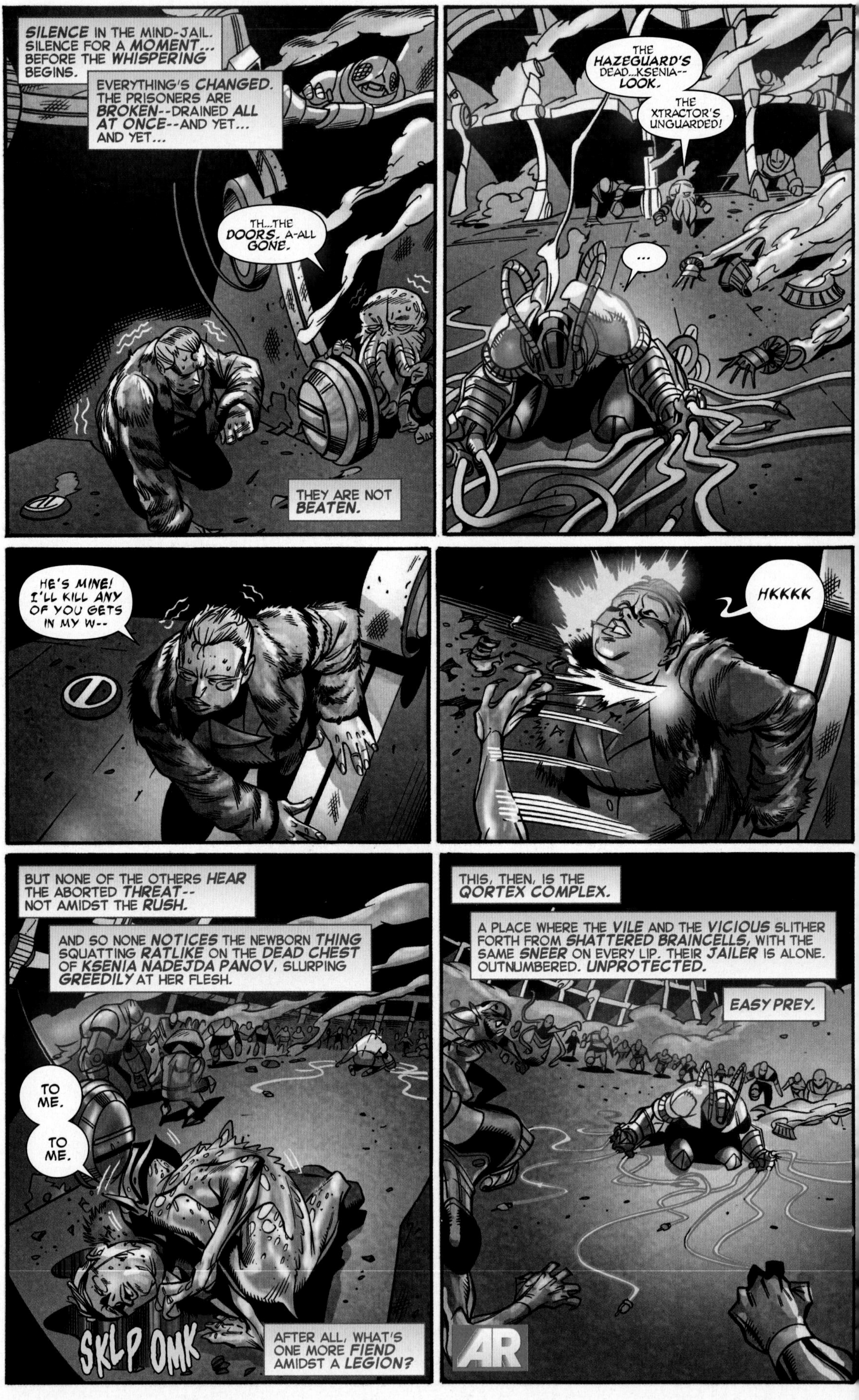
SILENCE IN THE MIND-JAIL. SILENCE FOR A MOMENT... BEFORE THE WHISPERING BEGINS.
EVERYTHING'S CHANGED. THE PRISONERS ARE BROKEN--DRAINED ALL AT ONCE--AND YET... AND YET...
TH...THE DOORS. A-ALL GONE.
THEY ARE NOT BEATEN.
THE HAZEGUARD'S DEAD...KSENIA--LOOK.
THE XTRACTOR'S UNGUARDED!
...
HE'S MINE! I'LL KILL ANY OF YOU GETS IN MY W--
HKKKK
BUT NONE OF THE OTHERS HEAR THE ABORTED THREAT-- NOT AMIDST THE RUSH.
AND SO NONE NOTICES THE NEWBORN THING SQUATTING RATLIKE ON THE DEAD CHEST OF KSENIA NADEJDA PANOV, SLURPING GREEDILY AT HER FLESH.
TO ME.
TO ME.
SKLP OMK
AFTER ALL, WHAT'S ONE MORE FIEND AMIDST A LEGION?
THIS, THEN, IS THE QORTEX COMPLEX.
A PLACE WHERE THE VILE AND THE VICIOUS SLITHER FORTH FROM SHATTERED BRAINCELLS, WITH THE SAME SNEER ON EVERY LIP. THEIR JAILER IS ALONE. OUTNUMBERED. UNPROTECTED.
EASY PREY.
AR

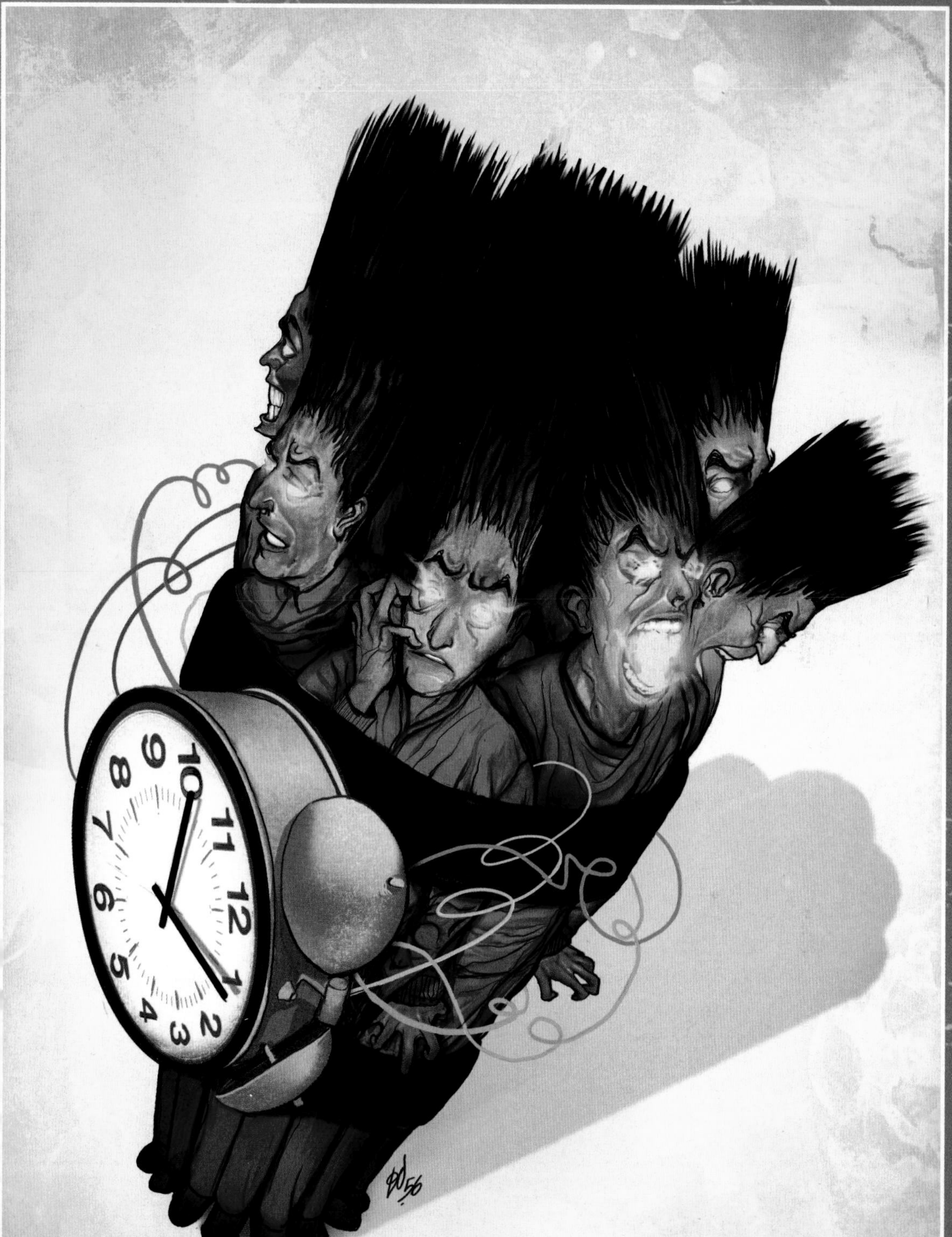

TWO

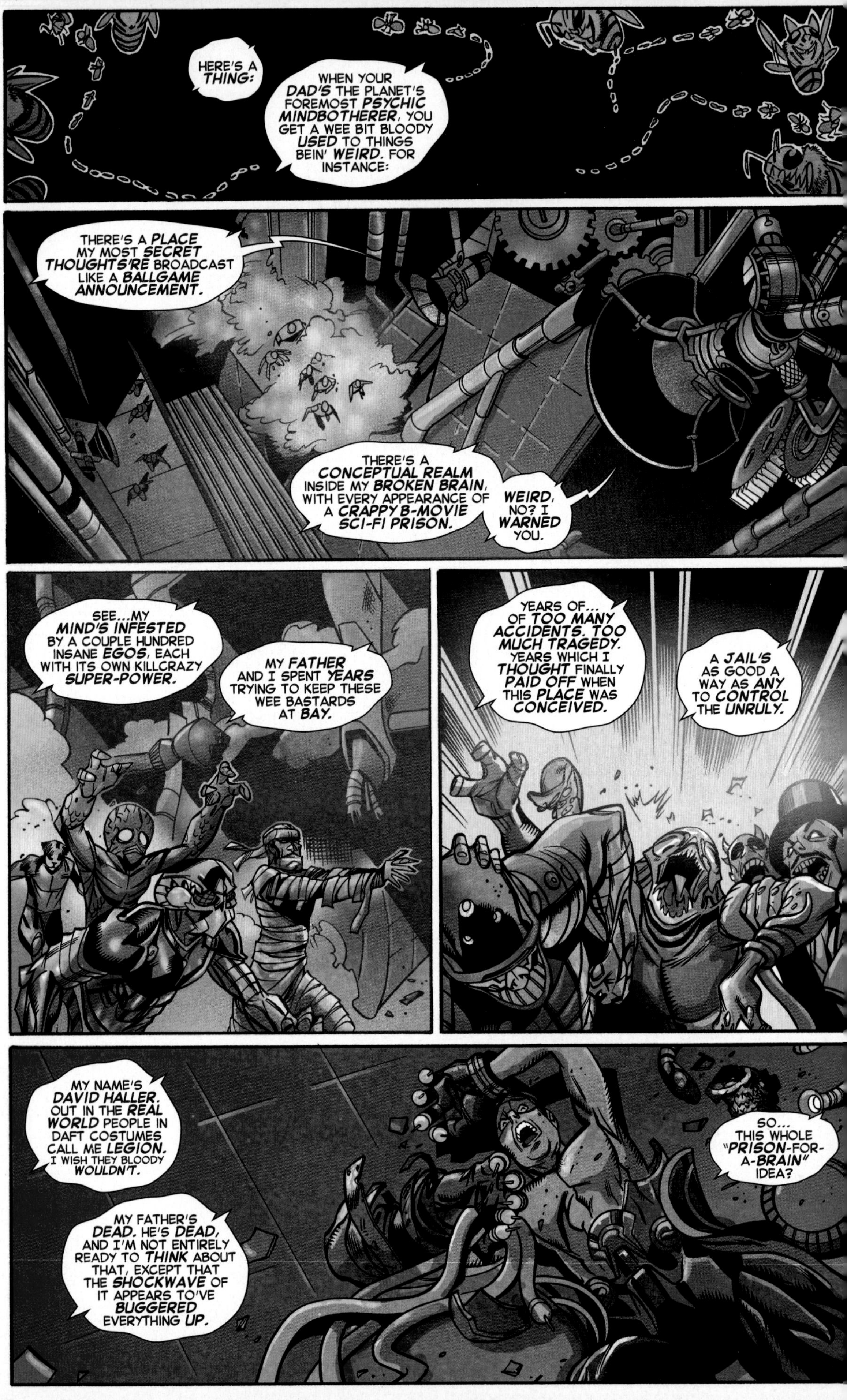

HERE'S A THING:
WHEN YOUR DAD'S THE PLANET'S FOREMOST PSYCHIC MINDBOTHERER, YOU GET A WEE BIT BLOODY USED TO THINGS BEIN' WEIRD. FOR INSTANCE:
THERE'S A PLACE MY MOST SECRET THOUGHTS'RE BROADCAST LIKE A BALLGAME ANNOUNCEMENT.
THERE'S A CONCEPTUAL REALM INSIDE MY BROKEN BRAIN, WITH EVERY APPEARANCE OF A CRAPPY B-MOVIE SCI-FI PRISON.
WEIRD, NO? I WARNED YOU.
SEE...MY MIND'S INFESTED BY A COUPLE HUNDRED INSANE EGOS, EACH WITH ITS OWN KILLCRAZY SUPER-POWER.
MY FATHER AND I SPENT YEARS TRYING TO KEEP THESE WEE BASTARDS AT BAY.
YEARS OF... OF TOO MANY ACCIDENTS. TOO MUCH TRAGEDY. YEARS WHICH I THOUGHT FINALLY PAID OFF WHEN THIS PLACE WAS CONCEIVED.
A JAIL'S AS GOOD A WAY AS ANY TO CONTROL THE UNRULY.
MY NAME'S DAVID HALLER. OUT IN THE REAL WORLD PEOPLE IN DAFT COSTUMES CALL ME LEGION. I WISH THEY BLOODY WOULDN'T.
MY FATHER'S DEAD. HE'S DEAD, AND I'M NOT ENTIRELY READY TO THINK ABOUT THAT, EXCEPT THAT THE SHOCKWAVE OF IT APPEARS TO'VE BUGGERED EVERYTHING UP.
SO... THIS WHOLE "PRISON-FOR-A-BRAIN" IDEA?

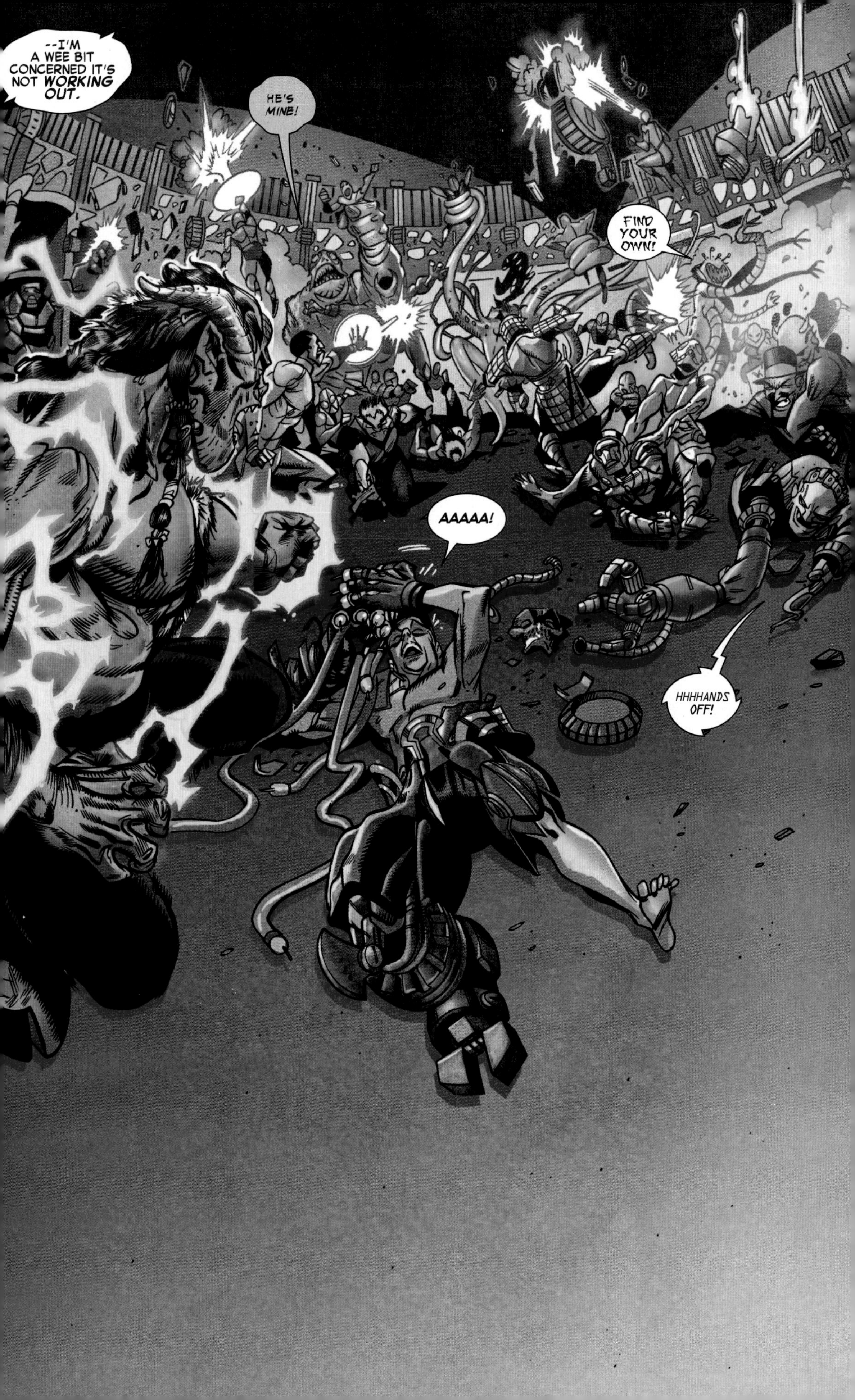
--I'M A WEE BIT CONCERNED IT'S NOT WORKING OUT.
HE'S MINE!
FIND YOUR OWN!
AAAAA!
HHHHANDS OFF!

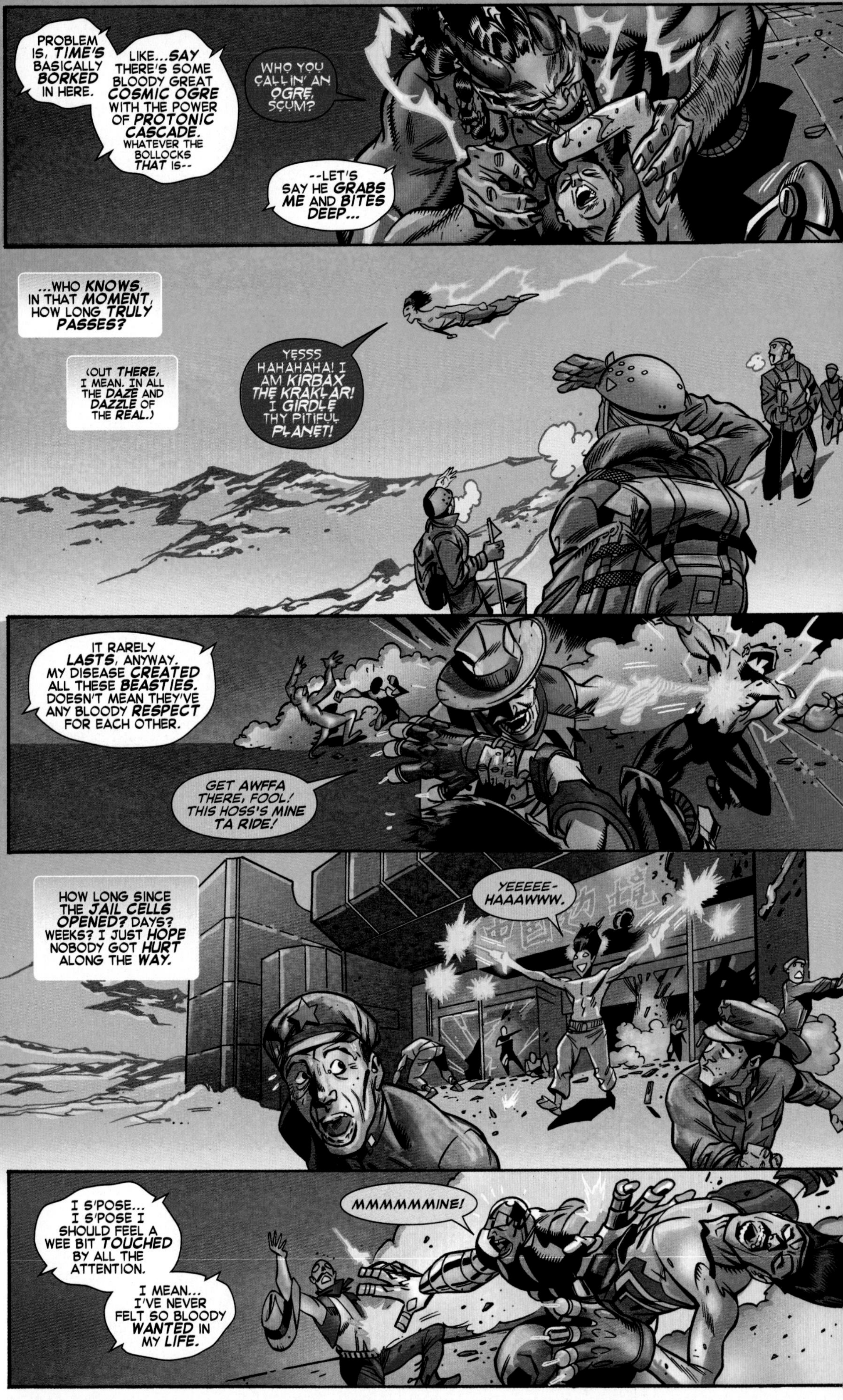
PROBLEM IS, TIME'S BASICALLY BORKED IN HERE.
LIKE...SAY THERE'S SOME BLOODY GREAT COSMIC OGRE WITH THE POWER OF PROTONIC CASCADE. WHATEVER THE BOLLOCKS THAT IS--
WHO YOU CALLIN' AN OGRE, SCUM?
--LET'S SAY HE GRABS ME AND BITES DEEP...
...WHO KNOWS, IN THAT MOMENT, HOW LONG TRULY PASSES?
(OUT THERE, I MEAN. IN ALL THE DAZE AND DAZZLE OF THE REAL.)
YESSS HAHAHAHA! I AM KIRBAX THE KRAKLAR! I GIRDLE THY PITIFUL PLANET!
IT RARELY LASTS, ANYWAY. MY DISEASE CREATED ALL THESE BEASTIES. DOESN'T MEAN THEY'VE ANY BLOODY RESPECT FOR EACH OTHER.
GET AWFFA THERE, FOOL! THIS HOSS'S MINE TA RIDE!
HOW LONG SINCE THE JAIL CELLS OPENED? DAYS? WEEKS? I JUST HOPE NOBODY GOT HURT ALONG THE WAY.
YEEEEE-HAAAWWW.
I S'POSE... I S'POSE I SHOULD FEEL A WEE BIT TOUCHED BY ALL THE ATTENTION.
MMMMMMMINE!
I MEAN... I'VE NEVER FELT SO BLOODY WANTED IN MY LIFE.

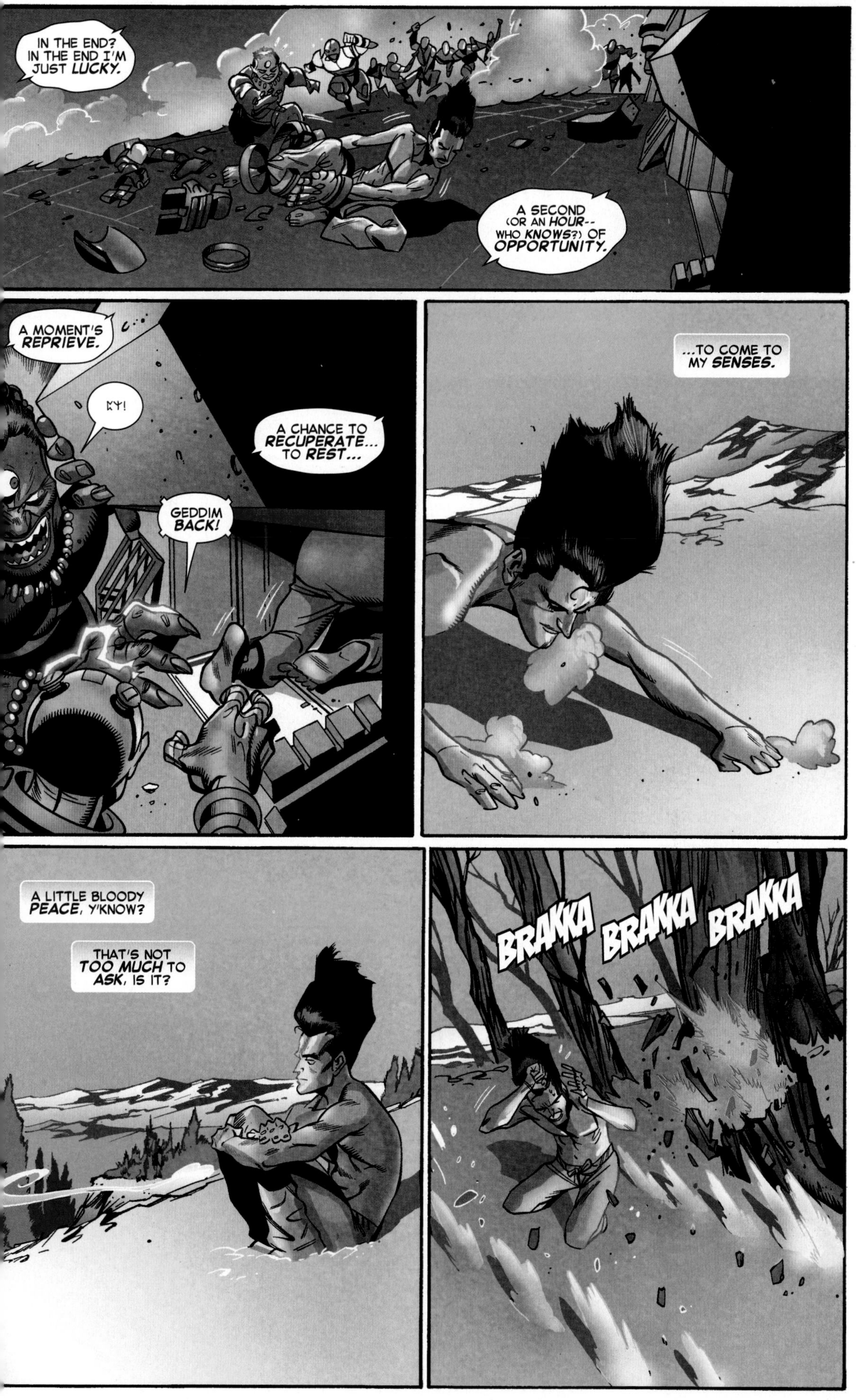
IN THE END? IN THE END I'M JUST LUCKY.
A SECOND (OR AN HOUR-- WHO KNOWS?) OF OPPORTUNITY.
A MOMENT'S REPRIEVE.
A CHANCE TO RECUPERATE... TO REST...
GEDDIM BACK!
...TO COME TO MY SENSES.
A LITTLE BLOODY PEACE, Y'KNOW?
THAT'S NOT TOO MUCH TO ASK, IS IT?
BRAKKA BRAKKA BRAKKA

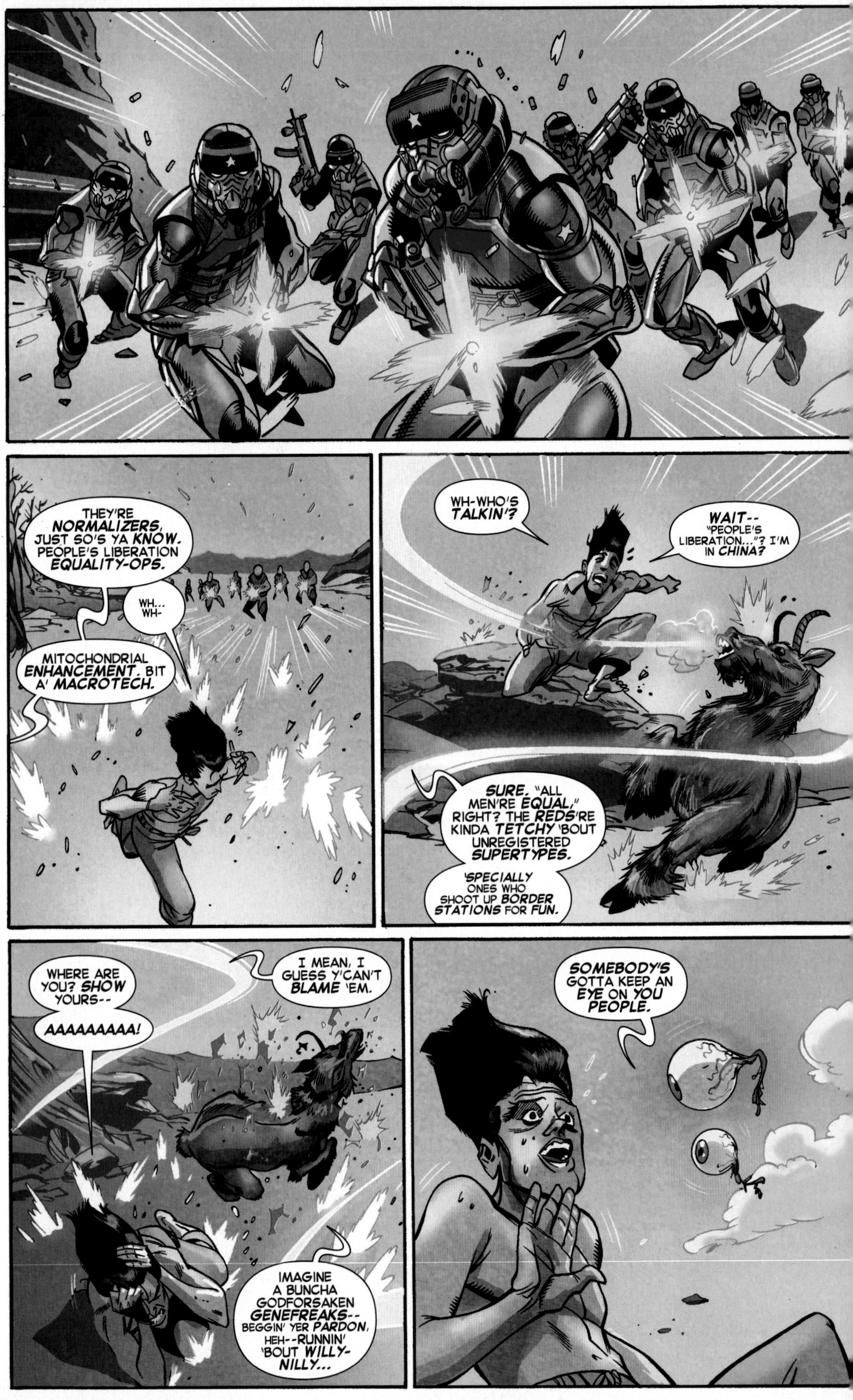
THEY'RE NORMALIZERS, JUST SO'S YA KNOW. PEOPLE'S LIBERATION EQUALITY-OPS.
WH... WH-
MITOCHONDRIAL ENHANCEMENT. BIT A' MACROTECH.
WH-WHO'S TALKIN'?
WAIT-- "PEOPLE'S LIBERATION..."? I'M IN CHINA?
SURE. "ALL MEN'RE EQUAL," RIGHT? THE REDS'RE KINDA TETCHY 'BOUT UNREGISTERED SUPERTYPES.
'SPECIALLY ONES WHO SHOOT UP BORDER STATIONS FOR FUN.
WHERE ARE YOU? SHOW YOURS--
AAAAAAAAA!
I MEAN, I GUESS Y'CAN'T BLAME 'EM.
IMAGINE A BUNCHA GODFORSAKEN GENEFREAKS-- BEGGIN' YER PARDON, HEH--RUNNIN' 'BOUT WILLY-NILLY...
SOMEBODY'S GOTTA KEEP AN EYE ON YOU PEOPLE.

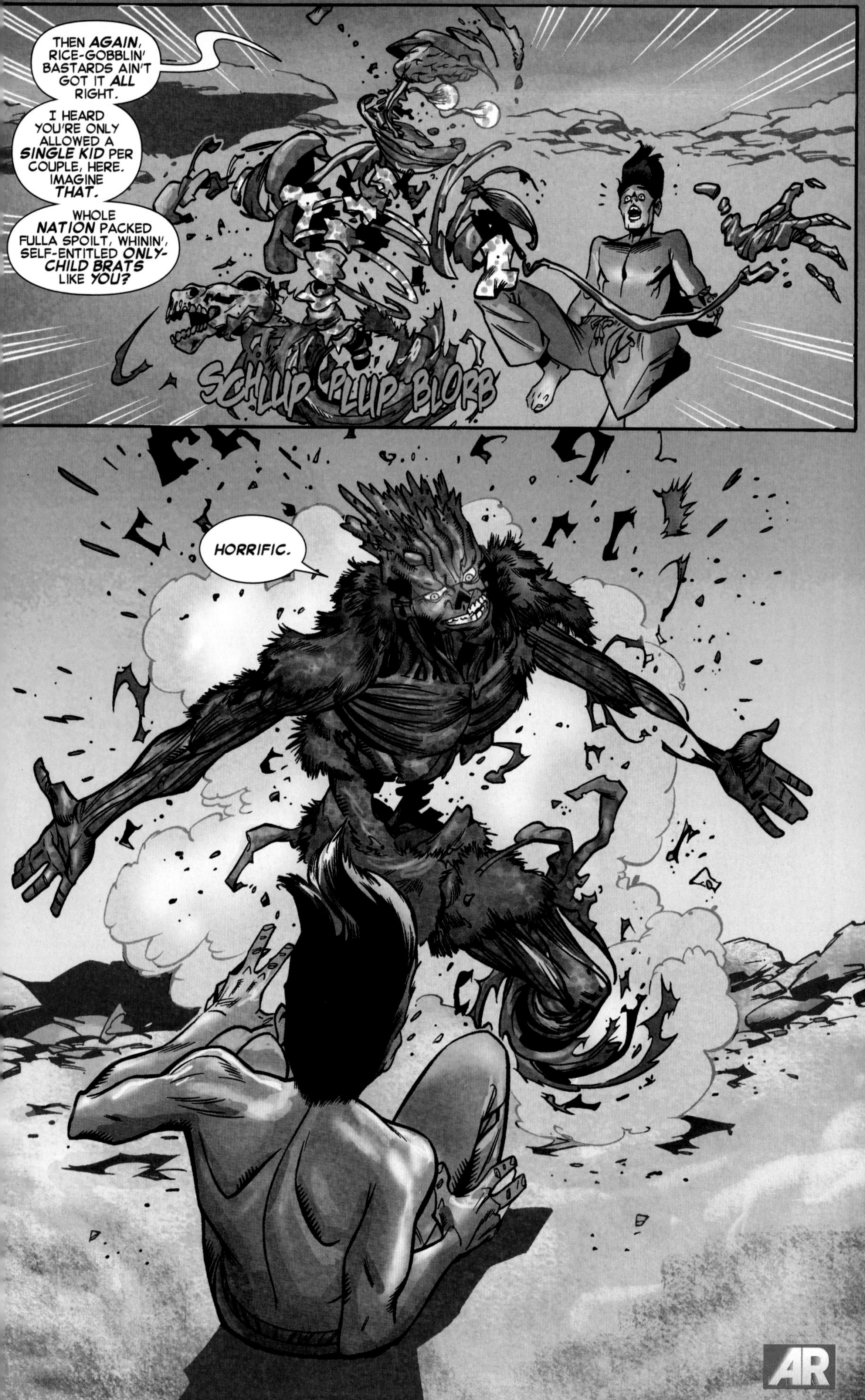
THEN AGAIN, RICE-GOBBLIN' BASTARDS AIN'T GOT IT ALL RIGHT.
I HEARD YOU'RE ONLY ALLOWED A SINGLE KID PER COUPLE, HERE. IMAGINE THAT.
WHOLE NATION PACKED FULLA SPOILT, WHININ', SELF-ENTITLED ONLY-CHILD BRATS LIKE YOU?
SCHLUP PLUP BLORB
HORRIFIC.

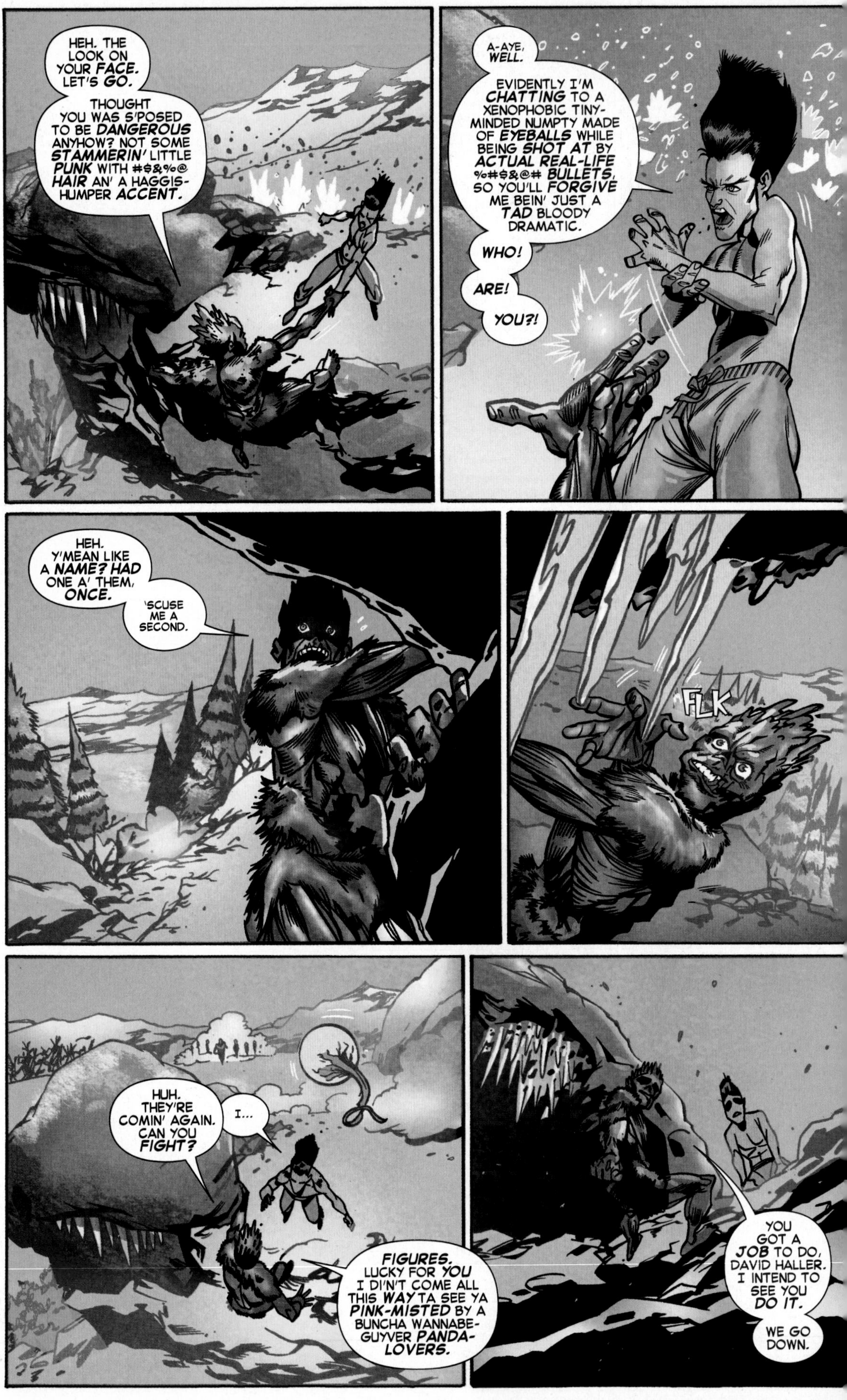

HEH. THE LOOK ON YOUR FACE. LET'S GO.
THOUGHT YOU WAS S'POSED TO BE DANGEROUS ANYHOW? NOT SOME STAMMERIN' LITTLE PUNK WITH #$&%@ HAIR AN' A HAGGIS-HUMPER ACCENT.
A-AYE, WELL.
EVIDENTLY I'M CHATTING TO A XENOPHOBIC TINY-MINDED NUMPTY MADE OF EYEBALLS WHILE BEING SHOT AT BY ACTUAL REAL-LIFE %#$&@# BULLETS, SO YOU'LL FORGIVE ME BEIN' JUST A TAD BLOODY DRAMATIC.
WHO!
ARE!
YOU?!
HEH. Y'MEAN LIKE A NAME? HAD ONE A' THEM, ONCE.
'SCUSE ME A SECOND.
FLK
HUH. THEY'RE COMIN' AGAIN. CAN YOU FIGHT?
I...
FIGURES. LUCKY FOR YOU I DI'N'T COME ALL THIS WAY TA SEE YA PINK-MISTED BY A BUNCHA WANNABE-GUYVER PANDA-LOVERS.
YOU GOT A JOB TO DO, DAVID HALLER. I INTEND TO SEE YOU DO IT.
WE GO DOWN.

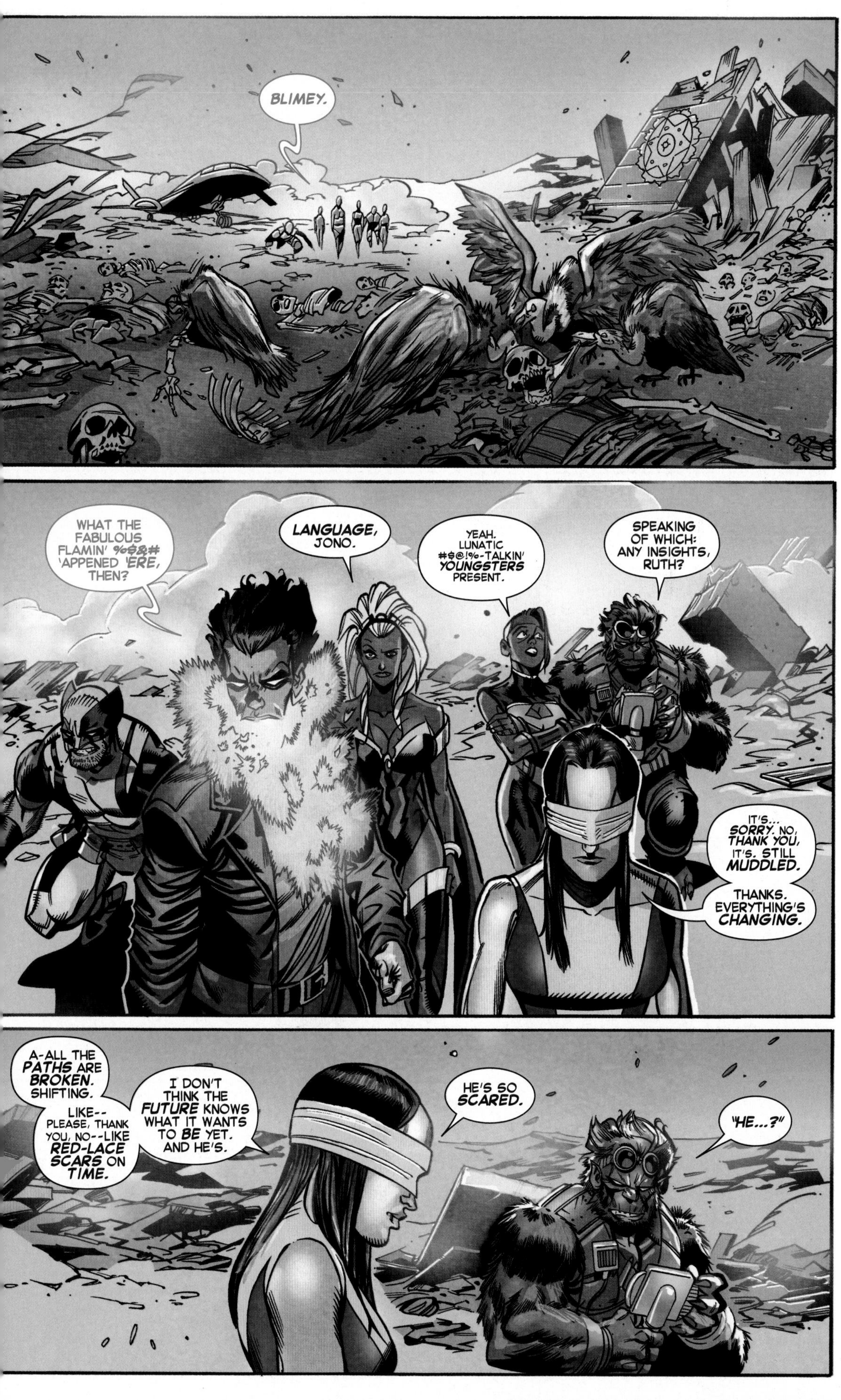

BLIMEY.
WHAT THE FABULOUS FLAMIN' %@$&# 'APPENED 'ERE, THEN?
LANGUAGE, JONO.
YEAH. LUNATIC #$@!%-TALKIN' YOUNGSTERS PRESENT.
SPEAKING OF WHICH: ANY INSIGHTS, RUTH?
IT'S... SORRY. NO, THANK YOU, IT'S. STILL MUDDLED.
THANKS. EVERYTHING'S CHANGING.
A-ALL THE PATHS ARE BROKEN. SHIFTING.
LIKE-- PLEASE, THANK YOU, NO--LIKE RED-LACE SCARS ON TIME.
I DON'T THINK THE FUTURE KNOWS WHAT IT WANTS TO BE YET. AND HE'S.
HE'S SO SCARED.
"HE...?"

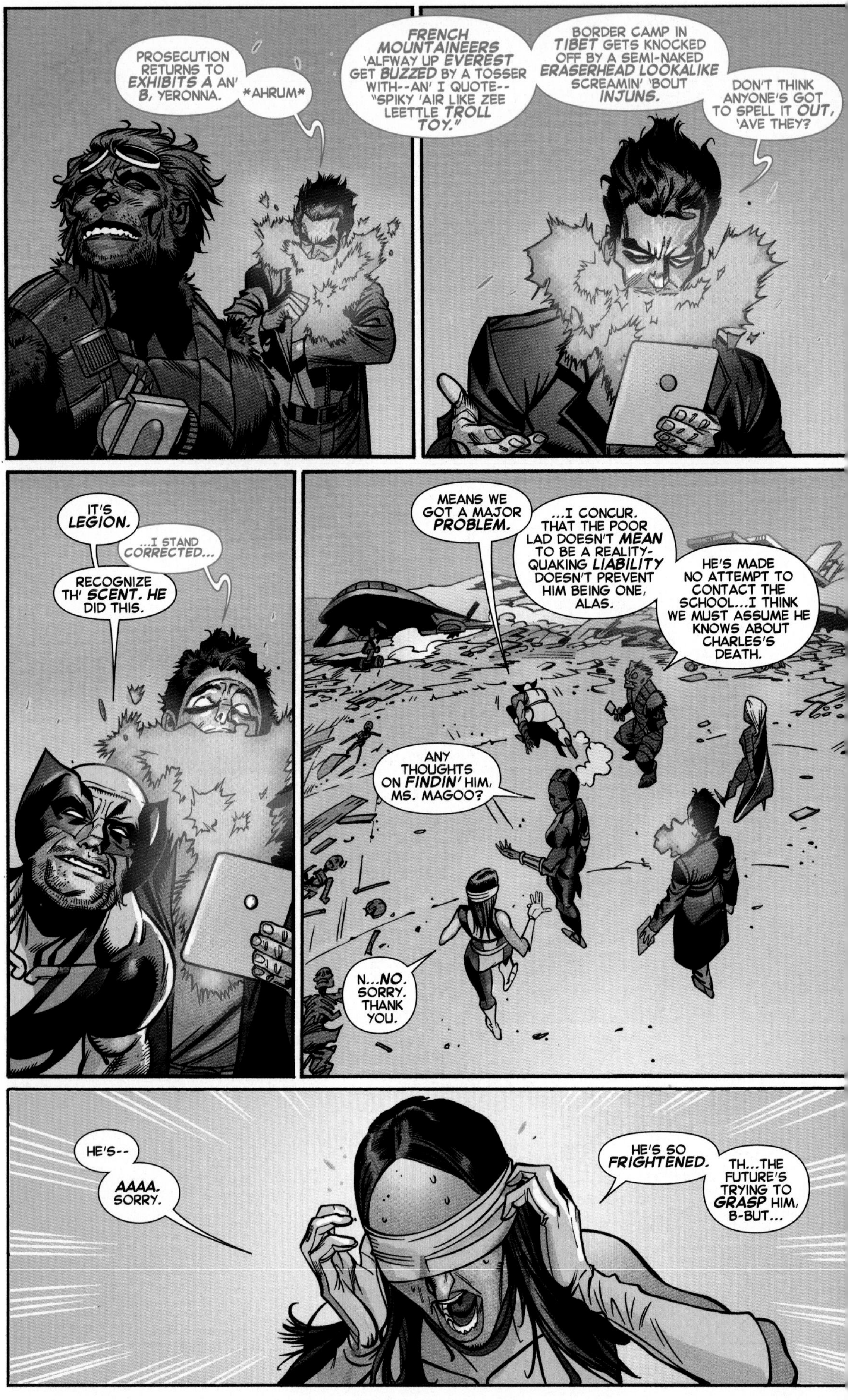
PROSECUTION RETURNS TO EXHIBITS A AN' B, YERONNA.
AHRUM
FRENCH MOUNTAINEERS 'ALFWAY UP EVEREST GET BUZZED BY A TOSSER WITH--AN' I QUOTE-- "SPIKY 'AIR LIKE ZEE LEETTLE TROLL TOY."
BORDER CAMP IN TIBET GETS KNOCKED OFF BY A SEMI-NAKED ERASERHEAD LOOKALIKE SCREAMIN' 'BOUT INJUNS.
DON'T THINK ANYONE'S GOT TO SPELL IT OUT, 'AVE THEY?
IT'S LEGION.
...I STAND CORRECTED...
RECOGNIZE TH' SCENT. HE DID THIS.
MEANS WE GOT A MAJOR PROBLEM.
...I CONCUR. THAT THE POOR LAD DOESN'T MEAN TO BE A REALITY-QUAKING LIABILITY DOESN'T PREVENT HIM BEING ONE, ALAS.
HE'S MADE NO ATTEMPT TO CONTACT THE SCHOOL...I THINK WE MUST ASSUME HE KNOWS ABOUT CHARLES'S DEATH.
ANY THOUGHTS ON FINDIN' HIM, MS. MAGOO?
N...NO. SORRY. THANK YOU.
HE'S--
AAAA. SORRY.
HE'S SO FRIGHTENED.
TH...THE FUTURE'S TRYING TO GRASP HIM, B-BUT...

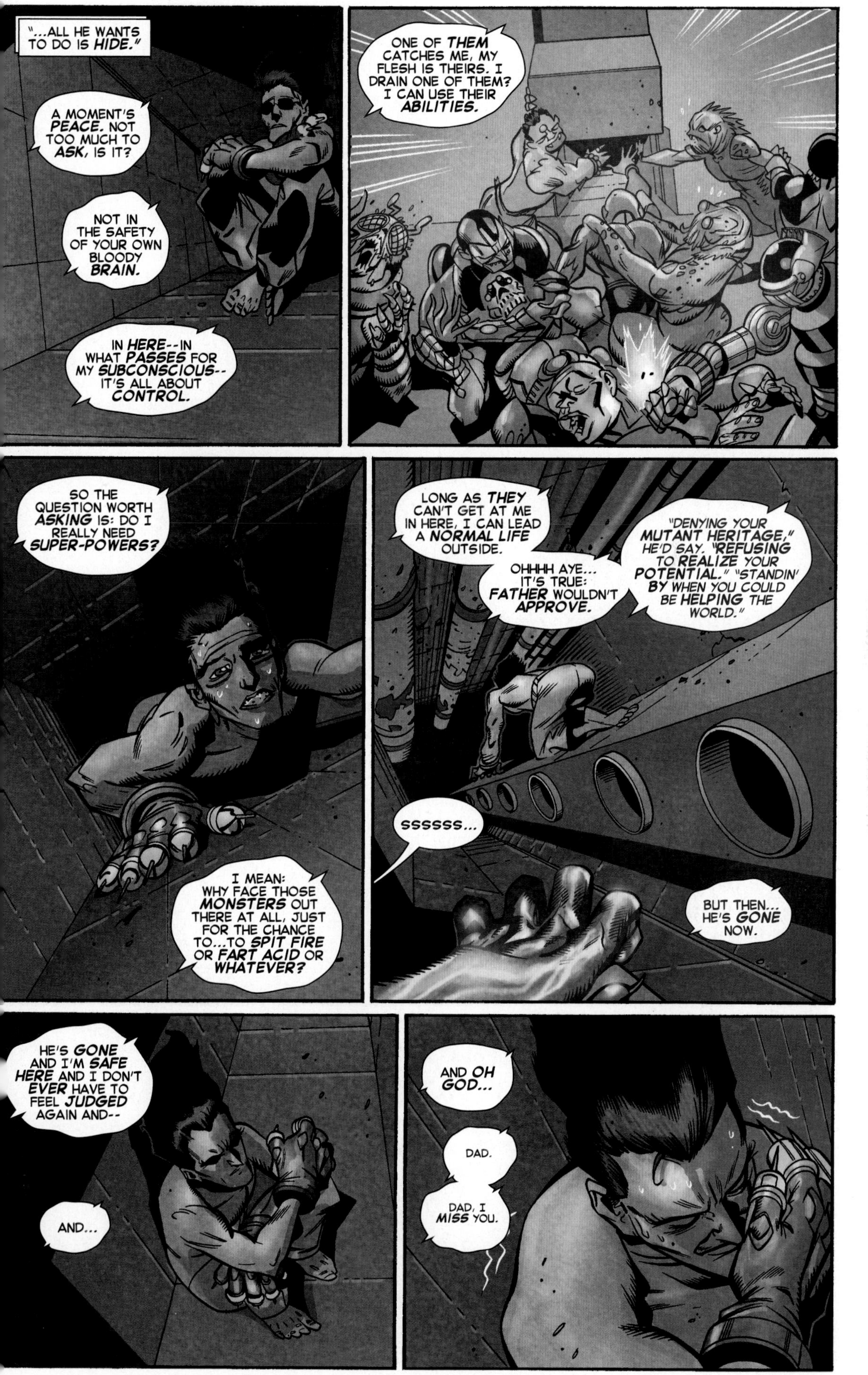
"...ALL HE WANTS TO DO IS HIDE."
A MOMENT'S PEACE. NOT TOO MUCH TO ASK, IS IT?
NOT IN THE SAFETY OF YOUR OWN BLOODY BRAIN.
IN HERE--IN WHAT PASSES FOR MY SUBCONSCIOUS--IT'S ALL ABOUT CONTROL.
ONE OF THEM CATCHES ME, MY FLESH IS THEIRS. I DRAIN ONE OF THEM? I CAN USE THEIR ABILITIES.
SO THE QUESTION WORTH ASKING IS: DO I REALLY NEED SUPER-POWERS?
I MEAN: WHY FACE THOSE MONSTERS OUT THERE AT ALL, JUST FOR THE CHANCE TO...TO SPIT FIRE OR FART ACID OR WHATEVER?
LONG AS THEY CAN'T GET AT ME IN HERE, I CAN LEAD A NORMAL LIFE OUTSIDE.
OHHHH AYE... IT'S TRUE: FATHER WOULDN'T APPROVE.
"DENYING YOUR MUTANT HERITAGE," HE'D SAY. "REFUSING TO REALIZE YOUR POTENTIAL." "STANDIN' BY WHEN YOU COULD BE HELPING THE WORLD."
SSSSSS...
BUT THEN... HE'S GONE NOW.
HE'S GONE AND I'M SAFE HERE AND I DON'T EVER HAVE TO FEEL JUDGED AGAIN AND--
AND...
AND OH GOD...
DAD.
DAD, I MISS YOU.

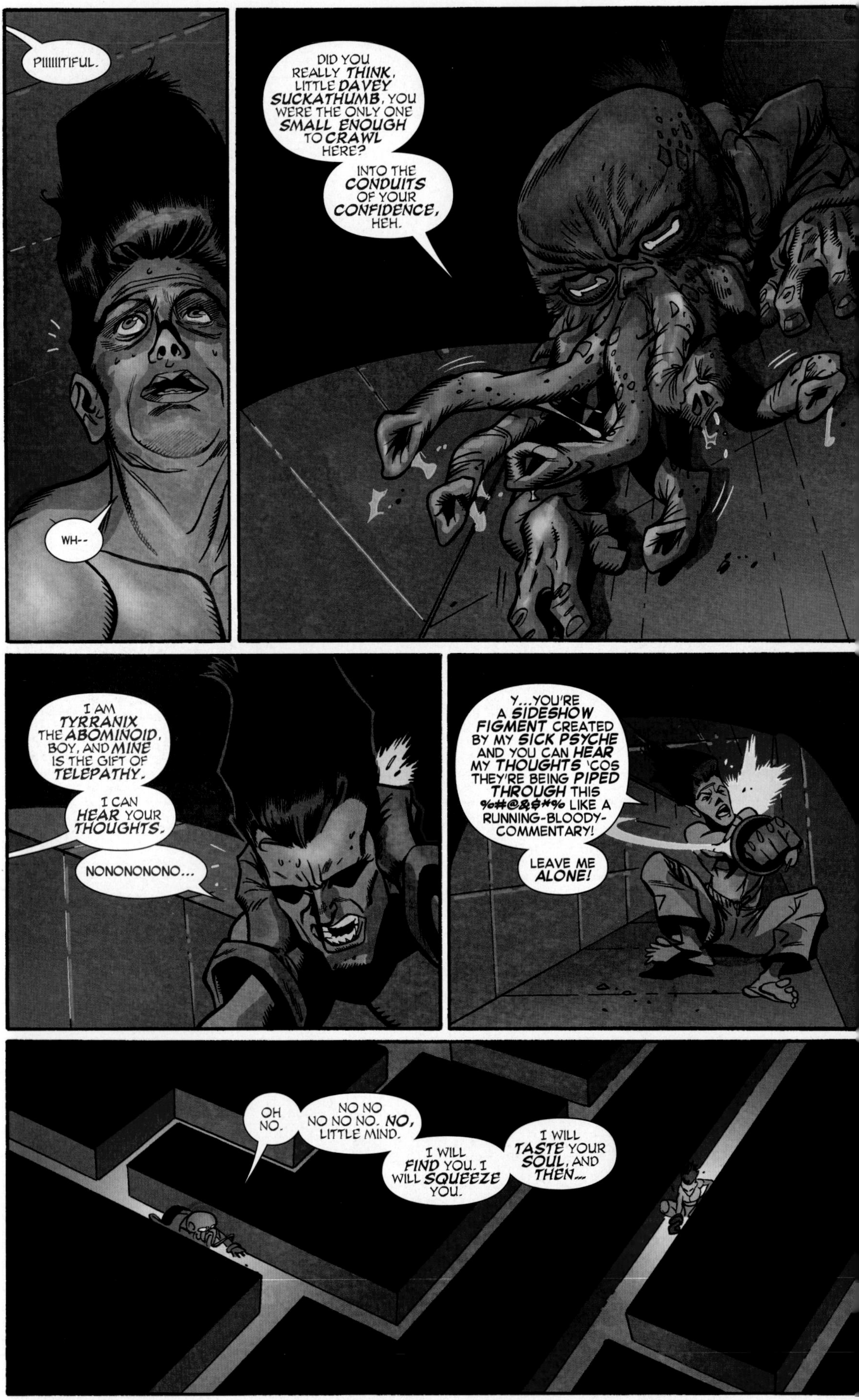
PIIIIITIFUL.
WH--
DID YOU REALLY THINK, LITTLE DAVEY SUCKATHUMB, YOU WERE THE ONLY ONE SMALL ENOUGH TO CRAWL HERE?
INTO THE CONDUITS OF YOUR CONFIDENCE, HEH.
I AM TYRRANIX THE ABOMINOID, BOY, AND MINE IS THE GIFT OF TELEPATHY.
I CAN HEAR YOUR THOUGHTS.
NONONONONO...
Y...YOU'RE A SIDESHOW FIGMENT CREATED BY MY SICK PSYCHE AND YOU CAN HEAR MY THOUGHTS 'COS THEY'RE BEING PIPED THROUGH THIS %#@&$*% LIKE A RUNNING-BLOODY-COMMENTARY!
LEAVE ME ALONE!
OH NO.
NO NO NO NO NO. NO, LITTLE MIND.
I WILL FIND YOU. I WILL SQUEEZE YOU.
I WILL TASTE YOUR SOUL, AND THEN...

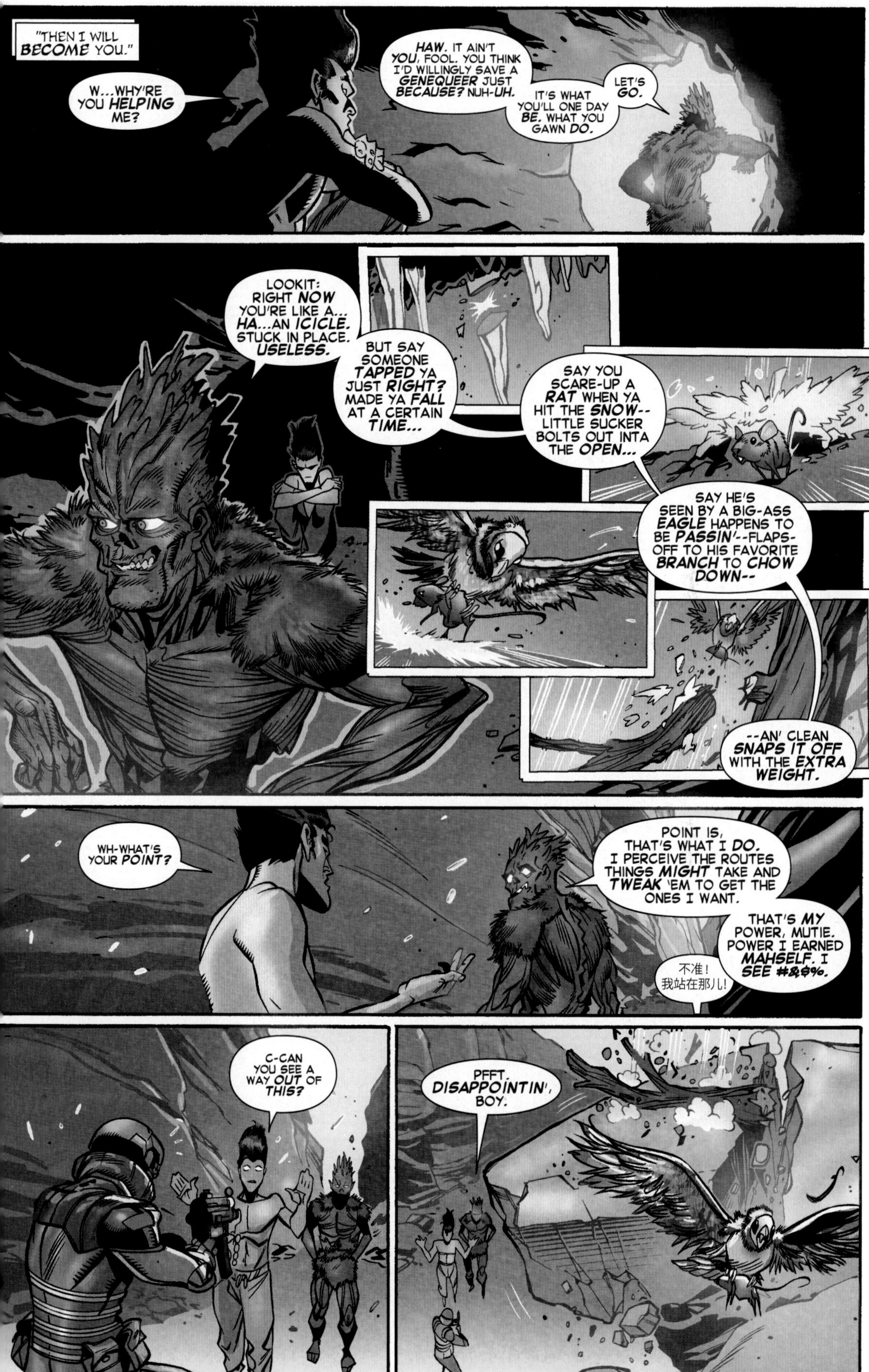
"THEN I WILL BECOME YOU."
W...WHY'RE YOU HELPING ME?
HAW. IT AIN'T YOU, FOOL. YOU THINK I'D WILLINGLY SAVE A GENEQUEER JUST BECAUSE? NUH-UH.
IT'S WHAT YOU'LL ONE DAY BE. WHAT YOU GAWN DO.
LET'S GO.
LOOKIT: RIGHT NOW YOU'RE LIKE A... HA...AN ICICLE. STUCK IN PLACE. USELESS.
BUT SAY SOMEONE TAPPED YA JUST RIGHT? MADE YA FALL AT A CERTAIN TIME...
SAY YOU SCARE-UP A RAT WHEN YA HIT THE SNOW-- LITTLE SUCKER BOLTS OUT INTA THE OPEN...
SAY HE'S SEEN BY A BIG-ASS EAGLE HAPPENS TO BE PASSIN'--FLAPS-OFF TO HIS FAVORITE BRANCH TO CHOW DOWN--
--AN' CLEAN SNAPS IT OFF WITH THE EXTRA WEIGHT.
WH-WHAT'S YOUR POINT?
POINT IS, THAT'S WHAT I DO. I PERCEIVE THE ROUTES THINGS MIGHT TAKE AND TWEAK 'EM TO GET THE ONES I WANT.
THAT'S MY POWER, MUTIE. POWER I EARNED MAHSELF. I SEE #&$%.
不准！我站在那儿!
C-CAN YOU SEE A WAY OUT OF THIS?
PFFT. DISAPPOINTIN', BOY.

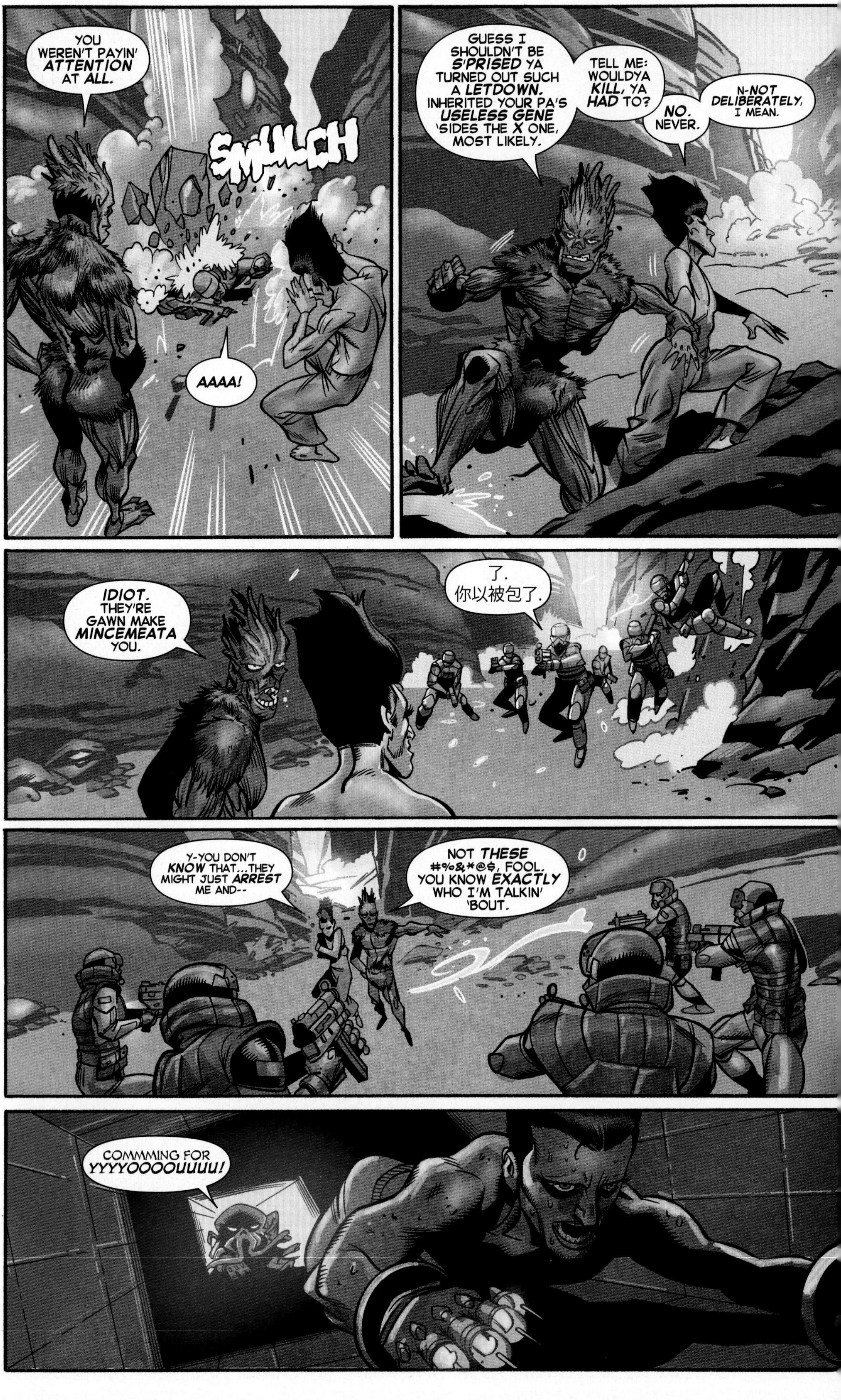
YOU WEREN'T PAYIN' ATTENTION AT ALL.
SMULCH
AAAA!
GUESS I SHOULDN'T BE S'PRISED YA TURNED OUT SUCH A LETDOWN. INHERITED YOUR PA'S USELESS GENE 'SIDES THE X ONE, MOST LIKELY.
TELL ME: WOULDYA KILL, YA HAD TO?
NO. NEVER.
N-NOT DELIBERATELY, I MEAN.
IDIOT. THEY'RE GAWN MAKE MINCEMEATA YOU.
了.
你以被包了.
Y-YOU DON'T KNOW THAT...THEY MIGHT JUST ARREST ME AND--
NOT THESE #%&*@$, FOOL. YOU KNOW EXACTLY WHO I'M TALKIN' 'BOUT.
COMMMING FOR YYYYOOOOUUUU!

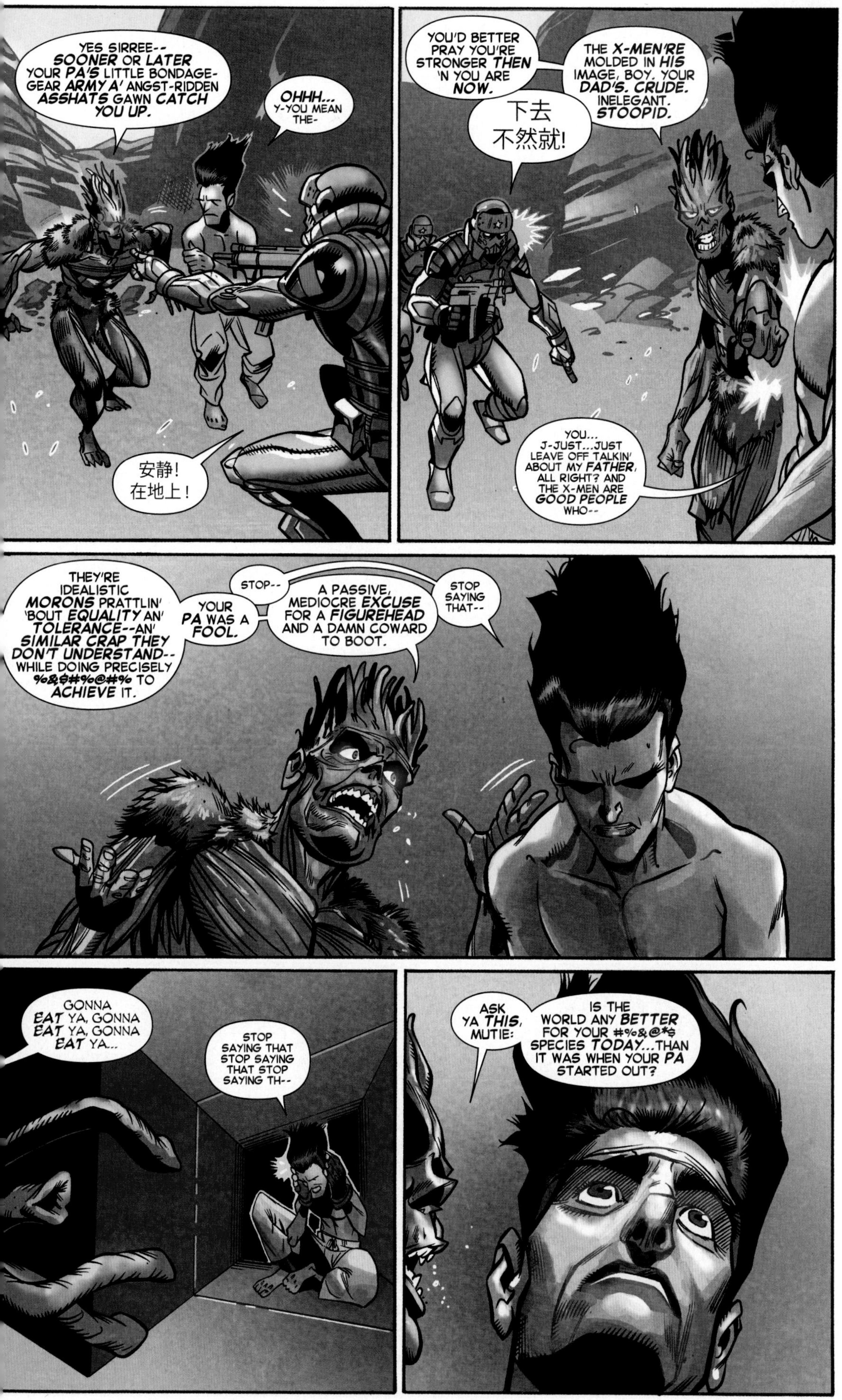
YES SIRREE-- SOONER OR LATER YOUR PA'S LITTLE BONDAGE-GEAR ARMY A' ANGST-RIDDEN ASSHATS GAWN CATCH YOU UP.
OHHH... Y-YOU MEAN THE-
安静! 在地上!
YOU'D BETTER PRAY YOU'RE STRONGER THEN 'N YOU ARE NOW.
THE X-MEN'RE MOLDED IN HIS IMAGE, BOY. YOUR DAD'S. CRUDE. INELEGANT. STOOPID.
下去 不然就!
YOU... J-JUST...JUST LEAVE OFF TALKIN' ABOUT MY FATHER, ALL RIGHT? AND THE X-MEN ARE GOOD PEOPLE WHO--
THEY'RE IDEALISTIC MORONS PRATTLIN' 'BOUT EQUALITY AN' TOLERANCE--AN' SIMILAR CRAP THEY DON'T UNDERSTAND--WHILE DOING PRECISELY %&$#%@#% TO ACHIEVE IT.
YOUR PA WAS A FOOL.
STOP--
A PASSIVE, MEDIOCRE EXCUSE FOR A FIGUREHEAD AND A DAMN COWARD TO BOOT.
STOP SAYING THAT--
GONNA EAT YA, GONNA EAT YA, GONNA EAT YA...
STOP SAYING THAT STOP SAYING THAT STOP SAYING TH--
ASK YA THIS, MUTIE:
IS THE WORLD ANY BETTER FOR YOUR #%&@*$ SPECIES TODAY...THAN IT WAS WHEN YOUR PA STARTED OUT?

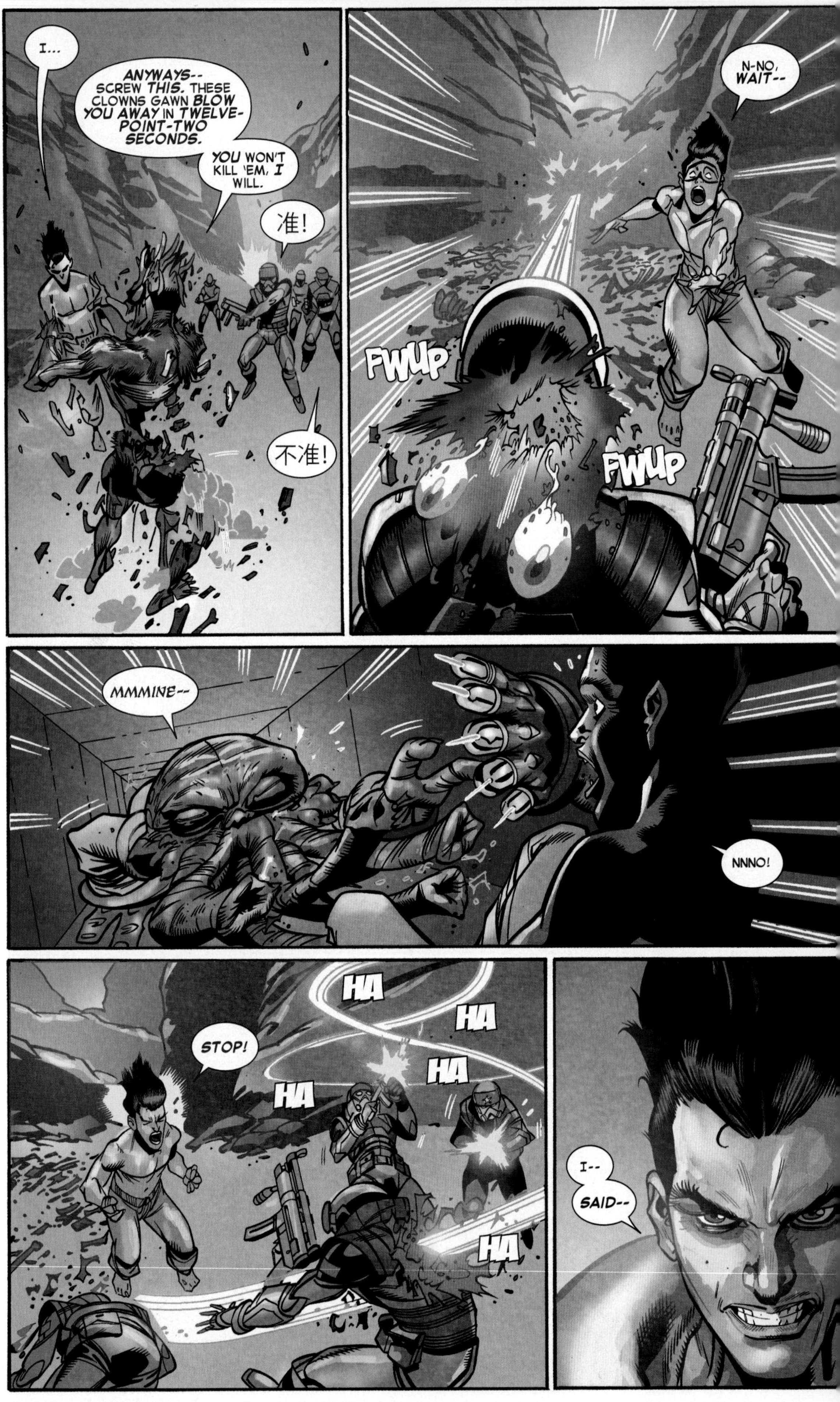
I...
ANYWAYS-- SCREW THIS. THESE CLOWNS GAWN BLOW YOU AWAY IN TWELVE-POINT-TWO SECONDS.
YOU WON'T KILL 'EM, I WILL.
准!
不准!
N-NO, WAIT--
FWUP
FWUP
MMMINE--
NNNO!
STOP!
HA
HA
HA
HA
HA
I--
SAID--

STOP!

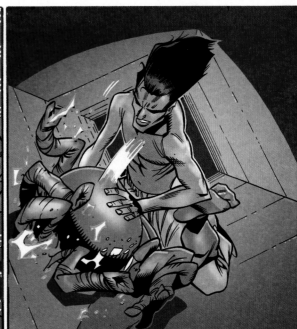

Y.

YOU'RE MEANT TO BE *SCARED.*

YOU'RE MEANT TO BE SCARED OF *YOURSE--*

SLURP

MINE IS THE GIFT OF *TELEPATHY.*

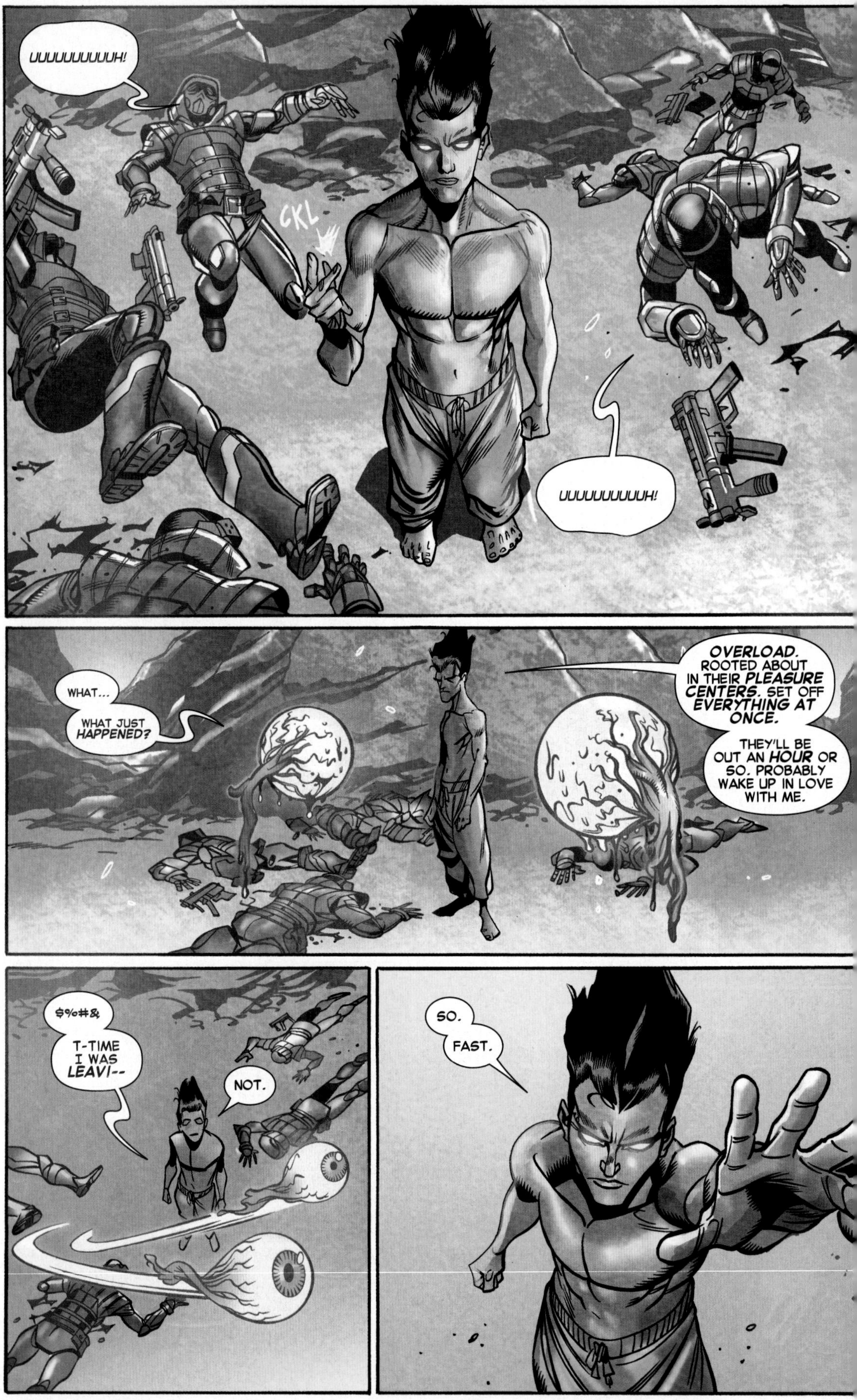
UUUUUUUUUUH!
CKL
UUUUUUUUUUH!
WHAT... WHAT JUST HAPPENED?
OVERLOAD. ROOTED ABOUT IN THEIR PLEASURE CENTERS. SET OFF EVERYTHING AT ONCE.
THEY'LL BE OUT AN HOUR OR SO. PROBABLY WAKE UP IN LOVE WITH ME.
$%#&
T-TIME I WAS LEAVI--
NOT.
SO.
FAST.

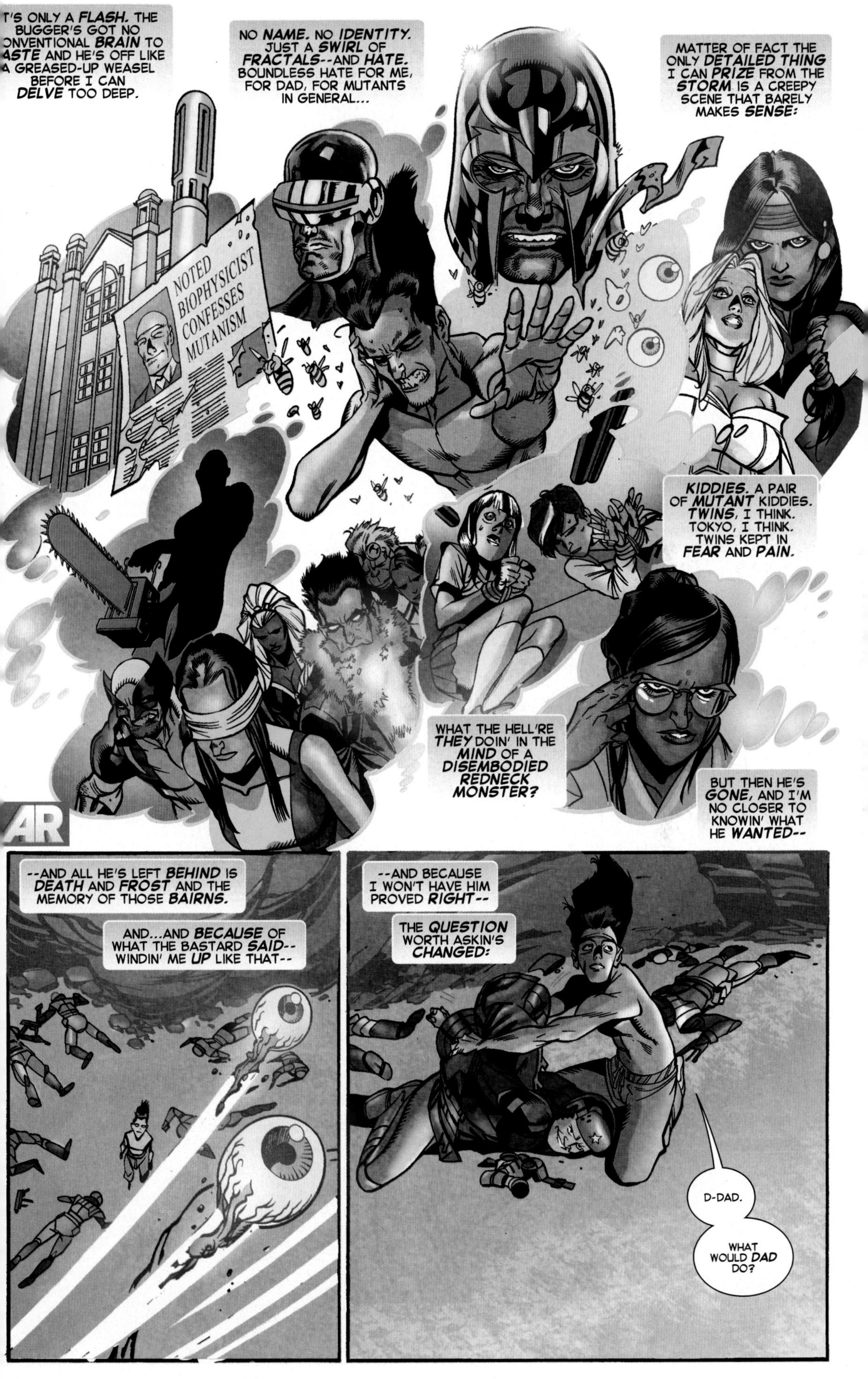
T'S ONLY A FLASH. THE BUGGER'S GOT NO ONVENTIONAL BRAIN TO ASTE AND HE'S OFF LIKE A GREASED-UP WEASEL BEFORE I CAN DELVE TOO DEEP.
NO NAME. NO IDENTITY. JUST A SWIRL OF FRACTALS--AND HATE. BOUNDLESS HATE FOR ME, FOR DAD, FOR MUTANTS IN GENERAL...
MATTER OF FACT THE ONLY DETAILED THING I CAN PRIZE FROM THE STORM IS A CREEPY SCENE THAT BARELY MAKES SENSE:
NOTED BIOPHYSICIST CONFESSES MUTANISM
KIDDIES. A PAIR OF MUTANT KIDDIES. TWINS, I THINK. TOKYO, I THINK. TWINS KEPT IN FEAR AND PAIN.
WHAT THE HELL'RE THEY DOIN' IN THE MIND OF A DISEMBODIED REDNECK MONSTER?
BUT THEN HE'S GONE, AND I'M NO CLOSER TO KNOWIN' WHAT HE WANTED--
--AND ALL HE'S LEFT BEHIND IS DEATH AND FROST AND THE MEMORY OF THOSE BAIRNS.
AND...AND BECAUSE OF WHAT THE BASTARD SAID--WINDIN' ME UP LIKE THAT--
--AND BECAUSE I WON'T HAVE HIM PROVED RIGHT--
THE QUESTION WORTH ASKIN'S CHANGED:
D-DAD.
WHAT WOULD DAD DO?

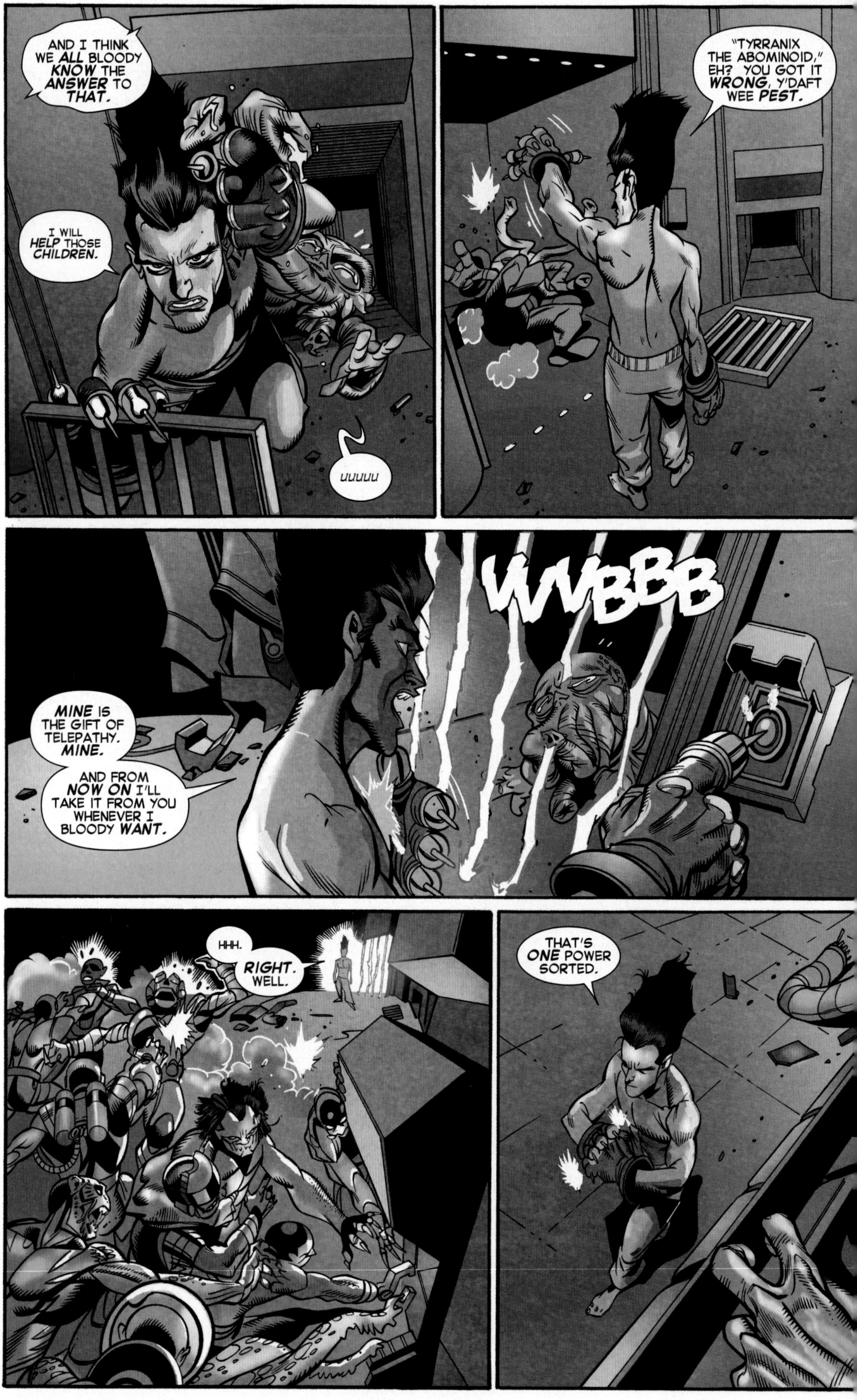
AND I THINK WE ALL BLOODY KNOW THE ANSWER TO THAT.
I WILL HELP THOSE CHILDREN.
uuuuu
"TYRRANIX THE ABOMINOID," EH? YOU GOT IT WRONG, Y'DAFT WEE PEST.
VVVBBB
MINE IS THE GIFT OF TELEPATHY. MINE.
AND FROM NOW ON I'LL TAKE IT FROM YOU WHENEVER I BLOODY WANT.
HHH. RIGHT. WELL.
THAT'S ONE POWER SORTED.

JUST A COUPLA HUNDRED TO GO.

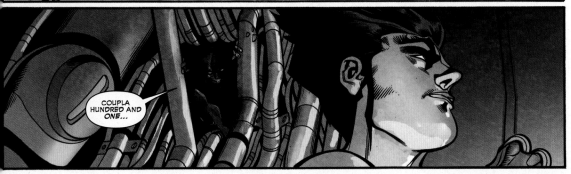

COUPLA HUNDRED AND ONE...

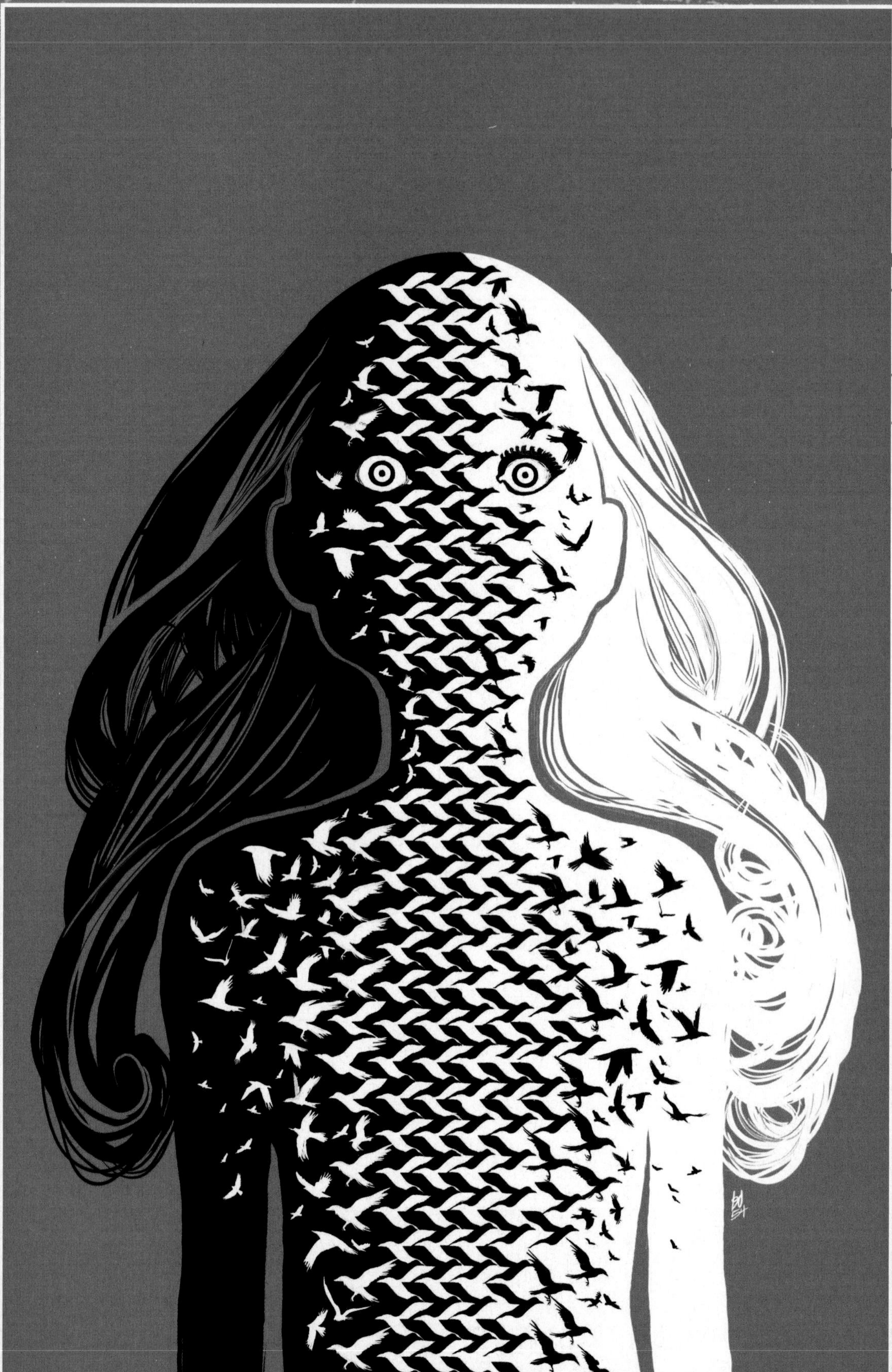

THREE

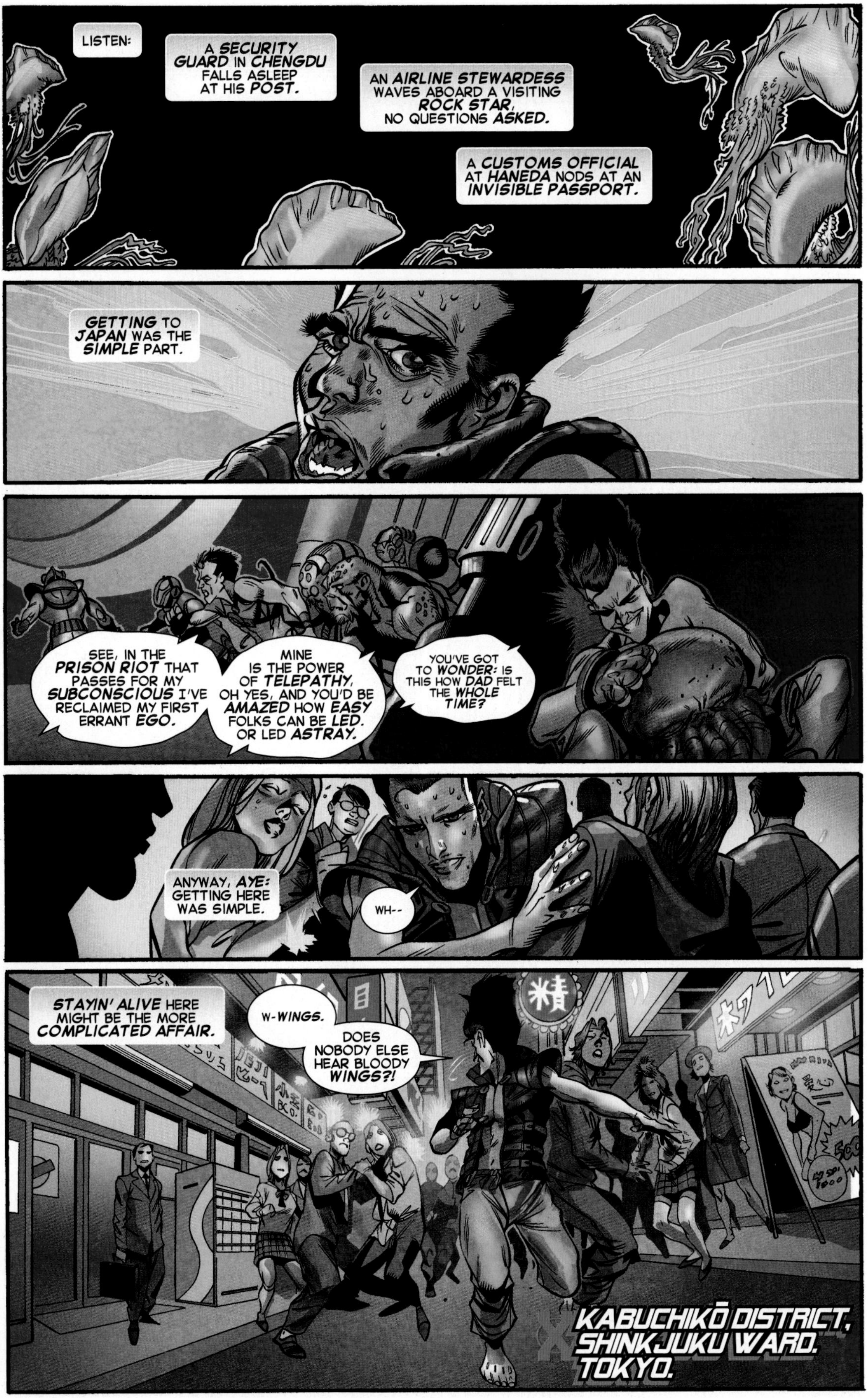
LISTEN:
A SECURITY GUARD IN CHENGDU FALLS ASLEEP AT HIS POST.
AN AIRLINE STEWARDESS WAVES ABOARD A VISITING ROCK STAR, NO QUESTIONS ASKED.
A CUSTOMS OFFICIAL AT HANEDA NODS AT AN INVISIBLE PASSPORT.
GETTING TO JAPAN WAS THE SIMPLE PART.
SEE, IN THE PRISON RIOT THAT PASSES FOR MY SUBCONSCIOUS I'VE RECLAIMED MY FIRST ERRANT EGO.
MINE IS THE POWER OF TELEPATHY, OH YES, AND YOU'D BE AMAZED HOW EASY FOLKS CAN BE LED. OR LED ASTRAY.
YOU'VE GOT TO WONDER: IS THIS HOW DAD FELT THE WHOLE TIME?
ANYWAY, AYE: GETTING HERE WAS SIMPLE.
WH--
STAYIN' ALIVE HERE MIGHT BE THE MORE COMPLICATED AFFAIR.
W-WINGS.
DOES NOBODY ELSE HEAR BLOODY WINGS?!
KABUCHIKŌ DISTRICT, SHINKJUKU WARD. TOKYO.

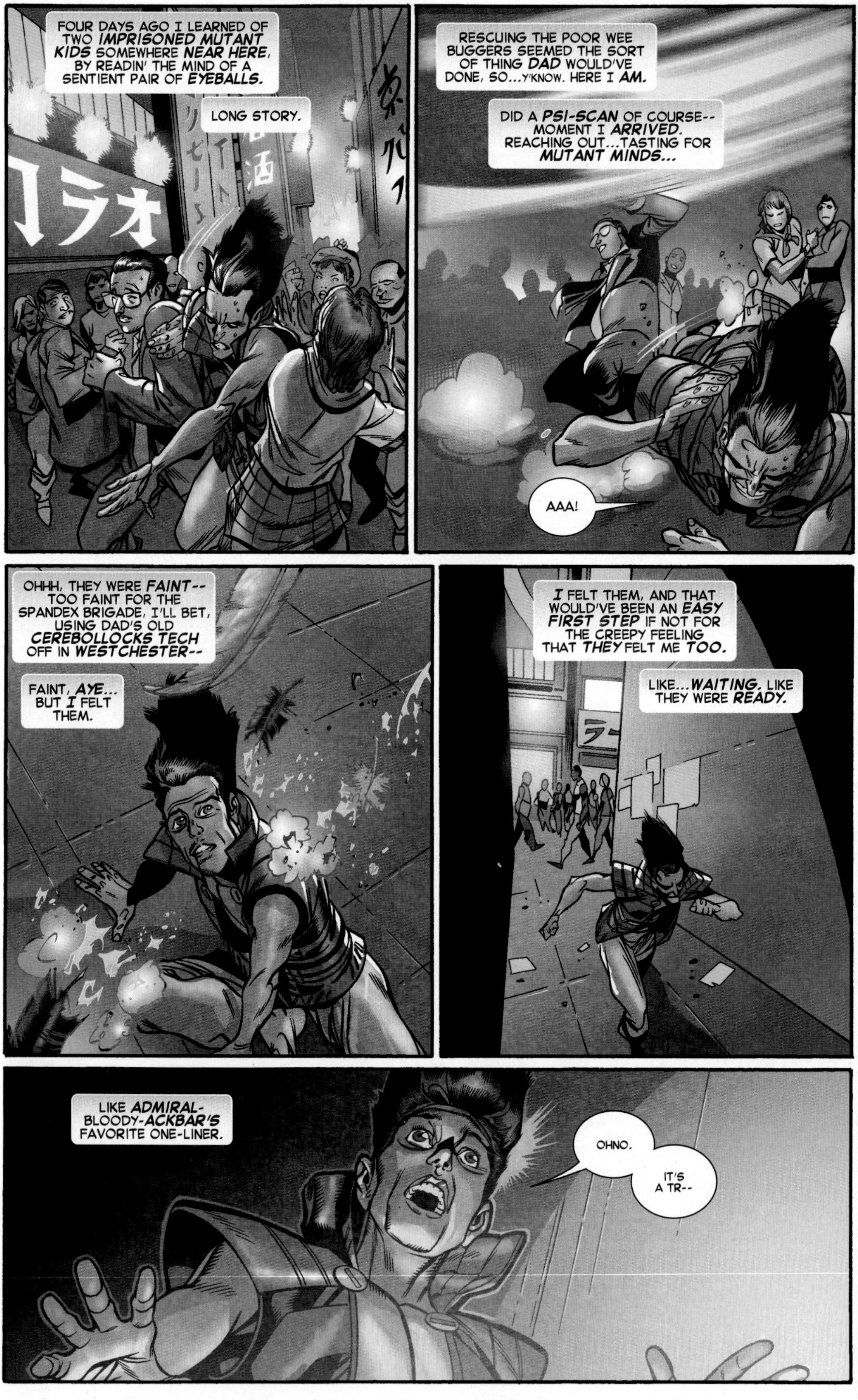
FOUR DAYS AGO I LEARNED OF TWO IMPRISONED MUTANT KIDS SOMEWHERE NEAR HERE, BY READIN' THE MIND OF A SENTIENT PAIR OF EYEBALLS.
LONG STORY.
RESCUING THE POOR WEE BUGGERS SEEMED THE SORT OF THING DAD WOULD'VE DONE, SO...Y'KNOW. HERE I AM.
DID A PSI-SCAN OF COURSE-- MOMENT I ARRIVED. REACHING OUT...TASTING FOR MUTANT MINDS...
AAA!
OHHH, THEY WERE FAINT-- TOO FAINT FOR THE SPANDEX BRIGADE, I'LL BET, USING DAD'S OLD CEREBOLLOCKS TECH OFF IN WESTCHESTER--
FAINT, AYE... BUT I FELT THEM.
I FELT THEM, AND THAT WOULD'VE BEEN AN EASY FIRST STEP IF NOT FOR THE CREEPY FEELING THAT THEY FELT ME TOO.
LIKE...WAITING. LIKE THEY WERE READY.
LIKE ADMIRAL-BLOODY-ACKBAR'S FAVORITE ONE-LINER.
OHNO.
IT'S A TR--

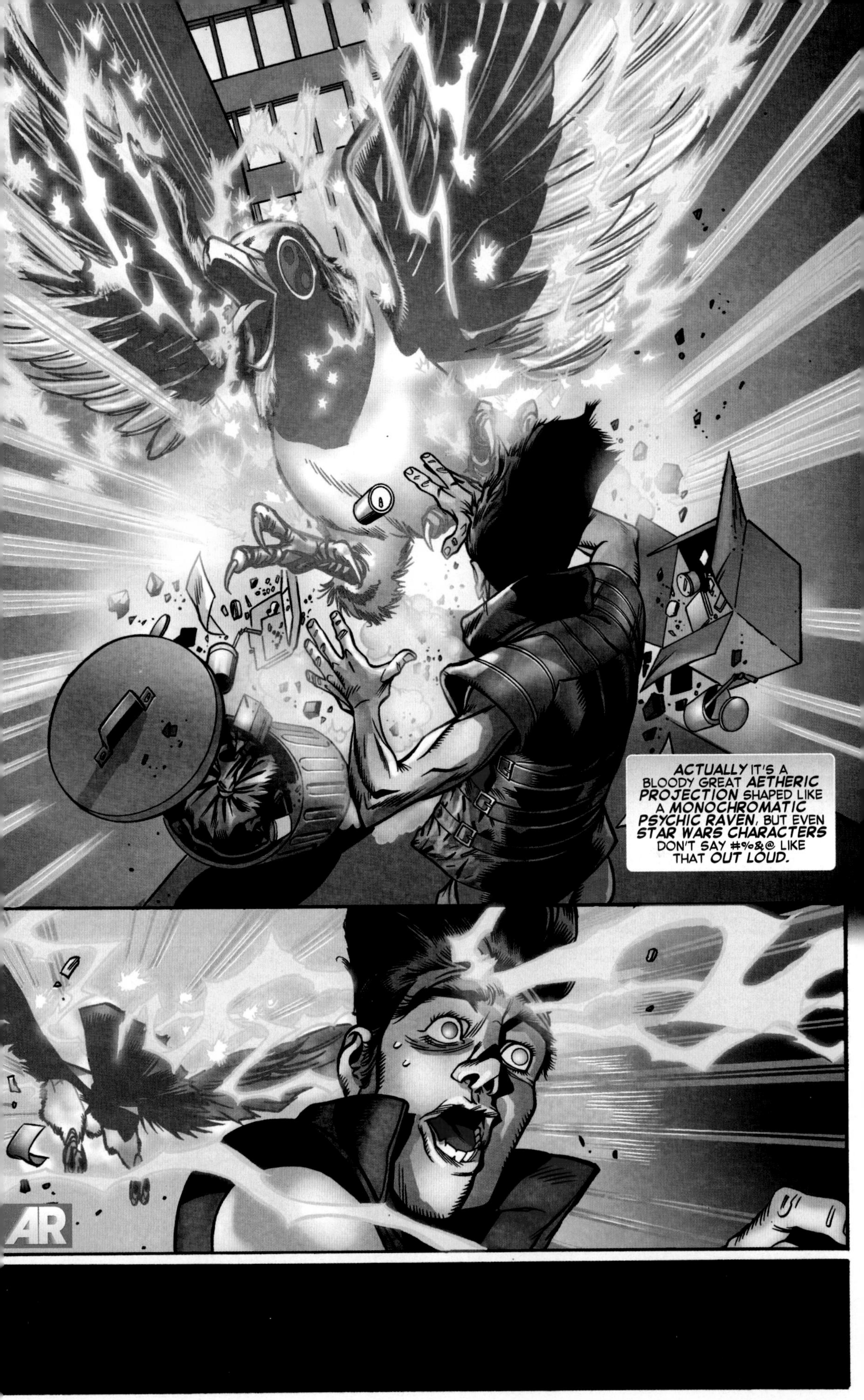
ACTUALLY IT'S A BLOODY GREAT AETHERIC PROJECTION SHAPED LIKE A MONOCHROMATIC PSYCHIC RAVEN, BUT EVEN STAR WARS CHARACTERS DON'T SAY #%&@ LIKE THAT OUT LOUD.

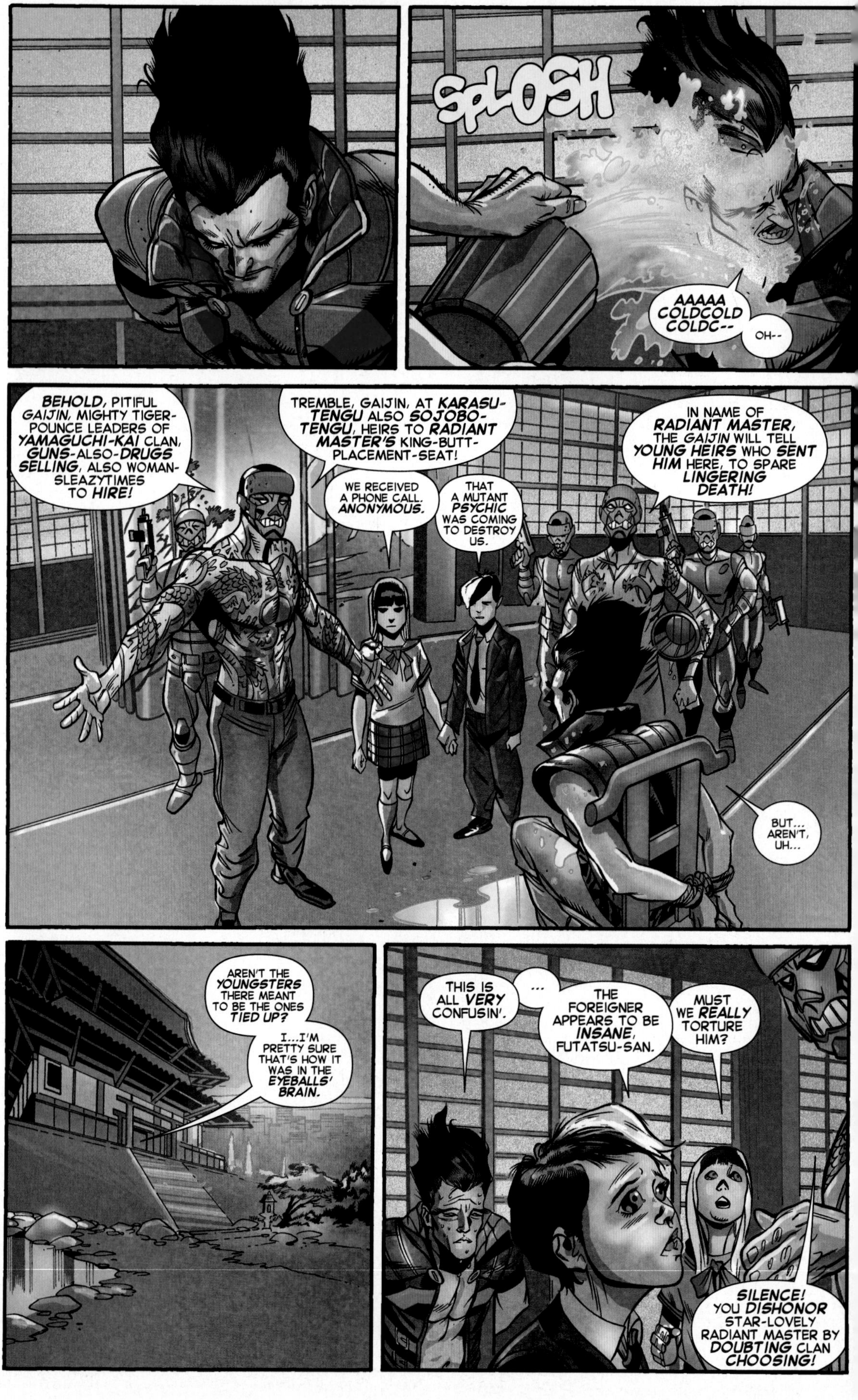

SPLOSH
AAAAA COLDCOLD COLDC--
OH--
BEHOLD, PITIFUL GAIJIN, MIGHTY TIGER-POUNCE LEADERS OF YAMAGUCHI-KAI CLAN, GUNS-ALSO-DRUGS SELLING, ALSO WOMAN-SLEAZYTIMES TO HIRE!
TREMBLE, GAIJIN, AT KARASU-TENGU ALSO SOJOBO-TENGU, HEIRS TO RADIANT MASTER'S KING-BUTT-PLACEMENT-SEAT!
WE RECEIVED A PHONE CALL. ANONYMOUS.
THAT A MUTANT PSYCHIC WAS COMING TO DESTROY US.
IN NAME OF RADIANT MASTER, THE GAIJIN WILL TELL YOUNG HEIRS WHO SENT HIM HERE, TO SPARE LINGERING DEATH!
BUT... AREN'T, UH...
AREN'T THE YOUNGSTERS THERE MEANT TO BE THE ONES TIED UP?
I...I'M PRETTY SURE THAT'S HOW IT WAS IN THE EYEBALLS' BRAIN.
THIS IS ALL VERY CONFUSIN'.
...
THE FOREIGNER APPEARS TO BE INSANE, FUTATSU-SAN.
MUST WE REALLY TORTURE HIM?
SILENCE! YOU DISHONOR STAR-LOVELY RADIANT MASTER BY DOUBTING CLAN CHOOSING!

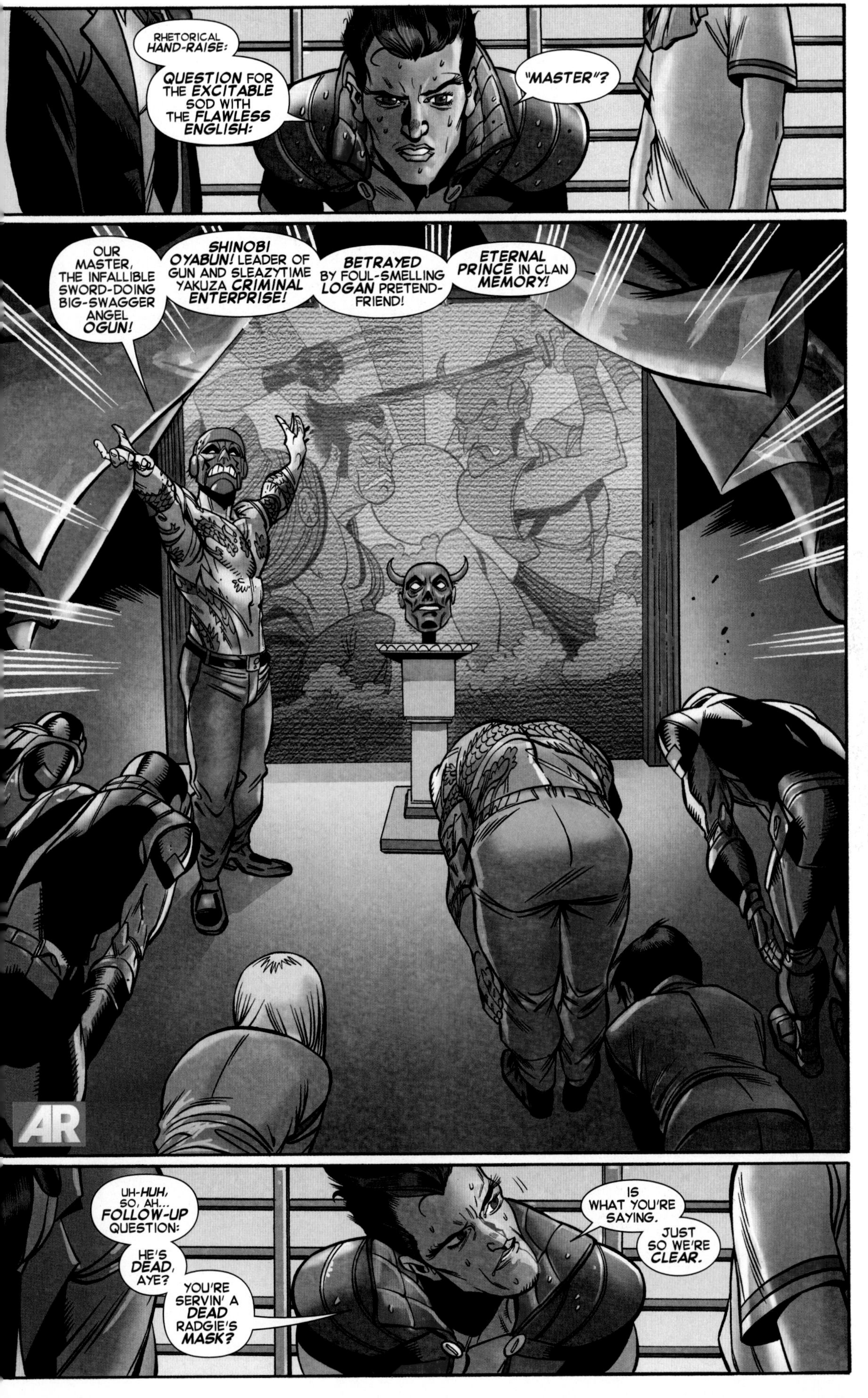
RHETORICAL HAND-RAISE:
QUESTION FOR THE EXCITABLE SOD WITH THE FLAWLESS ENGLISH:
"MASTER"?
OUR MASTER, THE INFALLIBLE SWORD-DOING BIG-SWAGGER ANGEL OGUN!
SHINOBI OYABUN! LEADER OF GUN AND SLEAZYTIME YAKUZA CRIMINAL ENTERPRISE!
BETRAYED BY FOUL-SMELLING LOGAN PRETEND-FRIEND!
ETERNAL PRINCE IN CLAN MEMORY!
UH-HUH, SO, AH... FOLLOW-UP QUESTION:
HE'S DEAD, AYE?
YOU'RE SERVIN' A DEAD RADGIE'S MASK?
IS WHAT YOU'RE SAYING.
JUST SO WE'RE CLEAR.

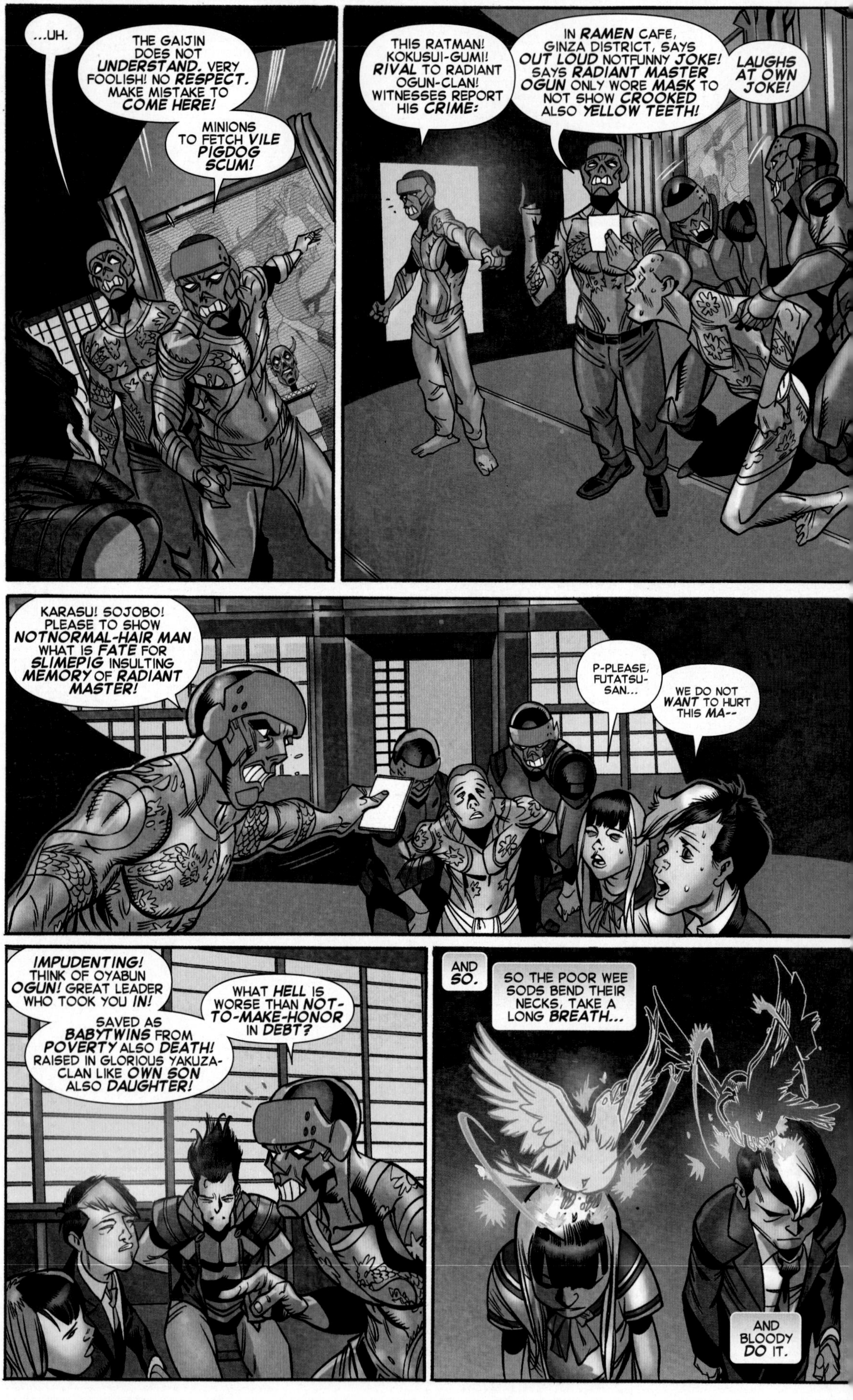

...UH.
THE GAIJIN DOES NOT UNDERSTAND. VERY FOOLISH! NO RESPECT. MAKE MISTAKE TO COME HERE!
MINIONS TO FETCH VILE PIGDOG SCUM!
THIS RATMAN! KOKUSUI-GUMI! RIVAL TO RADIANT OGUN-CLAN! WITNESSES REPORT HIS CRIME:
IN RAMEN CAFE, GINZA DISTRICT, SAYS OUT LOUD NOTFUNNY JOKE! SAYS RADIANT MASTER OGUN ONLY WORE MASK TO NOT SHOW CROOKED ALSO YELLOW TEETH!
LAUGHS AT OWN JOKE!
KARASU! SOJOBO! PLEASE TO SHOW NOTNORMAL-HAIR MAN WHAT IS FATE FOR SLIMEPIG INSULTING MEMORY OF RADIANT MASTER!
P-PLEASE, FUTATSU-SAN...
WE DO NOT WANT TO HURT THIS MA--
IMPUDENTING! THINK OF OYABUN OGUN! GREAT LEADER WHO TOOK YOU IN!
SAVED AS BABYTWINS FROM POVERTY ALSO DEATH! RAISED IN GLORIOUS YAKUZA-CLAN LIKE OWN SON ALSO DAUGHTER!
WHAT HELL IS WORSE THAN NOT-TO-MAKE-HONOR IN DEBT?
AND SO.
SO THE POOR WEE SODS BEND THEIR NECKS, TAKE A LONG BREATH...
AND BLOODY DO IT.

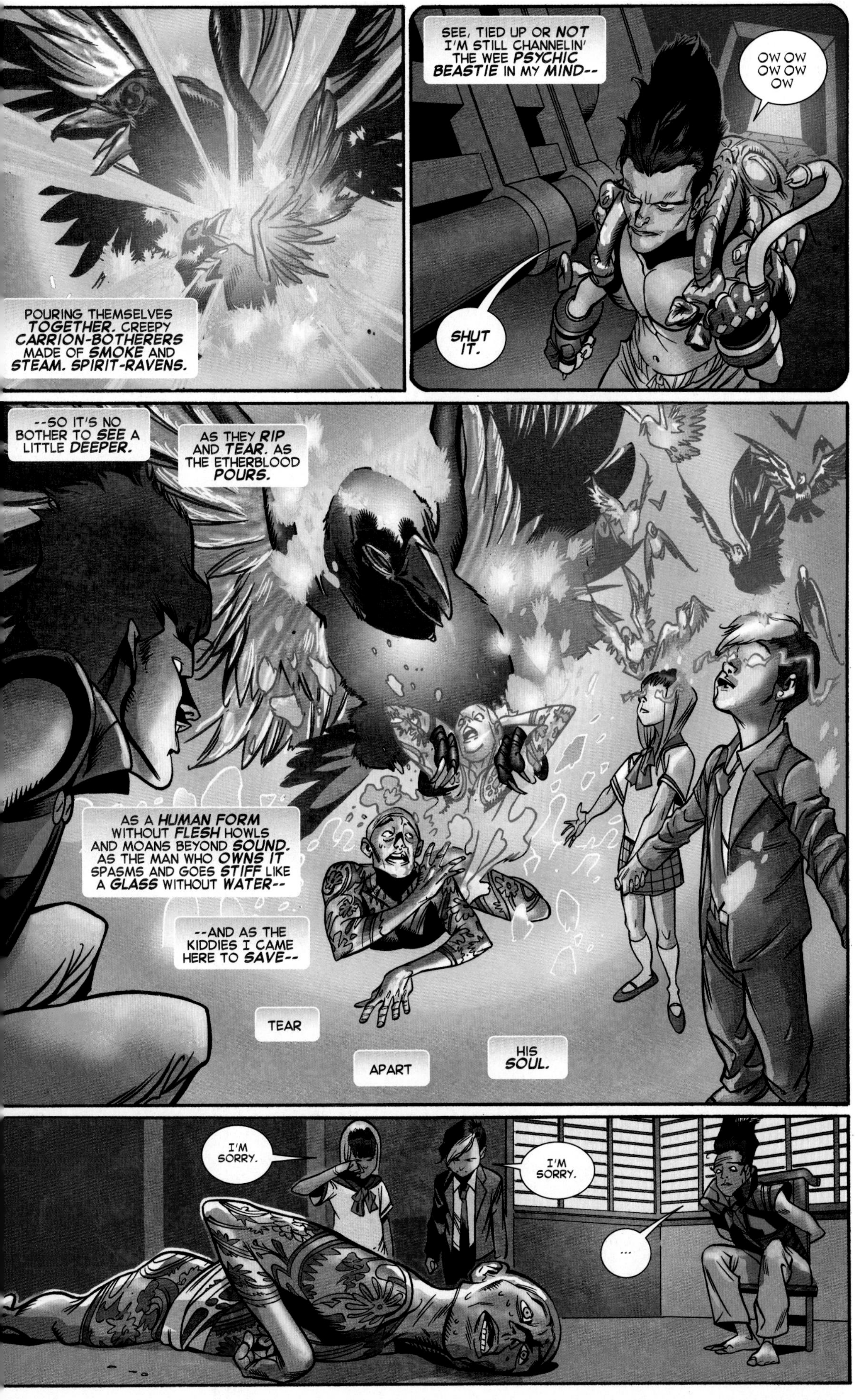
POURING THEMSELVES TOGETHER. CREEPY CARRION-BOTHERERS MADE OF SMOKE AND STEAM. SPIRIT-RAVENS.
SEE, TIED UP OR NOT I'M STILL CHANNELIN' THE WEE PSYCHIC BEASTIE IN MY MIND--
OW OW OW OW OW
SHUT IT.
--SO IT'S NO BOTHER TO SEE A LITTLE DEEPER.
AS THEY RIP AND TEAR. AS THE ETHERBLOOD POURS.
AS A HUMAN FORM WITHOUT FLESH HOWLS AND MOANS BEYOND SOUND. AS THE MAN WHO OWNS IT SPASMS AND GOES STIFF LIKE A GLASS WITHOUT WATER--
--AND AS THE KIDDIES I CAME HERE TO SAVE--
TEAR
APART
HIS SOUL.
I'M SORRY.
I'M SORRY.
...

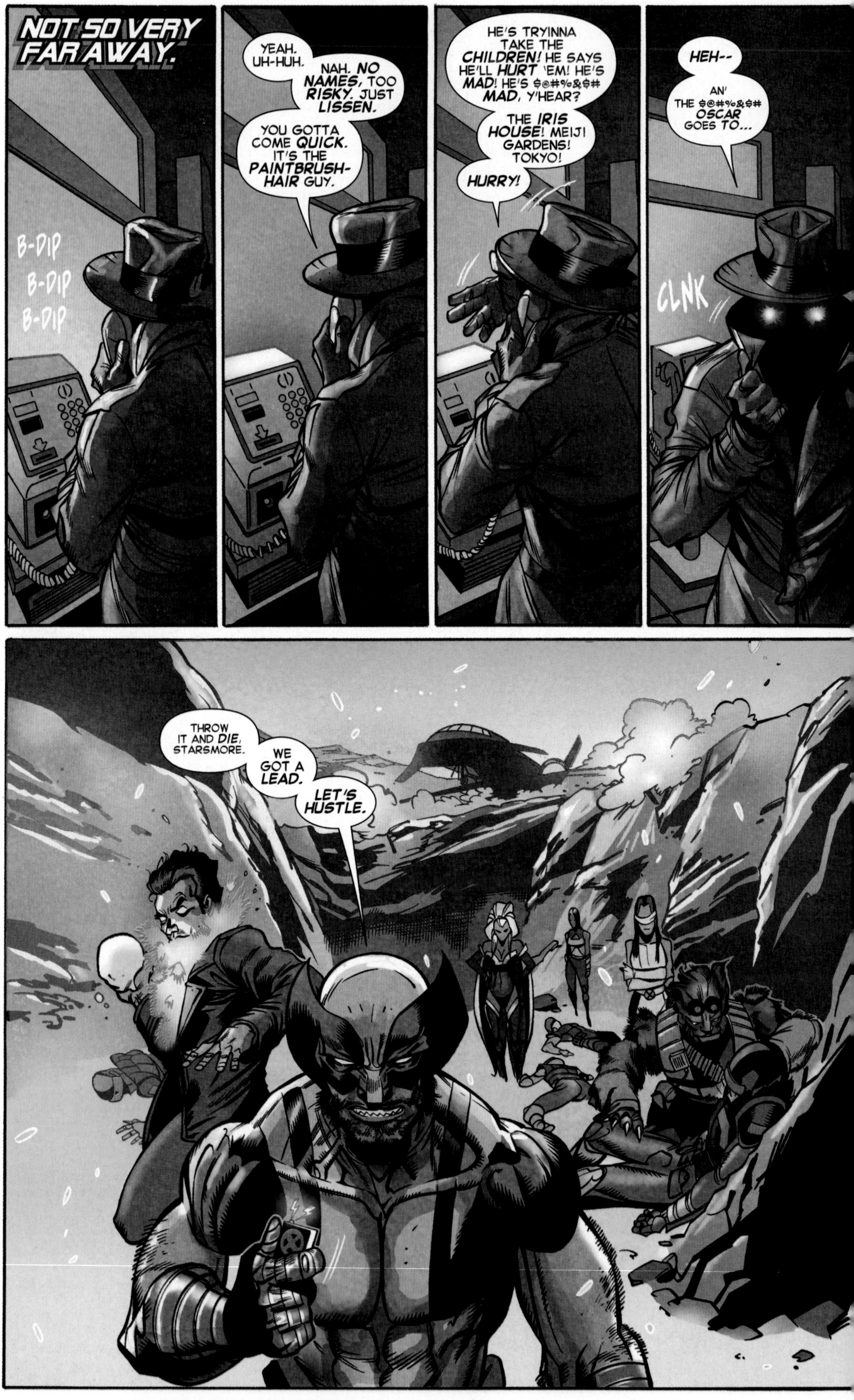
NOT SO VERY FAR AWAY.
B-DIP
B-DIP
B-DIP
YEAH. UH-HUH.
NAH. NO NAMES, TOO RISKY. JUST LISSEN.
YOU GOTTA COME QUICK. IT'S THE PAINTBRUSH-HAIR GUY.
HE'S TRYINNA TAKE THE CHILDREN! HE SAYS HE'LL HURT 'EM! HE'S MAD! HE'S $@#%&$# MAD, Y'HEAR?
THE IRIS HOUSE! MEIJI GARDENS! TOKYO!
HURRY!
HEH--
AN' THE $@#%&$# OSCAR GOES TO...
CLNK
THROW IT AND DIE, STARSMORE.
WE GOT A LEAD.
LET'S HUSTLE.

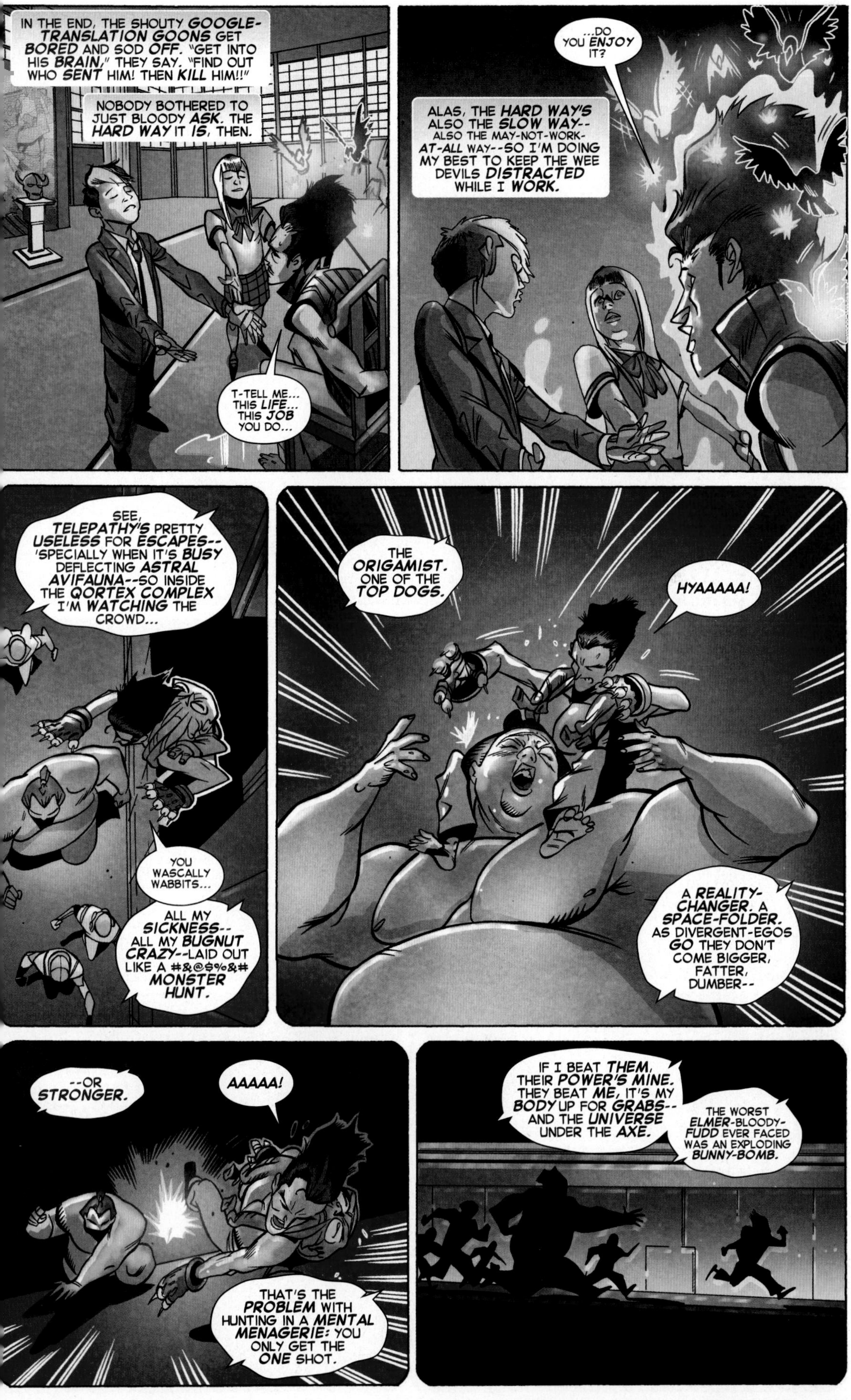
IN THE END, THE SHOUTY GOOGLE-TRANSLATION GOONS GET BORED AND SOD OFF. "GET INTO HIS BRAIN," THEY SAY. "FIND OUT WHO SENT HIM! THEN KILL HIM!!"
NOBODY BOTHERED TO JUST BLOODY ASK. THE HARD WAY IT IS, THEN.
T-TELL ME... THIS LIFE... THIS JOB YOU DO...
...DO YOU ENJOY IT?
ALAS, THE HARD WAY'S ALSO THE SLOW WAY-- ALSO THE MAY-NOT-WORK-AT-ALL WAY--SO I'M DOING MY BEST TO KEEP THE WEE DEVILS DISTRACTED WHILE I WORK.
SEE, TELEPATHY'S PRETTY USELESS FOR ESCAPES-- 'SPECIALLY WHEN IT'S BUSY DEFLECTING ASTRAL AVIFAUNA--SO INSIDE THE QORTEX COMPLEX I'M WATCHING THE CROWD...
YOU WASCALLY WABBITS...
ALL MY SICKNESS-- ALL MY BUGNUT CRAZY--LAID OUT LIKE A #&@$%&# MONSTER HUNT.
THE ORIGAMIST. ONE OF THE TOP DOGS.
HYAAAAA!
A REALITY-CHANGER. A SPACE-FOLDER. AS DIVERGENT-EGOS GO THEY DON'T COME BIGGER, FATTER, DUMBER--
--OR STRONGER.
AAAAA!
THAT'S THE PROBLEM WITH HUNTING IN A MENTAL MENAGERIE: YOU ONLY GET THE ONE SHOT.
IF I BEAT THEM, THEIR POWER'S MINE. THEY BEAT ME, IT'S MY BODY UP FOR GRABS-- AND THE UNIVERSE UNDER THE AXE.
THE WORST ELMER-BLOODY-FUDD EVER FACED WAS AN EXPLODING BUNNY-BOMB.

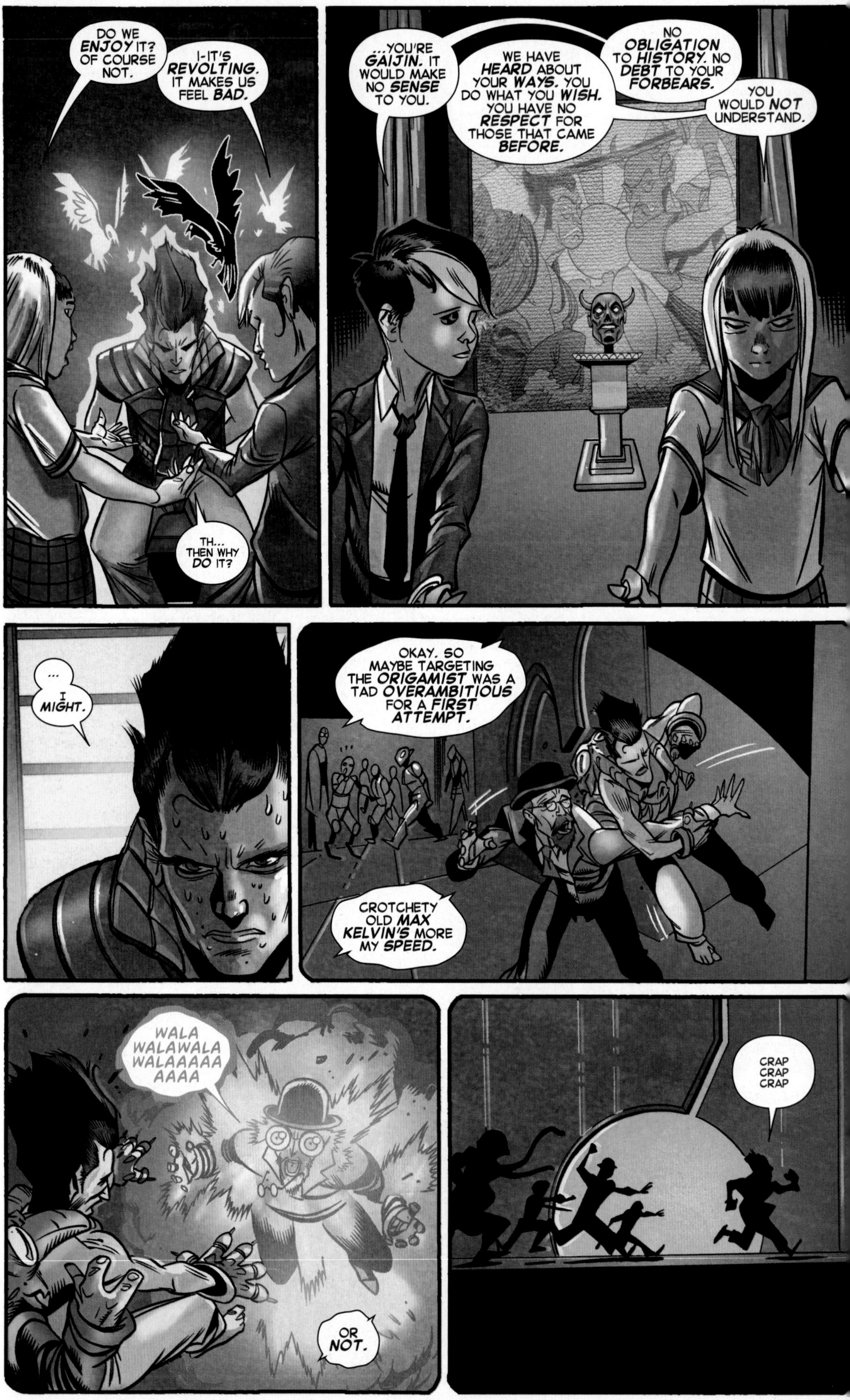

DO WE ENJOY IT? OF COURSE NOT.
I-IT'S REVOLTING. IT MAKES US FEEL BAD.
TH... THEN WHY DO IT?
...YOU'RE GAIJIN. IT WOULD MAKE NO SENSE TO YOU.
WE HAVE HEARD ABOUT YOUR WAYS. YOU DO WHAT YOU WISH. YOU HAVE NO RESPECT FOR THOSE THAT CAME BEFORE.
NO OBLIGATION TO HISTORY. NO DEBT TO YOUR FORBEARS.
YOU WOULD NOT UNDERSTAND.
... I MIGHT.
OKAY. SO MAYBE TARGETING THE ORIGAMIST WAS A TAD OVERAMBITIOUS FOR A FIRST ATTEMPT.
CROTCHETY OLD MAX KELVIN'S MORE MY SPEED.
WALA WALAWALA WALAAAAAA AAAA
OR NOT.
CRAP CRAP CRAP

L-LISTEN, *PLEASE.* SOMEONE'S WORKING *AGAINST* ME HERE. I'M NO *THREAT* TO YOU OR YOUR BLOODY *CLAN.* I...I CAME HERE TO *HELP.*

S-SEE, MY *FATHER*--HE'S *DEAD* NOW--HE LOOKED *AFTER* PEOPLE LIKE YOU.

PEOPLE LIKE *US.* S-SO I JUST THOUGHT I'D...Y'KNOW...

WE'RE VERY *CLOSE* TO *BREAKING IN,* MR. HALLER. WE CAN ALREADY *TASTE* YOUR *CONTRADICTIONS.* FOR INSTANCE:

IN WHAT WAY DID YOUR FATHER "LOOK AFTER" *YOU,* MR. HALLER?

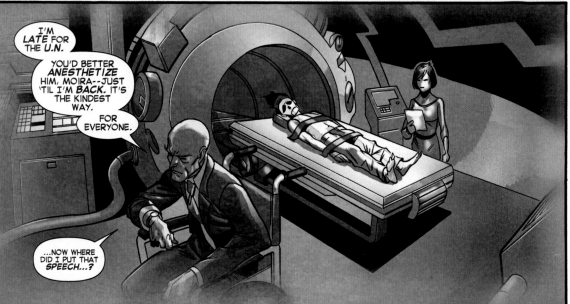

I'M *LATE* FOR THE *U.N.*

YOU'D BETTER *ANESTHETIZE* HIM, MOIRA--JUST 'TIL I'M *BACK.* IT'S THE *KINDEST* WAY. FOR *EVERYONE.*

...NOW WHERE DID I PUT THAT *SPEECH...?*

ATTEMPT *3.* TIME TO GET *SNEAKY.*

THE *CHRONODON* STUMBLES INTO A *DAVIDBAIT* TRAP.

...AND PROMPTLY STUMBLES DIRECTLY BACK *OUT.*

I CAN FEEL *WINGS* BEATING ON THE *WALLS* OF THE *PRISON.*

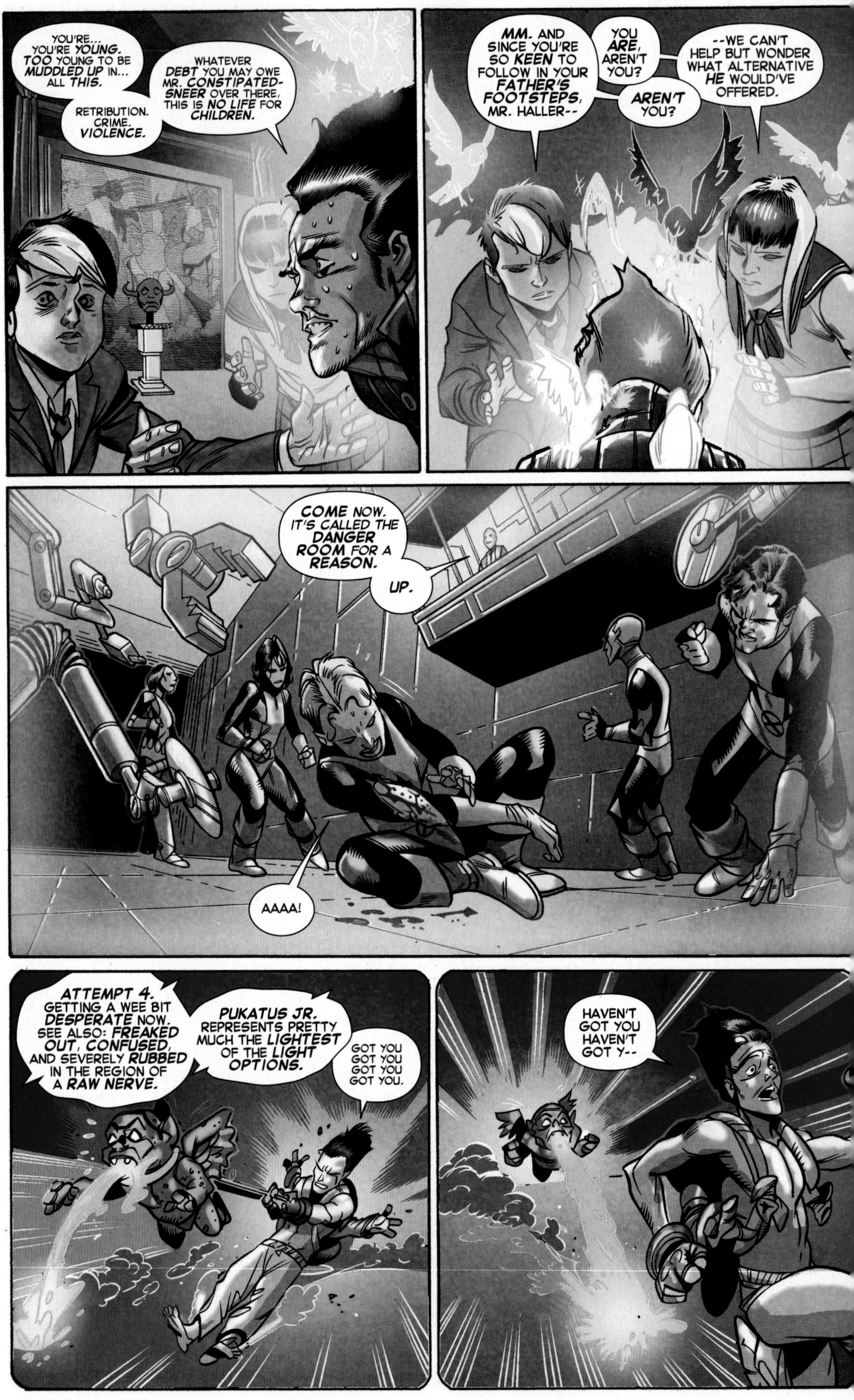
YOU'RE... YOU'RE YOUNG. TOO YOUNG TO BE MUDDLED UP IN... ALL THIS.
RETRIBUTION. CRIME. VIOLENCE.
WHATEVER DEBT YOU MAY OWE MR. CONSTIPATED-SNEER OVER THERE, THIS IS NO LIFE FOR CHILDREN.
MM. AND SINCE YOU'RE SO KEEN TO FOLLOW IN YOUR FATHER'S FOOTSTEPS, MR. HALLER--
YOU ARE, AREN'T YOU?
AREN'T YOU?
--WE CAN'T HELP BUT WONDER WHAT ALTERNATIVE HE WOULD'VE OFFERED.
COME NOW. IT'S CALLED THE DANGER ROOM FOR A REASON.
UP.
AAAA!
ATTEMPT 4. GETTING A WEE BIT DESPERATE NOW. SEE ALSO: FREAKED OUT, CONFUSED, AND SEVERELY RUBBED IN THE REGION OF A RAW NERVE.
PUKATUS JR. REPRESENTS PRETTY MUCH THE LIGHTEST OF THE LIGHT OPTIONS.
GOT YOU GOT YOU GOT YOU GOT YOU.
HAVEN'T GOT YOU HAVEN'T GOT Y--

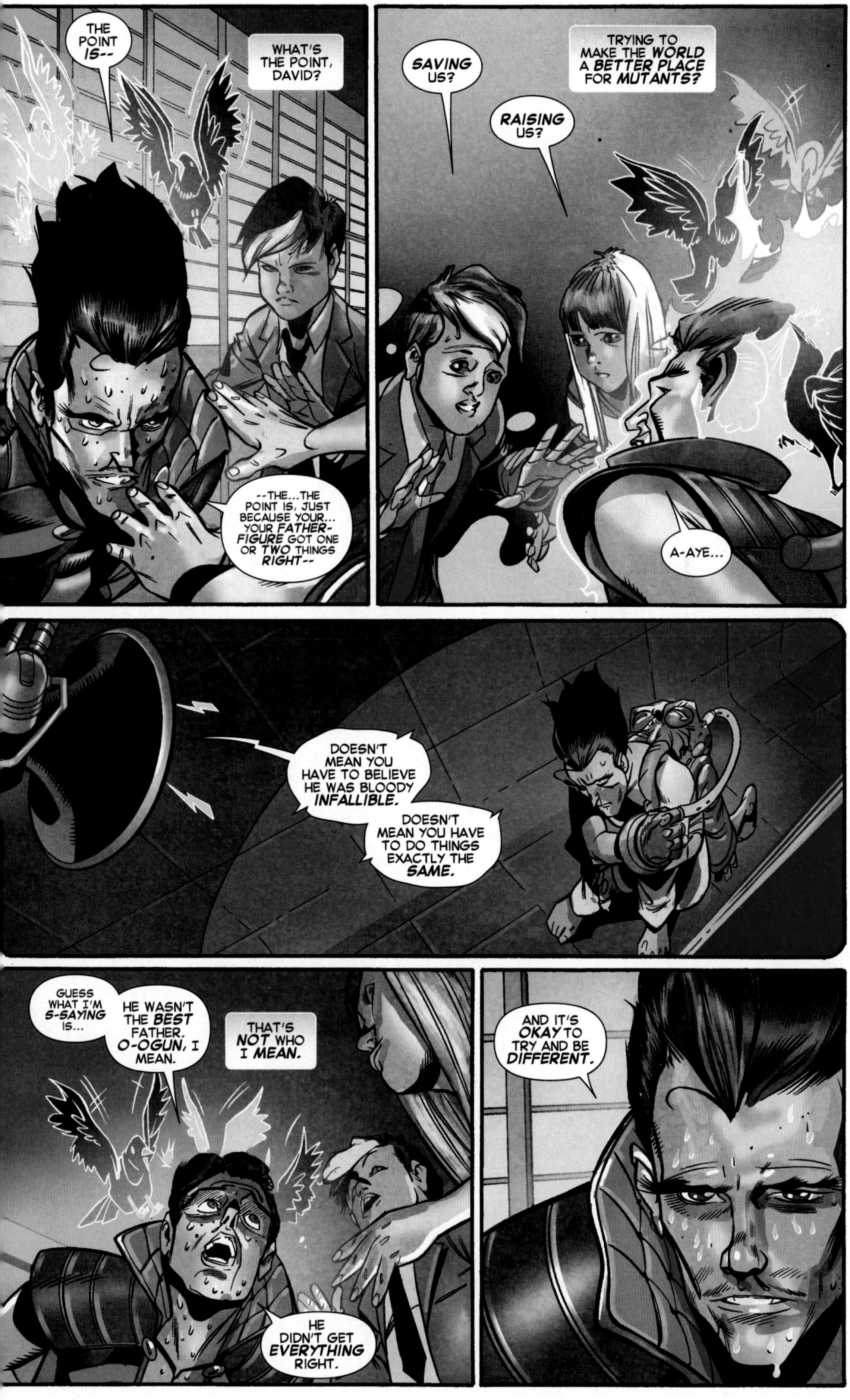
THE POINT IS--
WHAT'S THE POINT, DAVID?
--THE...THE POINT IS, JUST BECAUSE YOUR... YOUR FATHER-FIGURE GOT ONE OR TWO THINGS RIGHT--
SAVING US?
RAISING US?
TRYING TO MAKE THE WORLD A BETTER PLACE FOR MUTANTS?
A-AYE...
DOESN'T MEAN YOU HAVE TO BELIEVE HE WAS BLOODY INFALLIBLE.
DOESN'T MEAN YOU HAVE TO DO THINGS EXACTLY THE SAME.
GUESS WHAT I'M S-SAYING IS...
HE WASN'T THE BEST FATHER. O-OGUN, I MEAN.
THAT'S NOT WHO I MEAN.
HE DIDN'T GET EVERYTHING RIGHT.
AND IT'S OKAY TO TRY AND BE DIFFERENT.

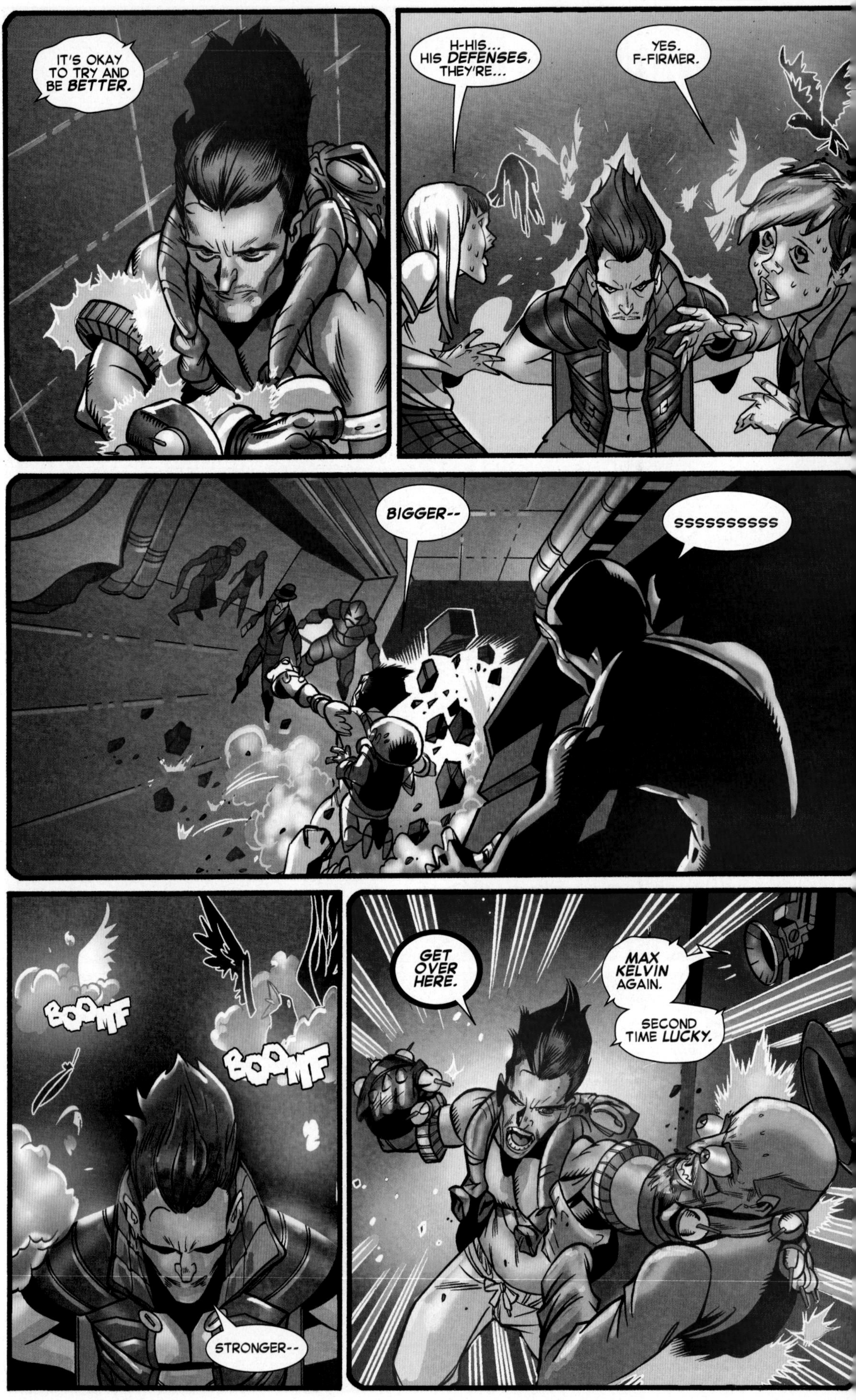
IT'S OKAY TO TRY AND BE BETTER.
H-HIS... HIS DEFENSES, THEY'RE...
YES. F-FIRMER.
BIGGER--
SSSSSSSSSS
BOOMF
BOOMF
STRONGER--
GET OVER HERE.
MAX KELVIN AGAIN.
SECOND TIME LUCKY.

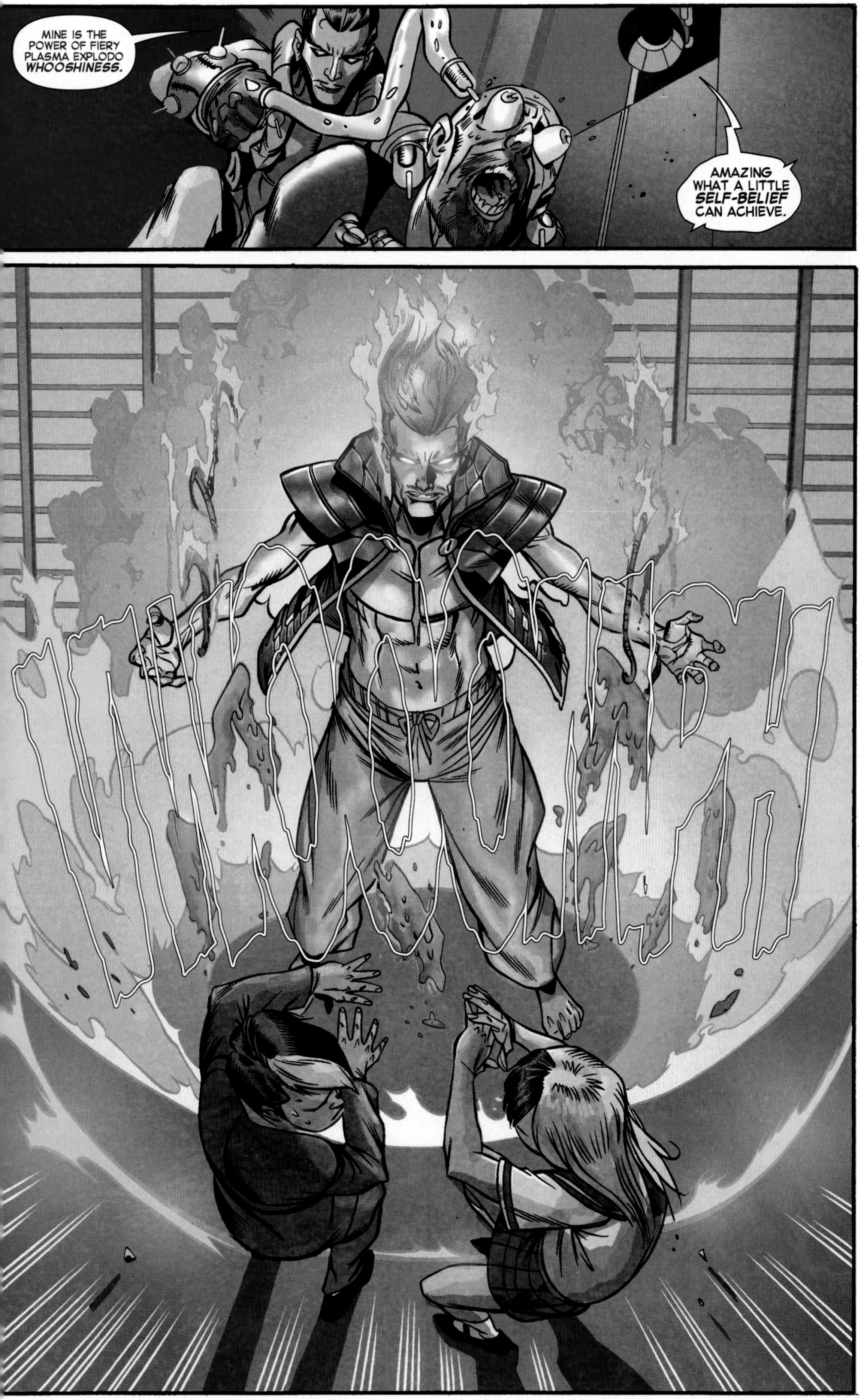
MINE IS THE POWER OF FIERY PLASMA EXPLODO WHOOSHINESS.
AMAZING WHAT A LITTLE SELF-BELIEF CAN ACHIEVE.

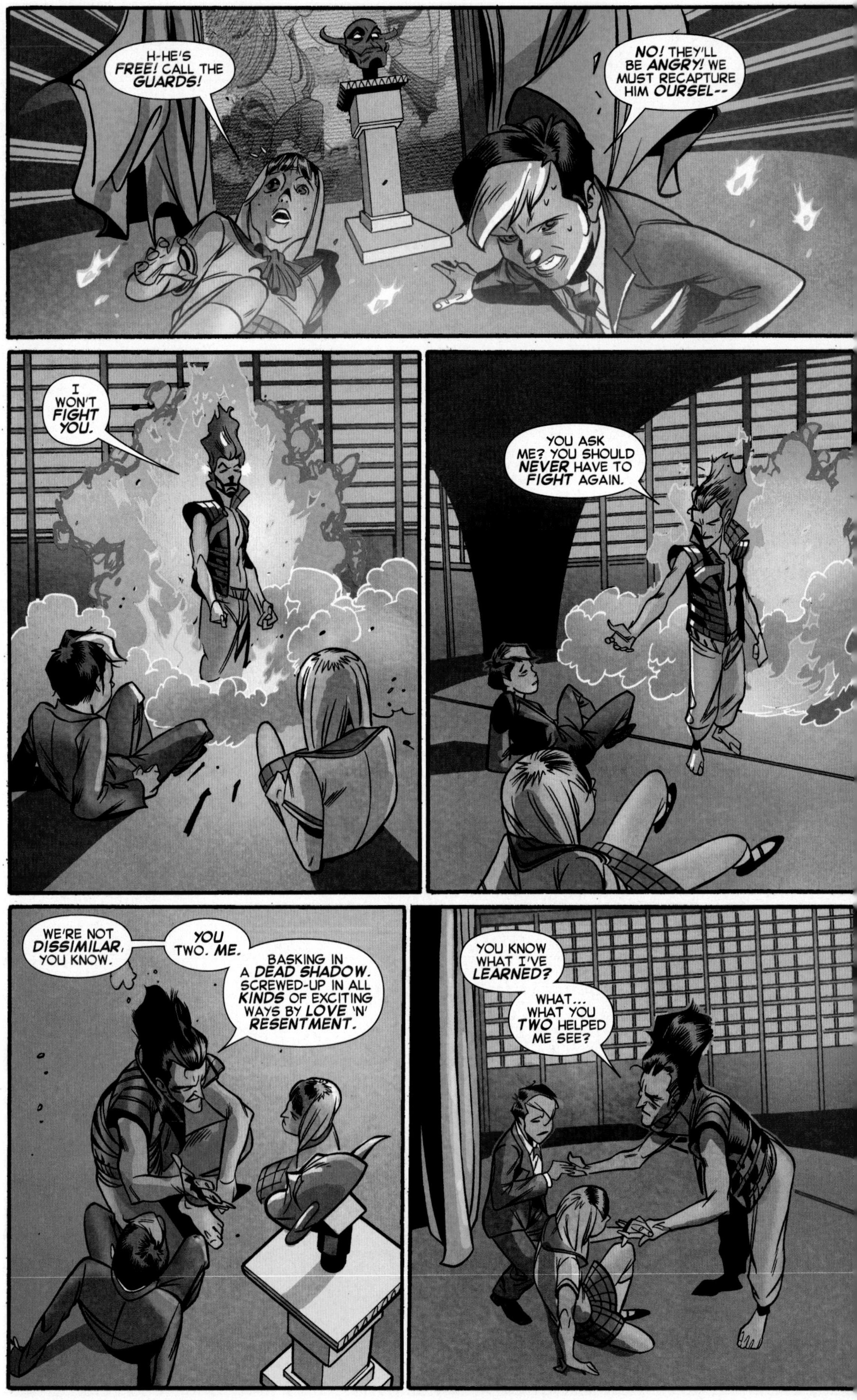
H-HE'S FREE! CALL THE GUARDS!
NO! THEY'LL BE ANGRY! WE MUST RECAPTURE HIM OURSEL--
I WON'T FIGHT YOU.
YOU ASK ME? YOU SHOULD NEVER HAVE TO FIGHT AGAIN.
WE'RE NOT DISSIMILAR, YOU KNOW.
YOU TWO. ME.
BASKING IN A DEAD SHADOW. SCREWED-UP IN ALL KINDS OF EXCITING WAYS BY LOVE 'N' RESENTMENT.
YOU KNOW WHAT I'VE LEARNED?
WHAT... WHAT YOU TWO HELPED ME SEE?

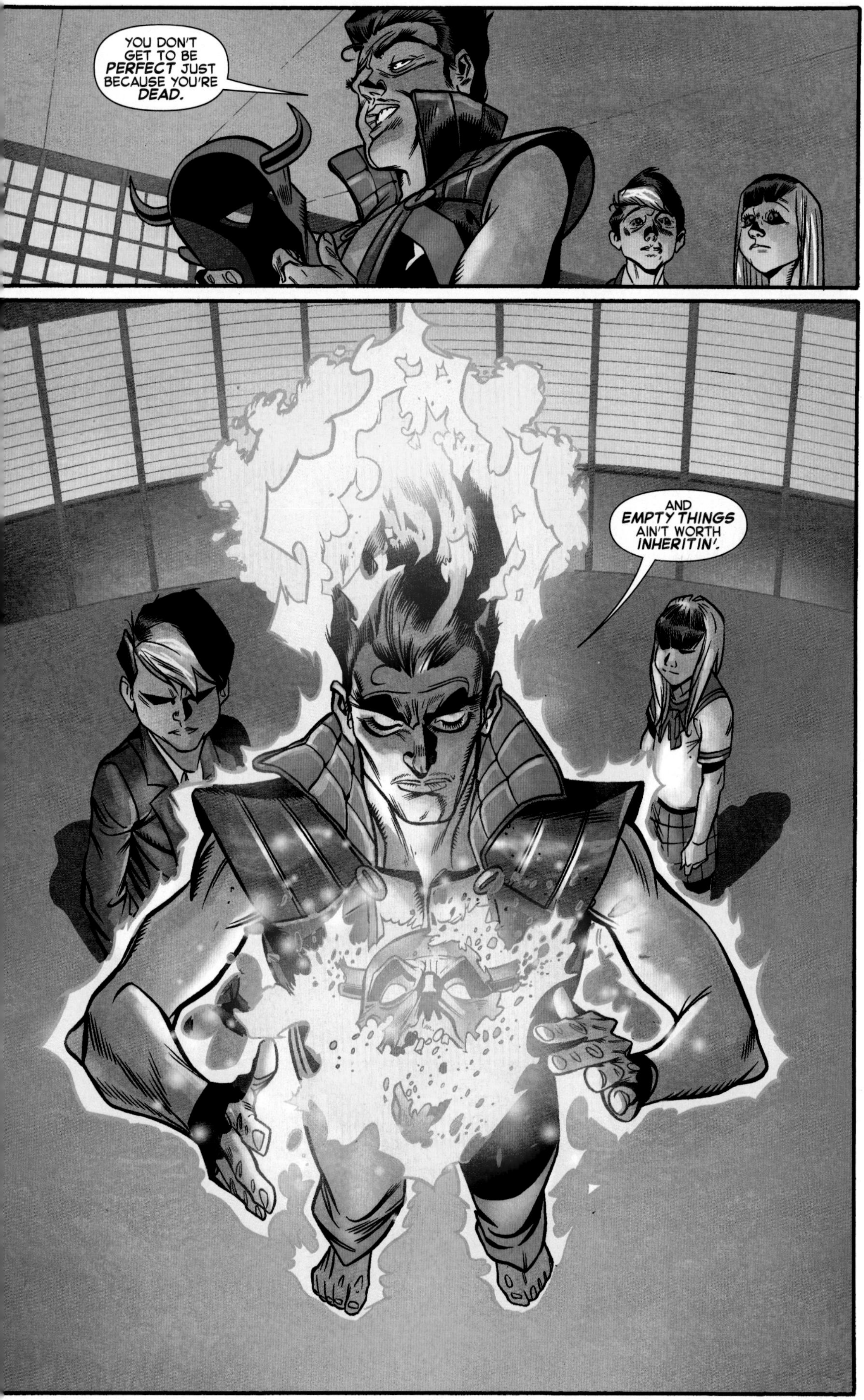
YOU DON'T GET TO BE PERFECT JUST BECAUSE YOU'RE DEAD.
AND EMPTY THINGS AIN'T WORTH INHERITIN'.

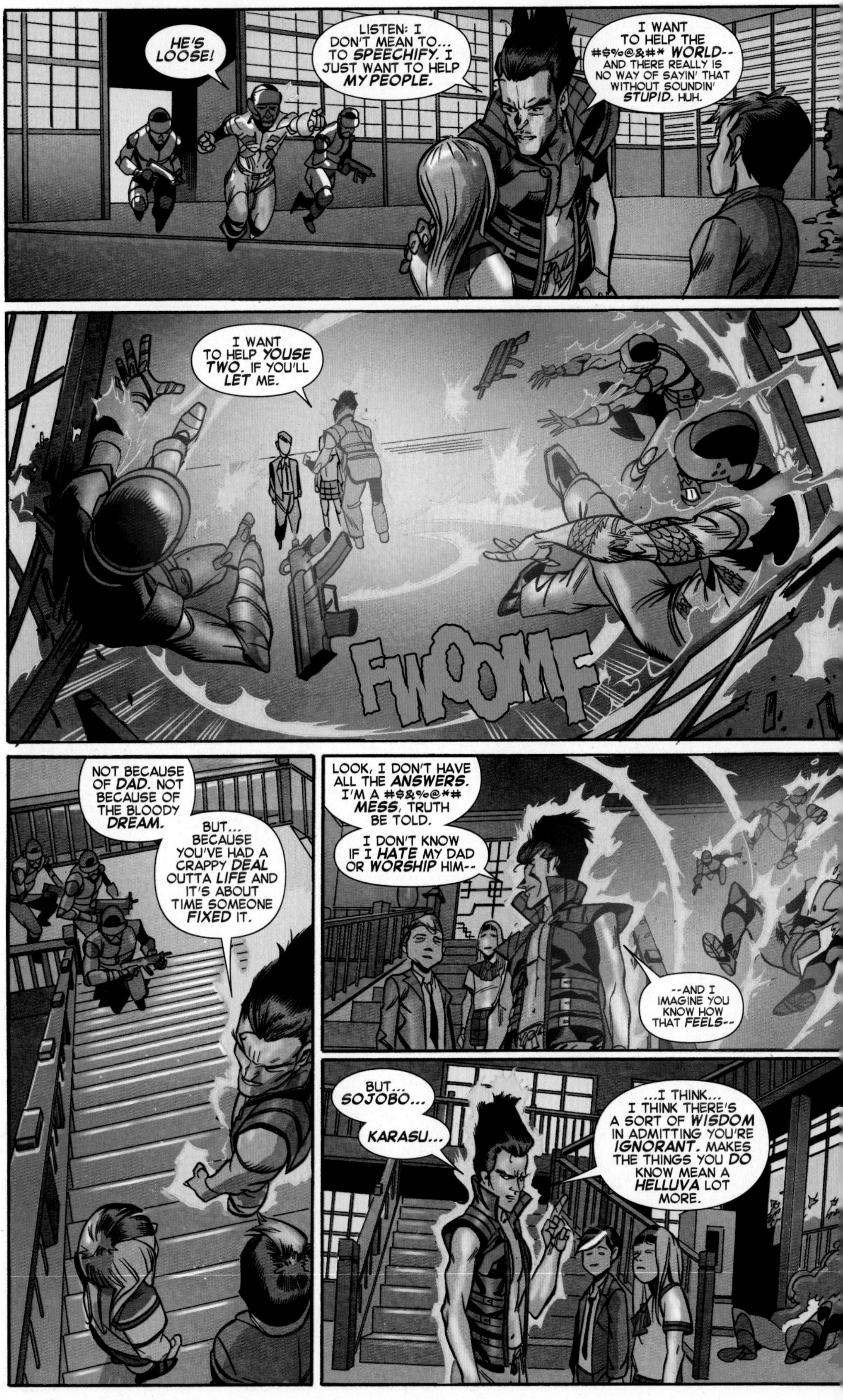
HE'S LOOSE!
LISTEN: I DON'T MEAN TO... TO SPEECHIFY. I JUST WANT TO HELP MY PEOPLE.
I WANT TO HELP THE #$%@&#* WORLD-- AND THERE REALLY IS NO WAY OF SAYIN' THAT WITHOUT SOUNDIN' STUPID. HUH.
I WANT TO HELP YOUSE TWO. IF YOU'LL LET ME.
FWOOMF
NOT BECAUSE OF DAD. NOT BECAUSE OF THE BLOODY DREAM.
BUT... BECAUSE YOU'VE HAD A CRAPPY DEAL OUTTA LIFE AND IT'S ABOUT TIME SOMEONE FIXED IT.
LOOK, I DON'T HAVE ALL THE ANSWERS. I'M A #$&%@*# MESS, TRUTH BE TOLD.
I DON'T KNOW IF I HATE MY DAD OR WORSHIP HIM--
--AND I IMAGINE YOU KNOW HOW THAT FEELS--
BUT... SOJOBO...
KARASU...
...I THINK... I THINK THERE'S A SORT OF WISDOM IN ADMITTING YOU'RE IGNORANT. MAKES THE THINGS YOU DO KNOW MEAN A HELLUVA LOT MORE.

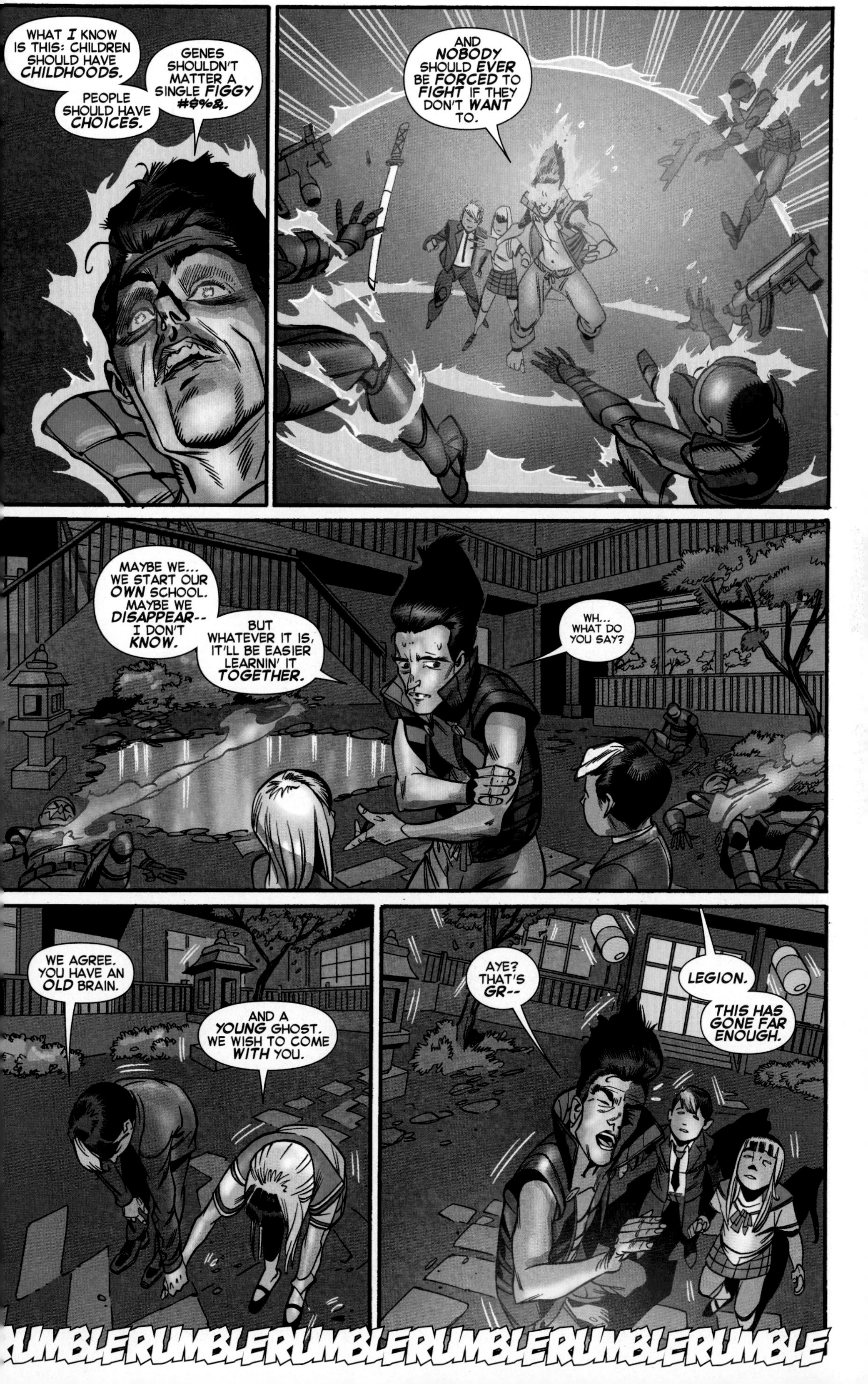

WHAT I KNOW IS THIS: CHILDREN SHOULD HAVE CHILDHOODS.
PEOPLE SHOULD HAVE CHOICES.
GENES SHOULDN'T MATTER A SINGLE FIGGY #$%&.
AND NOBODY SHOULD EVER BE FORCED TO FIGHT IF THEY DON'T WANT TO.
MAYBE WE... WE START OUR OWN SCHOOL. MAYBE WE DISAPPEAR-- I DON'T KNOW.
BUT WHATEVER IT IS, IT'LL BE EASIER LEARNIN' IT TOGETHER.
WH... WHAT DO YOU SAY?
WE AGREE. YOU HAVE AN OLD BRAIN.
AND A YOUNG GHOST. WE WISH TO COME WITH YOU.
AYE? THAT'S GR--
LEGION.
THIS HAS GONE FAR ENOUGH.
RUMBLERUMBLERUMBLERUMBLERUMBLERUMBLE

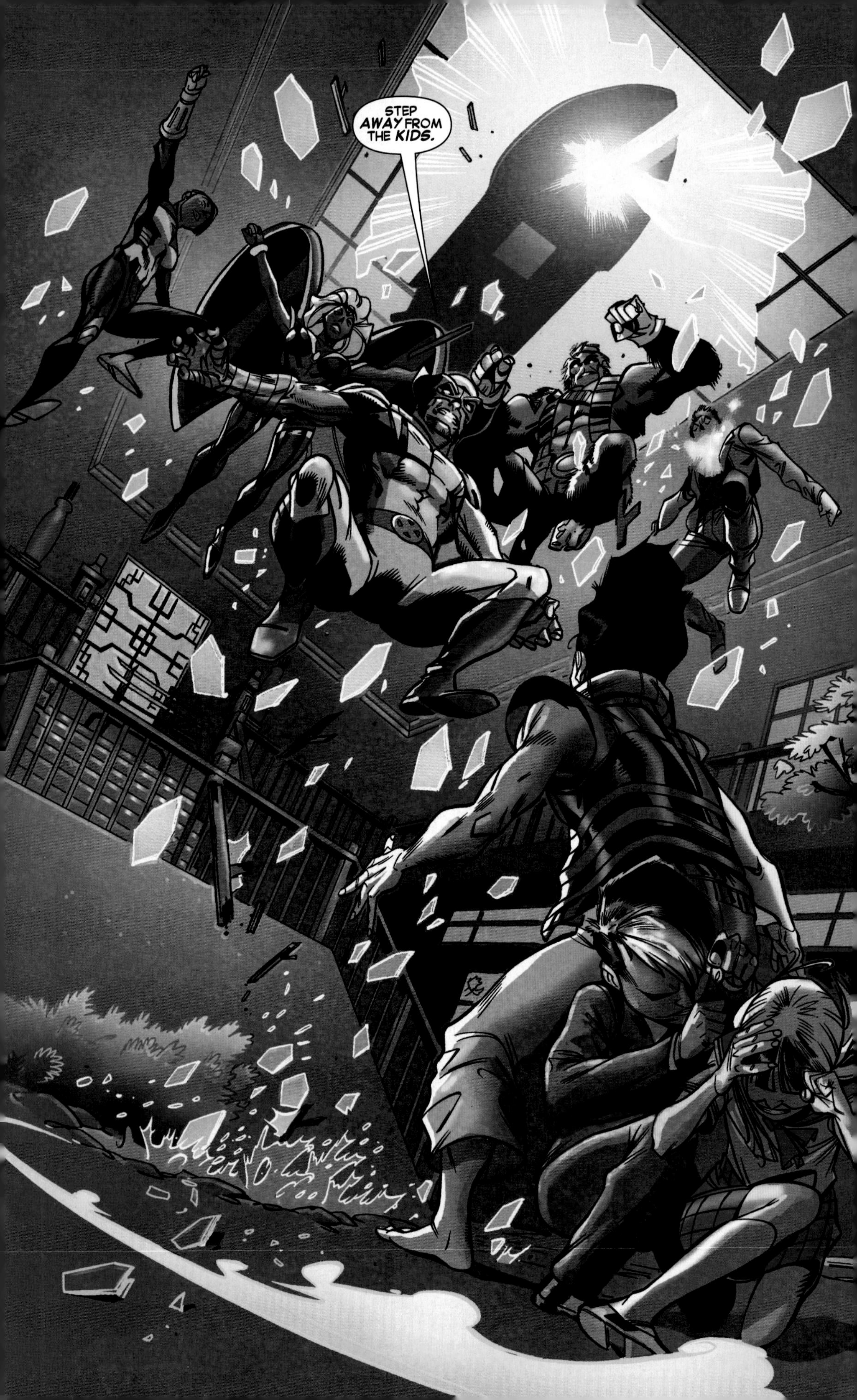
STEP AWAY FROM THE KIDS.

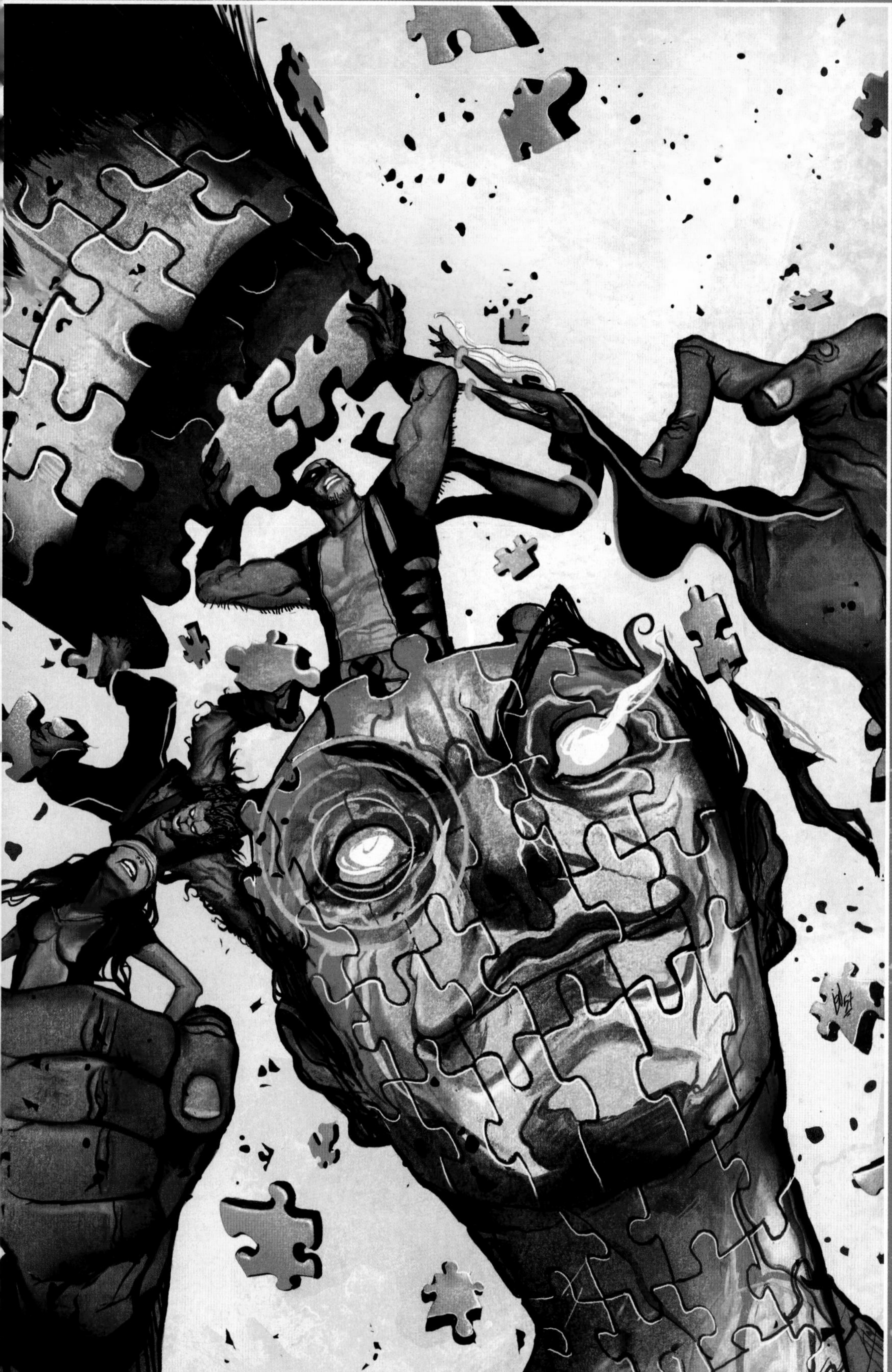

FOUR

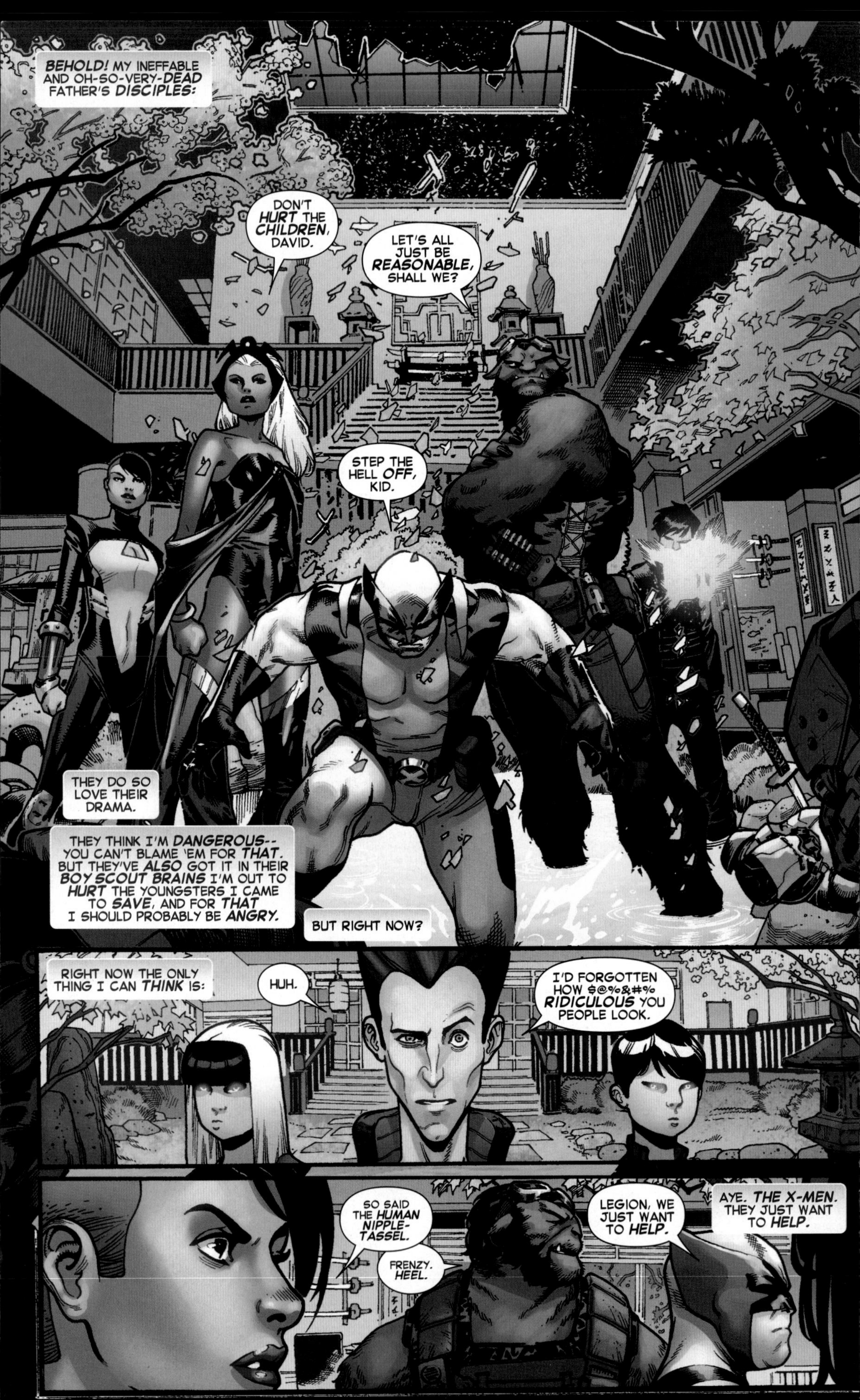
BEHOLD! MY INEFFABLE AND OH-SO-VERY-DEAD FATHER'S DISCIPLES:
DON'T HURT THE CHILDREN, DAVID.
LET'S ALL JUST BE REASONABLE, SHALL WE?
STEP THE HELL OFF, KID.
THEY DO SO LOVE THEIR DRAMA.
THEY THINK I'M DANGEROUS-- YOU CAN'T BLAME 'EM FOR THAT. BUT THEY'VE ALSO GOT IT IN THEIR BOY SCOUT BRAINS I'M OUT TO HURT THE YOUNGSTERS I CAME TO SAVE, AND FOR THAT I SHOULD PROBABLY BE ANGRY.
BUT RIGHT NOW?
RIGHT NOW THE ONLY THING I CAN THINK IS:
HUH.
I'D FORGOTTEN HOW $@%&#% RIDICULOUS YOU PEOPLE LOOK.
SO SAID THE HUMAN NIPPLE-TASSEL.
FRENZY. HEEL.
LEGION, WE JUST WANT TO HELP.
AYE. THE X-MEN. THEY JUST WANT TO HELP.

NOT CALLIN' ME BLOODY *"LEGION"* WOULD BE A GOOD *START.*

AND IF THE *LIVING TRACHEOTOMY* OVER THERE KEEPS SNEAKING ROUND THE BACK, I MIGHT JUST LOSE MY #%$& AND--WHO KNOWS-- *FRACTURE* THE *UNIVERSE* OR SOMETHIN'.

UH.

I'M *BLUFFING,* MOSTLY. CAN'T *ACCESS* ANY OF THE *MAJOR* POWERS JUST YET--MY *INNER ME'S* NOT *STRONG ENOUGH...*

...BUT *THESE* CLOWNS DON'T KNOW THAT.

DAVID, PLEASE--YOU'RE NOT *WELL.* WE CAN HELP YOU. WE CAN HELP YOUR *YOUNG FRIENDS.*

OH *AYE?* HELP THEM *HOW,* EXACTLY?

YOU *KNOW* HOW. WE GIVE THEM A *FUTURE.* HELP THEM *CONTROL* THEIR *POWERS.* TEACH THEM TO *FIGHT* FOR A *BETTER TO--*

THERE IT IS. *"FIGHT."*

THESE TWO'VE KNOWN NOTHING BUT *VIOLENCE* THEIR WHOLE BLOODY LIVES AND YOUSE WANT TO *FIX IT* AT *PARAMILITARY SPANDEX SCHOOL?*

SO WHADDAYA *SUGGEST,* BOY? KIDS SHOULD BE KIDS, BUT YOU'RE SAYIN' *MUTANTS SHOULDN'T* BE TAUGHT TO *DEFEND* 'EMSELVES?

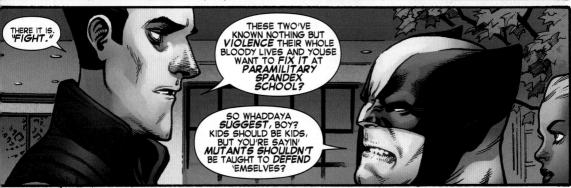

I'M SAYING THEY SHOULDN'T *HAVE* TO.

AND THEY *WOULDN'T,* IF YOU *NODDIES'D* EVER MADE A JOT OF *DIFFERENCE* TO THE *WORLD.*

THAT'S...THAT'S YOUR *FATHER'S DREAM* YOU'RE TALKING AB--

NO, IT'S NOT. THE *DREAM'S* FINE.

I JUST THINK... M-MAYBE THE WAY HE WENT *ABOUT* IT MIGHT'VE BEEN...

(SAYIT SAYIT SAYIT)

WRONG.

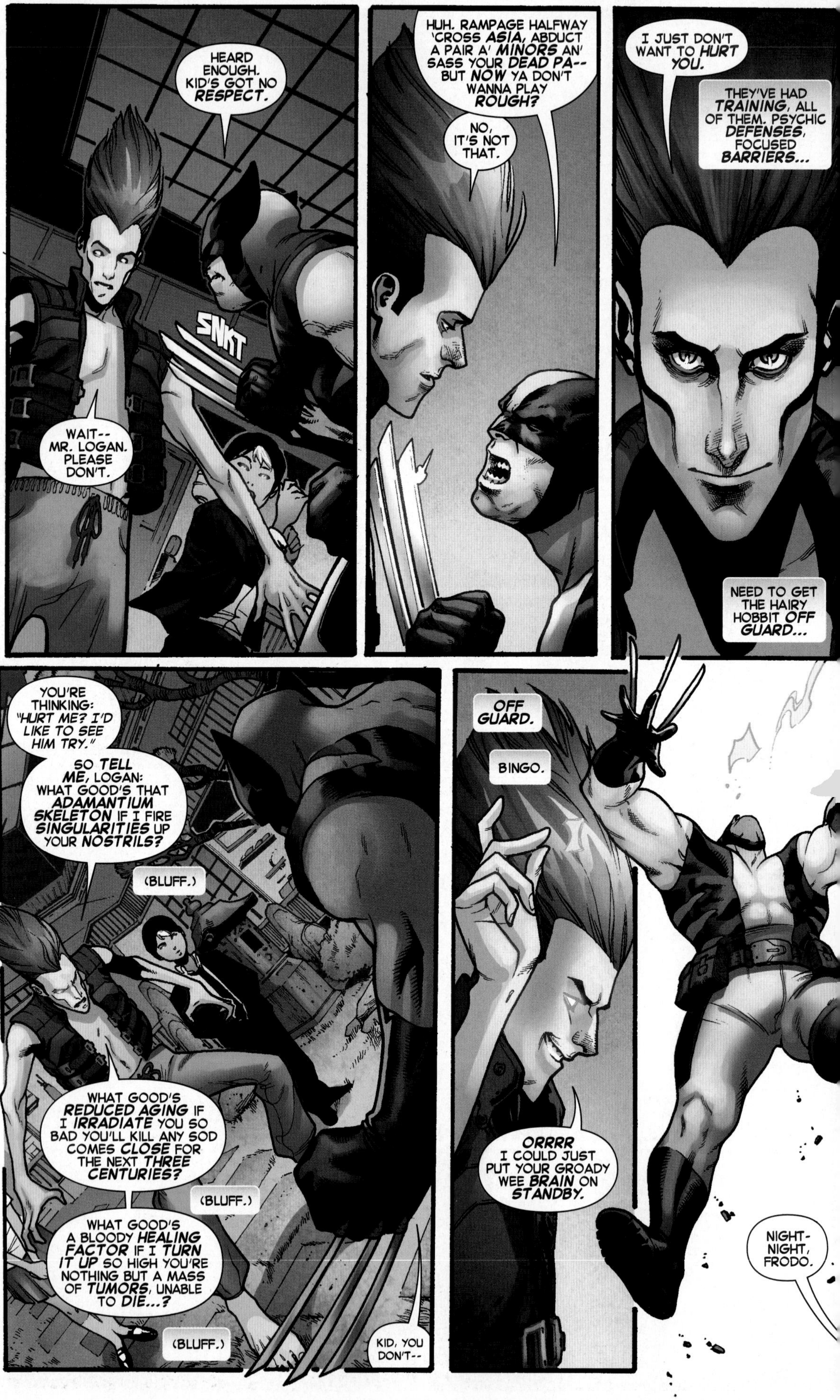

HEARD ENOUGH. KID'S GOT NO RESPECT.
SNKT
WAIT-- MR. LOGAN. PLEASE DON'T.
HUH. RAMPAGE HALFWAY 'CROSS ASIA, ABDUCT A PAIR A' MINORS AN' SASS YOUR DEAD PA-- BUT NOW YA DON'T WANNA PLAY ROUGH?
NO, IT'S NOT THAT.
I JUST DON'T WANT TO HURT YOU.
THEY'VE HAD TRAINING, ALL OF THEM. PSYCHIC DEFENSES, FOCUSED BARRIERS...
NEED TO GET THE HAIRY HOBBIT OFF GUARD...
YOU'RE THINKING: "HURT ME? I'D LIKE TO SEE HIM TRY."
SO TELL ME, LOGAN: WHAT GOOD'S THAT ADAMANTIUM SKELETON IF I FIRE SINGULARITIES UP YOUR NOSTRILS?
(BLUFF.)
WHAT GOOD'S REDUCED AGING IF I IRRADIATE YOU SO BAD YOU'LL KILL ANY SOD COMES CLOSE FOR THE NEXT THREE CENTURIES?
(BLUFF.)
WHAT GOOD'S A BLOODY HEALING FACTOR IF I TURN IT UP SO HIGH YOU'RE NOTHING BUT A MASS OF TUMORS, UNABLE TO DIE...?
(BLUFF.)
KID, YOU DON'T--
OFF GUARD.
BINGO.
ORRRR I COULD JUST PUT YOUR GROADY WEE BRAIN ON STANDBY.
NIGHT-NIGHT, FRODO.

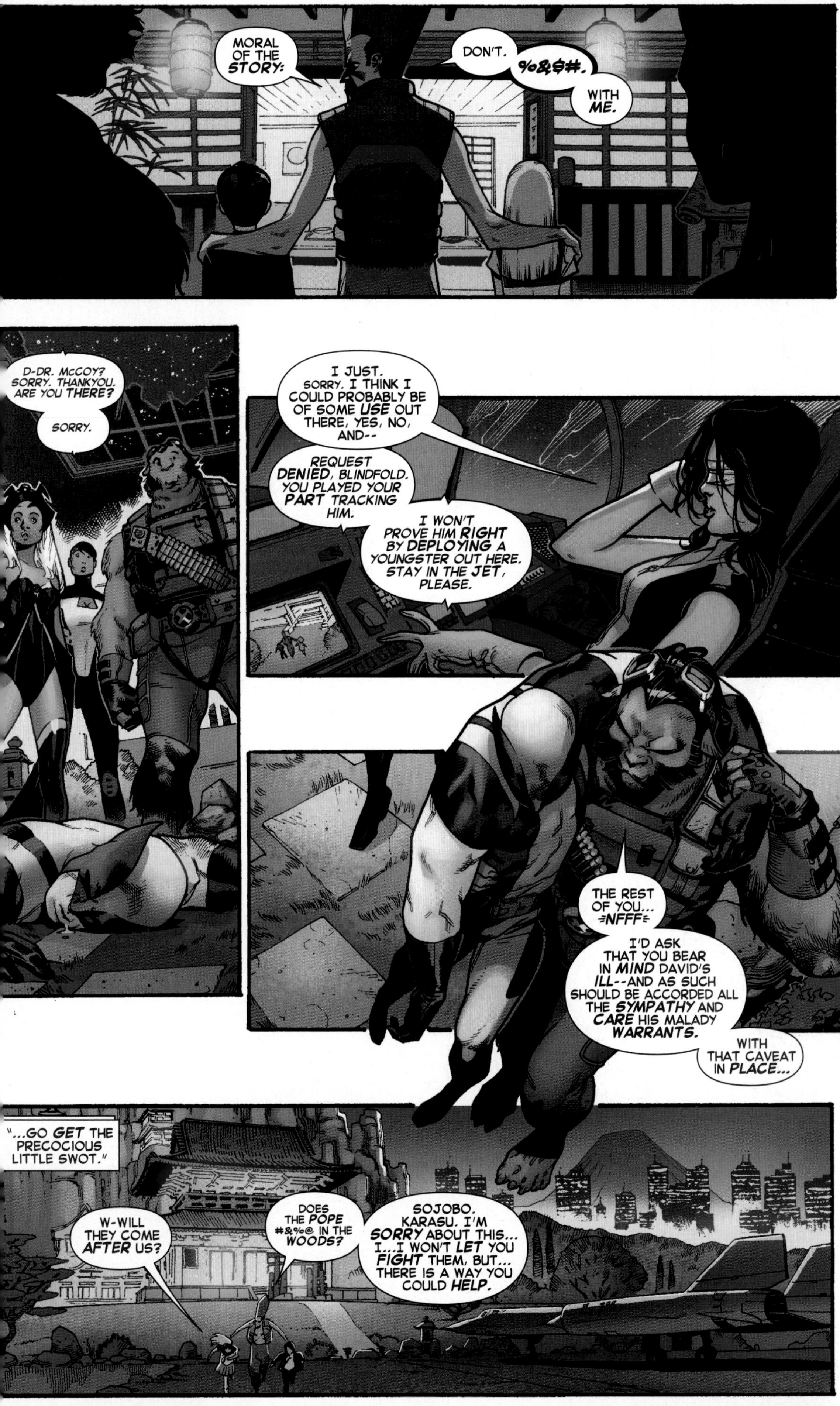

MORAL OF THE STORY:
DON'T.
%&$#.
WITH ME.
D-DR. McCOY? SORRY. THANKYOU. ARE YOU THERE?
SORRY.
I JUST. SORRY. I THINK I COULD PROBABLY BE OF SOME USE OUT THERE, YES, NO, AND--
REQUEST DENIED, BLINDFOLD. YOU PLAYED YOUR PART TRACKING HIM.
I WON'T PROVE HIM RIGHT BY DEPLOYING A YOUNGSTER OUT HERE. STAY IN THE JET, PLEASE.
THE REST OF YOU... NFFF
I'D ASK THAT YOU BEAR IN MIND DAVID'S ILL--AND AS SUCH SHOULD BE ACCORDED ALL THE SYMPATHY AND CARE HIS MALADY WARRANTS.
WITH THAT CAVEAT IN PLACE...
"...GO GET THE PRECOCIOUS LITTLE SWOT."
W-WILL THEY COME AFTER US?
DOES THE POPE #&%@ IN THE WOODS?
SOJOBO. KARASU. I'M SORRY ABOUT THIS... I...I WON'T LET YOU FIGHT THEM, BUT... THERE IS A WAY YOU COULD HELP.

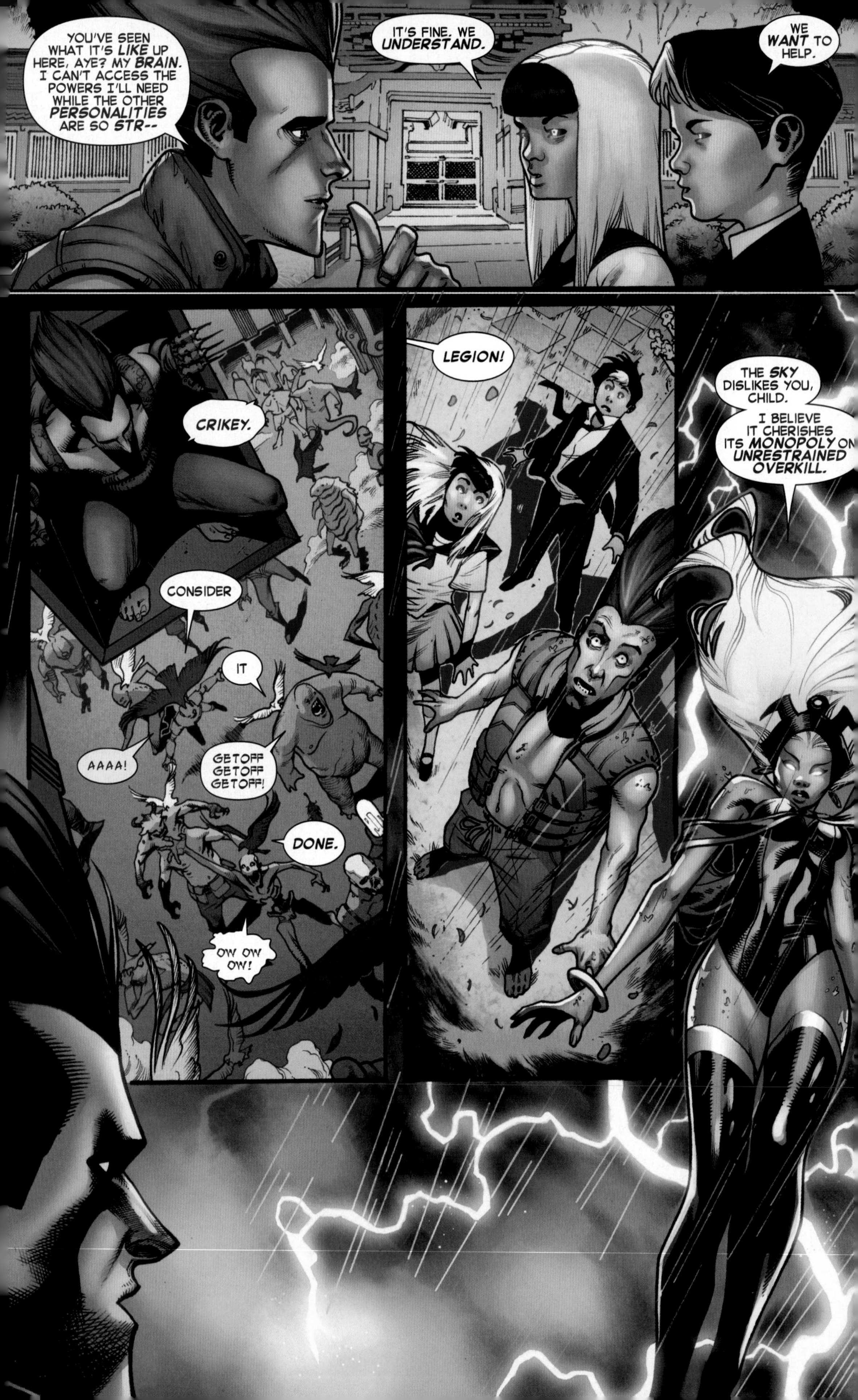

YOU'VE SEEN WHAT IT'S LIKE UP HERE, AYE? MY BRAIN. I CAN'T ACCESS THE POWERS I'LL NEED WHILE THE OTHER PERSONALITIES ARE SO STR--
IT'S FINE. WE UNDERSTAND.
WE WANT TO HELP.
CRIKEY.
CONSIDER
IT
AAAA!
GETOFF GETOFF GETOFF!
DONE.
OW OW OW!
LEGION!
THE SKY DISLIKES YOU, CHILD.
I BELIEVE IT CHERISHES ITS MONOPOLY ON UNRESTRAINED OVERKILL.

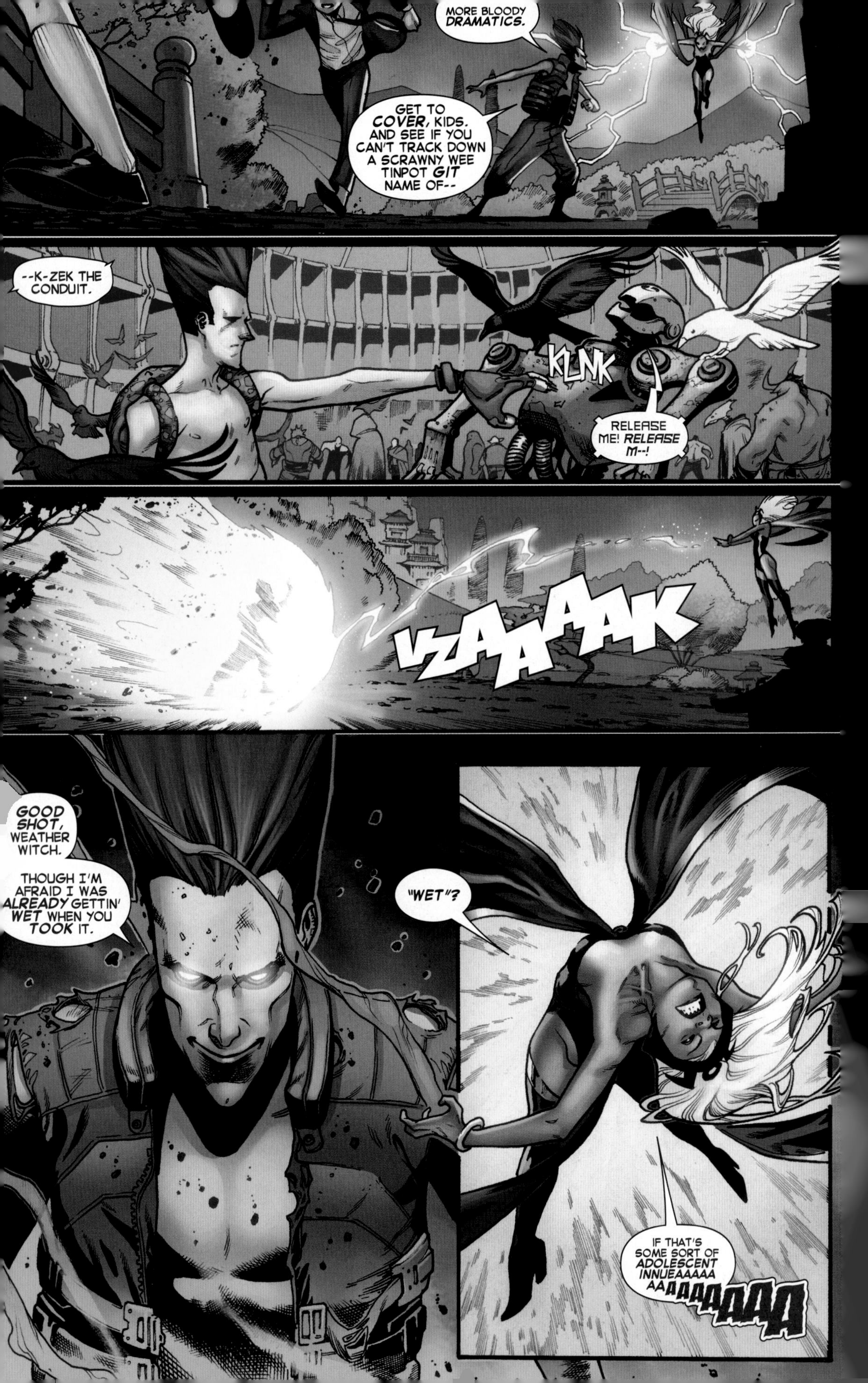
MORE BLOODY DRAMATICS.
GET TO COVER, KIDS. AND SEE IF YOU CAN'T TRACK DOWN A SCRAWNY WEE TINPOT GIT NAME OF--
--K-ZEK THE CONDUIT.
KLNK
RELEASE ME! RELEASE M--!
VZAAAAAK
GOOD SHOT, WEATHER WITCH.
THOUGH I'M AFRAID I WAS ALREADY GETTIN' WET WHEN YOU TOOK IT.
"WET"?
IF THAT'S SOME SORT OF ADOLESCENT INNUEAAAAA AAAAAAAAA

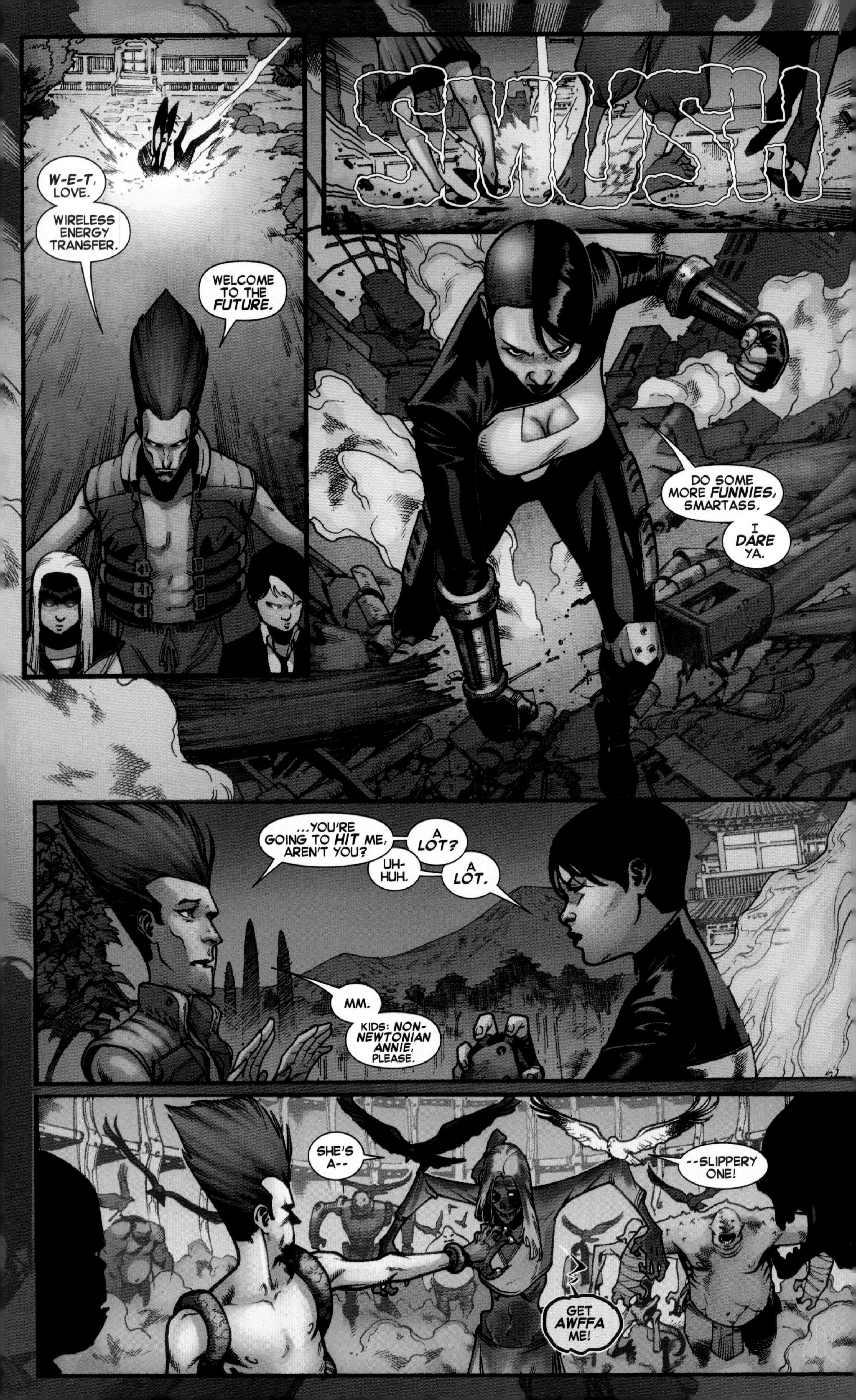
W-E-T, LOVE.
WIRELESS ENERGY TRANSFER.
WELCOME TO THE FUTURE.
SWOOSH
DO SOME MORE FUNNIES, SMARTASS.
I DARE YA.
...YOU'RE GOING TO HIT ME, AREN'T YOU?
A LOT?
UH-HUH.
A LOT.
MM.
KIDS: NON-NEWTONIAN ANNIE, PLEASE.
SHE'S A--
--SLIPPERY ONE!
GET AWFFA ME!

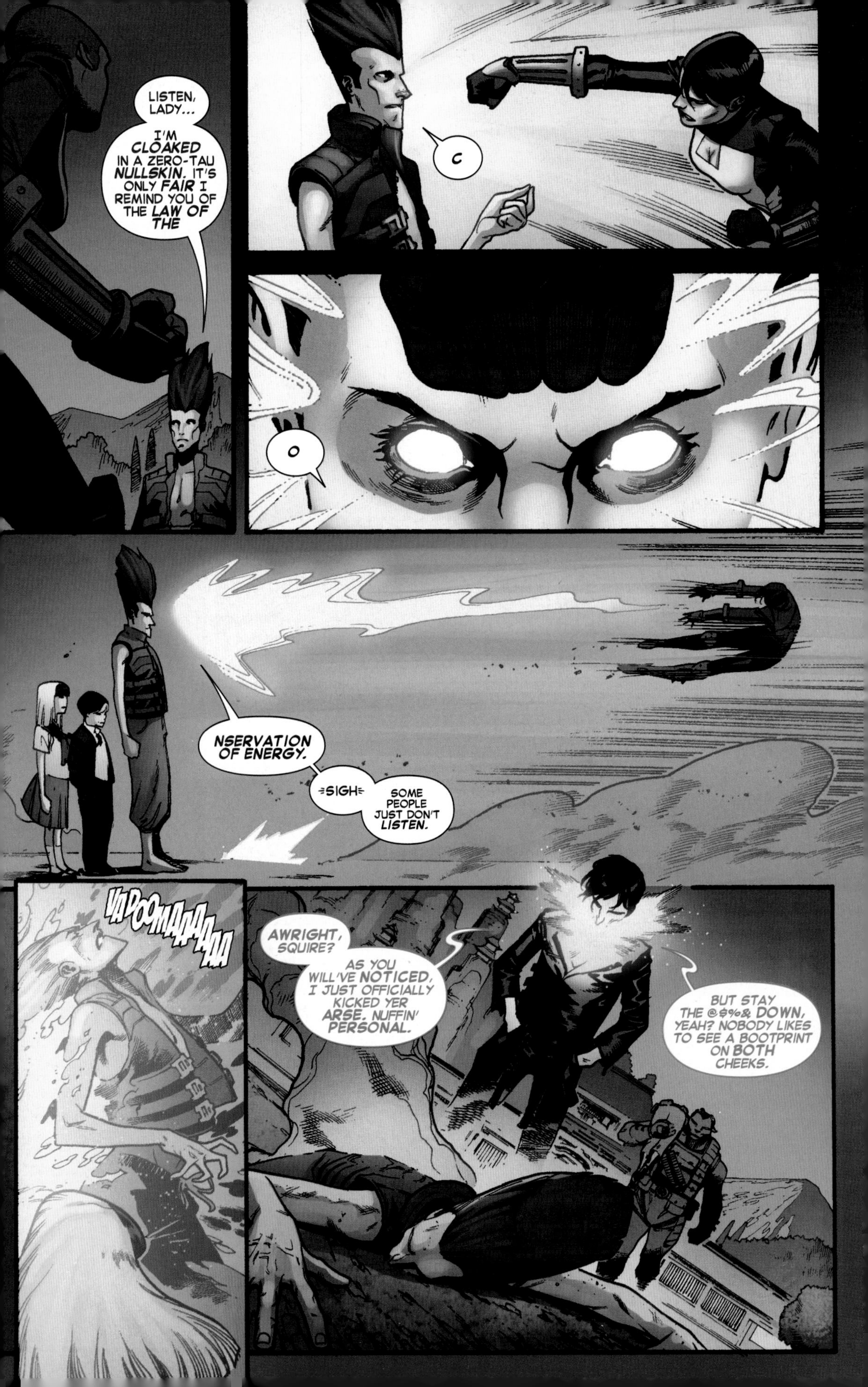
LISTEN, LADY...
I'M CLOAKED IN A ZERO-TAU NULLSKIN. IT'S ONLY FAIR I REMIND YOU OF THE LAW OF THE
C
O
NSERVATION OF ENERGY.
=SIGH=
SOME PEOPLE JUST DON'T LISTEN.
VADOOMAAAAAAA
AWRIGHT, SQUIRE?
AS YOU WILL'VE NOTICED, I JUST OFFICIALLY KICKED YER ARSE. NUFFIN' PERSONAL.
BUT STAY THE @$%& DOWN, YEAH? NOBODY LIKES TO SEE A BOOTPRINT ON BOTH CHEEKS.

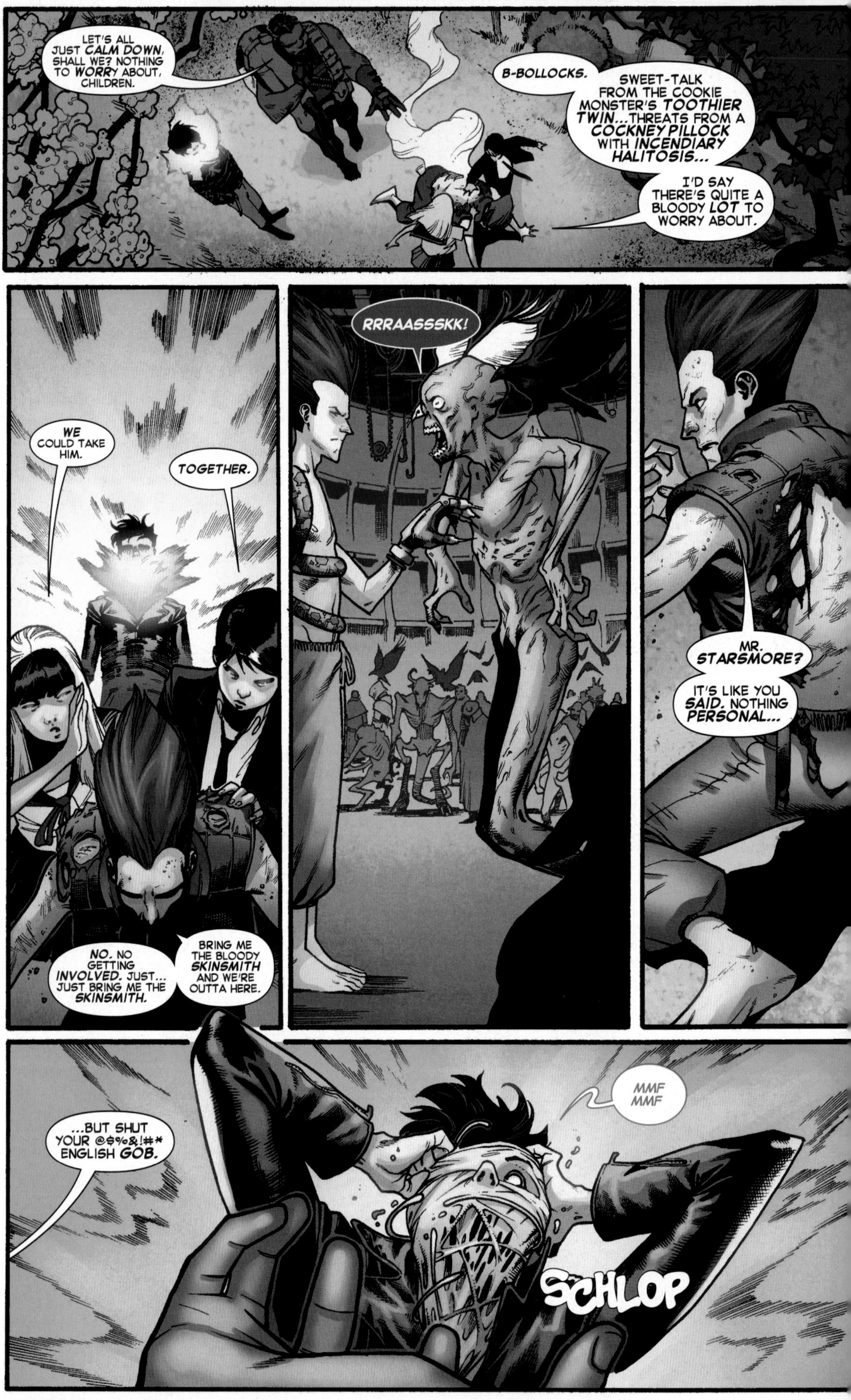
LET'S ALL JUST CALM DOWN, SHALL WE? NOTHING TO WORRY ABOUT, CHILDREN.
B-BOLLOCKS.
SWEET-TALK FROM THE COOKIE MONSTER'S TOOTHIER TWIN...THREATS FROM A COCKNEY PILLOCK WITH INCENDIARY HALITOSIS...
I'D SAY THERE'S QUITE A BLOODY LOT TO WORRY ABOUT.
WE COULD TAKE HIM.
TOGETHER.
NO. NO GETTING INVOLVED. JUST... JUST BRING ME THE SKINSMITH.
BRING ME THE BLOODY SKINSMITH AND WE'RE OUTTA HERE.
RRRAASSSKK!
MR. STARSMORE?
IT'S LIKE YOU SAID. NOTHING PERSONAL...
...BUT SHUT YOUR @$%&!#* ENGLISH GOB.
MMF MMF
SCHLOP

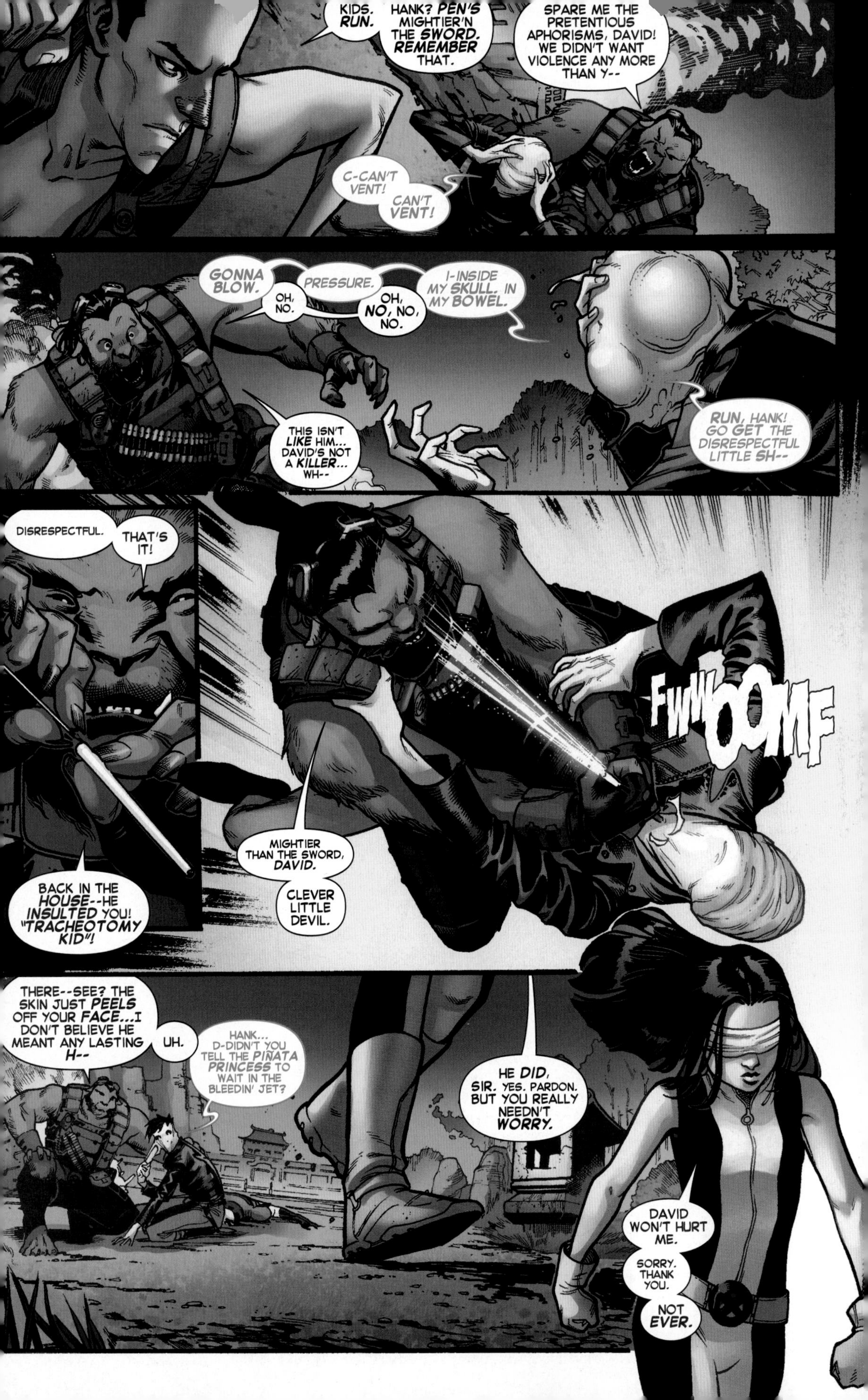
KIDS. RUN.
HANK? PEN'S MIGHTIER'N THE SWORD. REMEMBER THAT.
SPARE ME THE PRETENTIOUS APHORISMS, DAVID! WE DIDN'T WANT VIOLENCE ANY MORE THAN Y--
C-CAN'T VENT!
CAN'T VENT!
GONNA BLOW.
OH, NO.
PRESSURE.
OH, NO, NO, NO.
I-INSIDE MY SKULL. IN MY BOWEL.
THIS ISN'T LIKE HIM... DAVID'S NOT A KILLER... WH--
RUN, HANK! GO GET THE DISRESPECTFUL LITTLE SH--
DISRESPECTFUL.
THAT'S IT!
FWWOOMF
BACK IN THE HOUSE--HE INSULTED YOU! "TRACHEOTOMY KID"!
MIGHTIER THAN THE SWORD, DAVID.
CLEVER LITTLE DEVIL.
THERE--SEE? THE SKIN JUST PEELS OFF YOUR FACE...I DON'T BELIEVE HE MEANT ANY LASTING H--
UH.
HANK... D-DIDN'T YOU TELL THE PIÑATA PRINCESS TO WAIT IN THE BLEEDIN' JET?
HE DID, SIR. YES. PARDON. BUT YOU REALLY NEEDN'T WORRY.
DAVID WON'T HURT ME.
SORRY. THANK YOU.
NOT EVER.

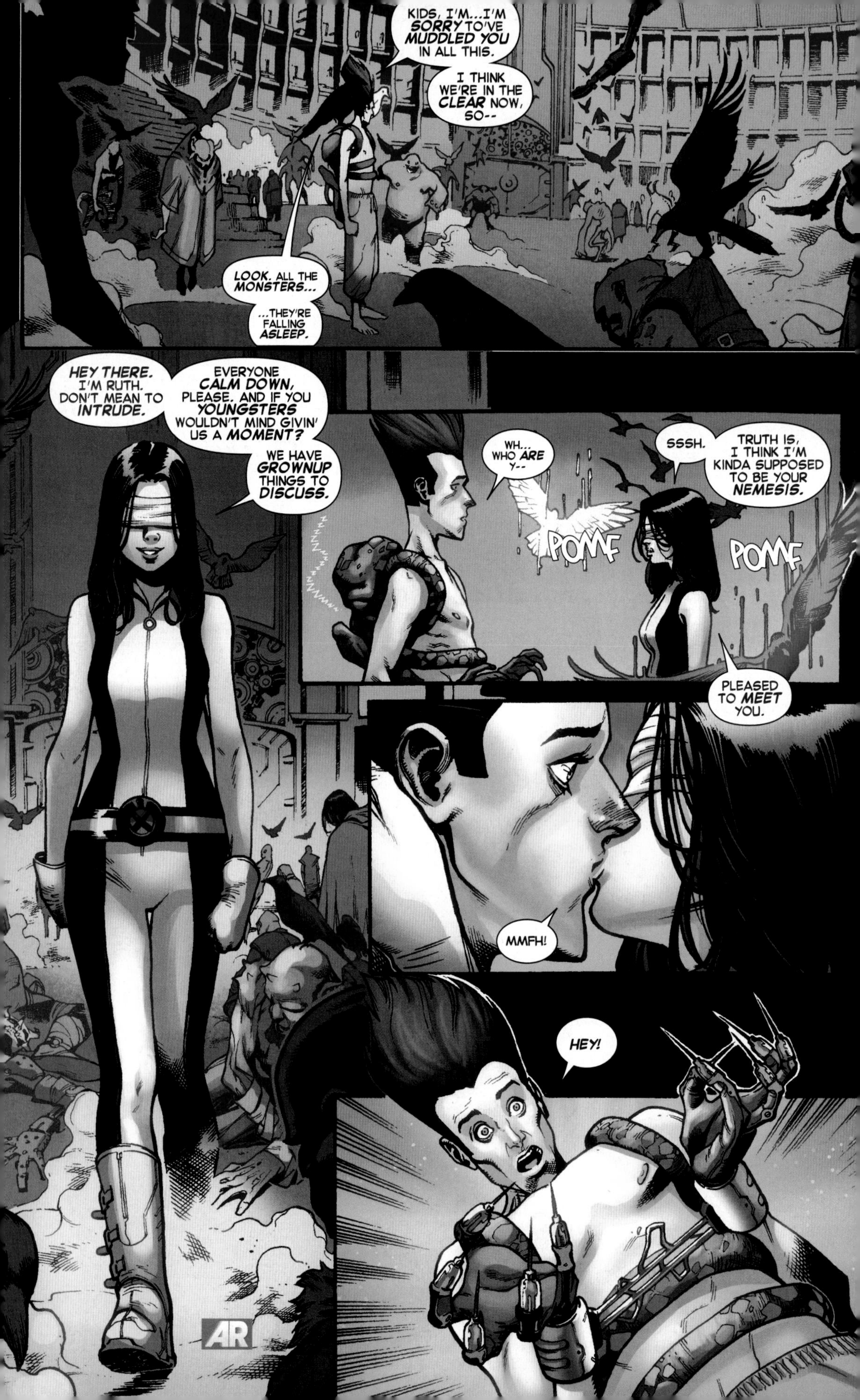
KIDS, I'M...I'M SORRY TO'VE MUDDLED YOU IN ALL THIS.
I THINK WE'RE IN THE CLEAR NOW, SO--
LOOK. ALL THE MONSTERS...
...THEY'RE FALLING ASLEEP.
HEY THERE. I'M RUTH. DON'T MEAN TO INTRUDE.
EVERYONE CALM DOWN, PLEASE. AND IF YOU YOUNGSTERS WOULDN'T MIND GIVIN' US A MOMENT?
WE HAVE GROWNUP THINGS TO DISCUSS.
WH... WHO ARE Y--
SSSH.
TRUTH IS, I THINK I'M KINDA SUPPOSED TO BE YOUR NEMESIS.
POMF
POMF
PLEASED TO MEET YOU.
MMFH!
HEY!
AR

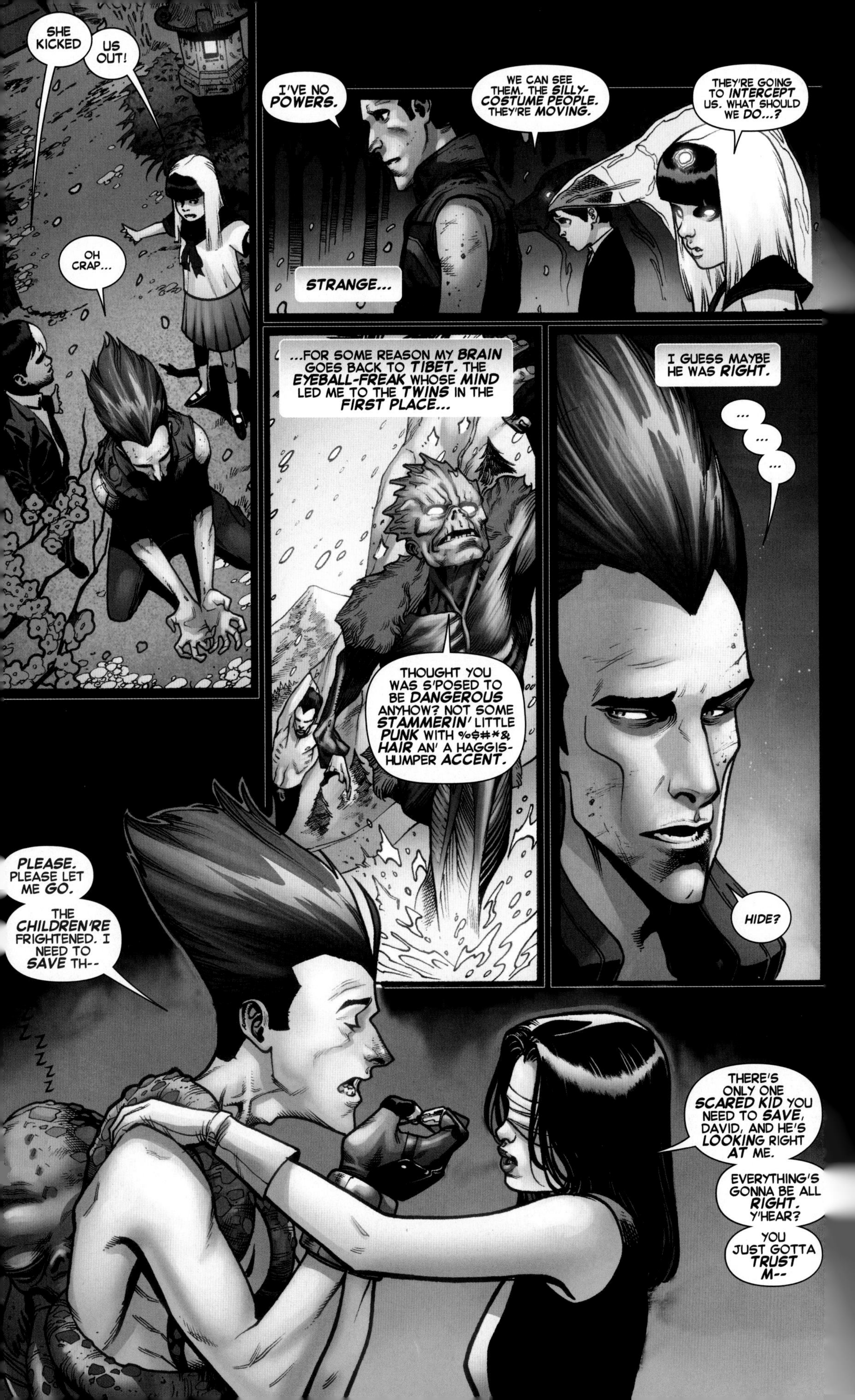
SHE KICKED
US OUT!
OH CRAP...
I'VE NO POWERS.
WE CAN SEE THEM. THE SILLY-COSTUME PEOPLE. THEY'RE MOVING.
THEY'RE GOING TO INTERCEPT US. WHAT SHOULD WE DO...?
STRANGE...
...FOR SOME REASON MY BRAIN GOES BACK TO TIBET. THE EYEBALL-FREAK WHOSE MIND LED ME TO THE TWINS IN THE FIRST PLACE...
THOUGHT YOU WAS S'POSED TO BE DANGEROUS ANYHOW? NOT SOME STAMMERIN' LITTLE PUNK WITH %$#*& HAIR AN' A HAGGIS-HUMPER ACCENT.
I GUESS MAYBE HE WAS RIGHT.
...
...
...
HIDE?
PLEASE. PLEASE LET ME GO.
THE CHILDREN'RE FRIGHTENED. I NEED TO SAVE TH--
THERE'S ONLY ONE SCARED KID YOU NEED TO SAVE, DAVID, AND HE'S LOOKING RIGHT AT ME.
EVERYTHING'S GONNA BE ALL RIGHT. Y'HEAR?
YOU JUST GOTTA TRUST M--

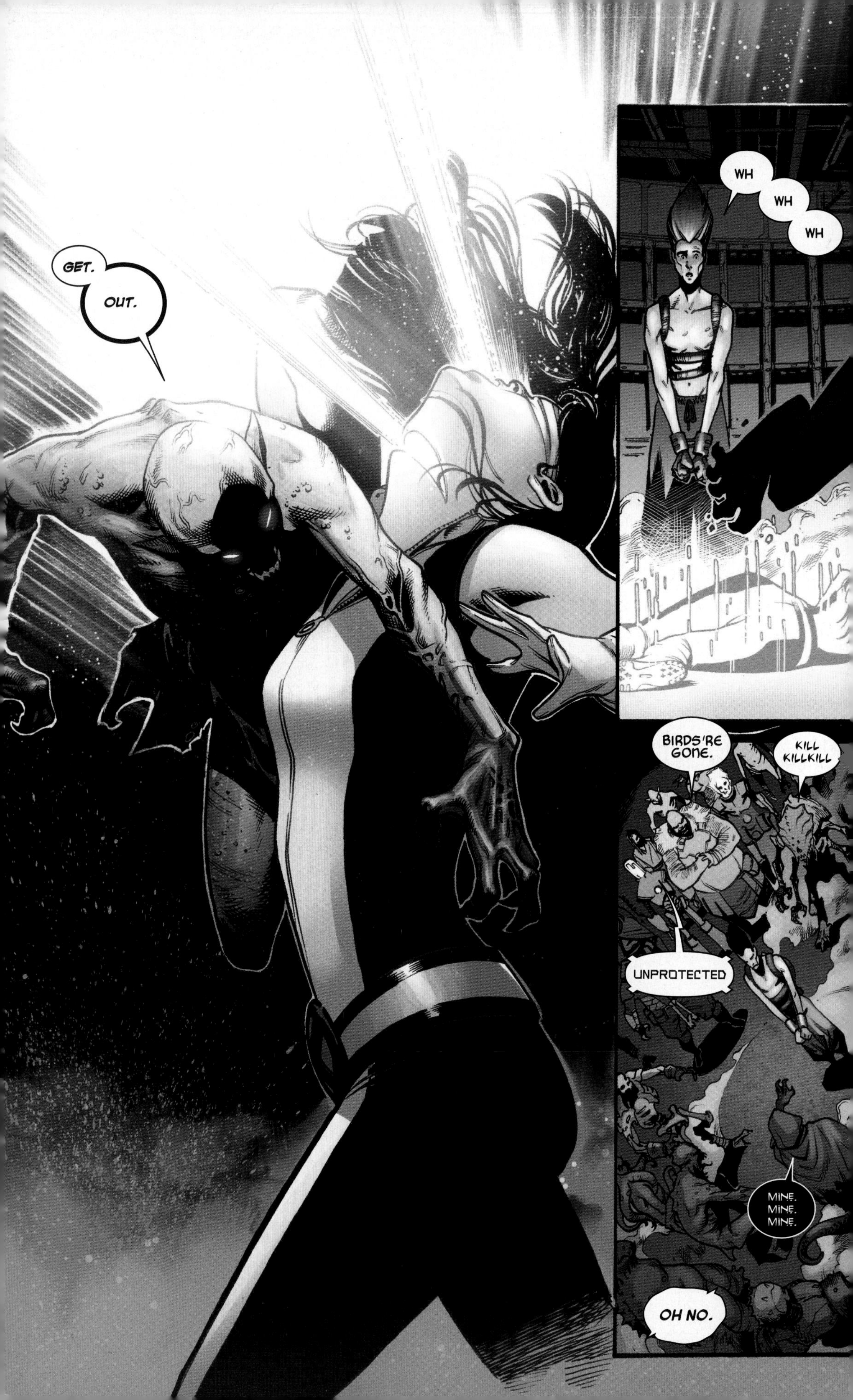
GET.
OUT.
WH
WH
WH
BIRDS'RE GONE.
KILL KILLKILL
UNPROTECTED
MINE. MINE. MINE.
OH NO.

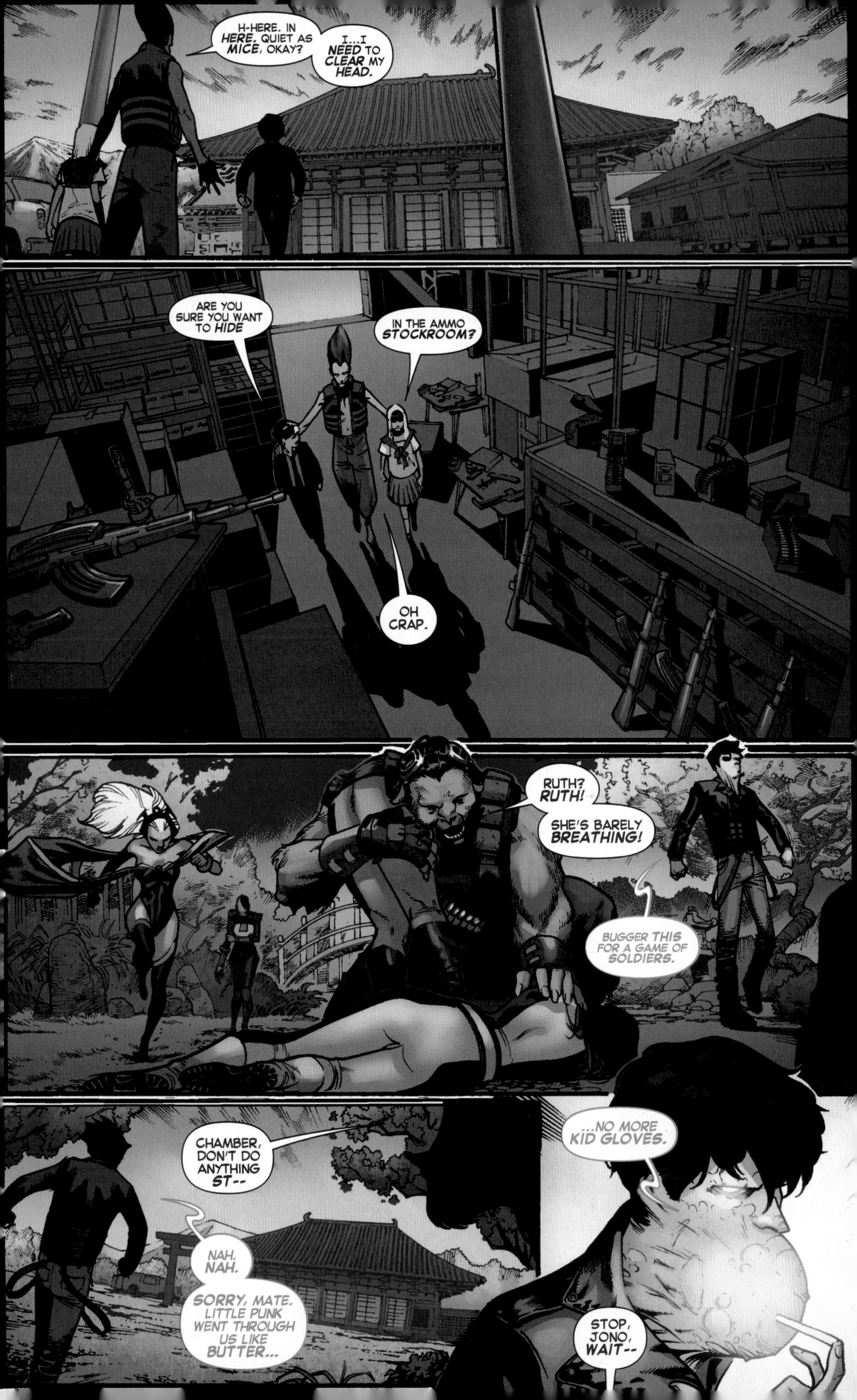

H-HERE. IN HERE. QUIET AS MICE, OKAY?
I...I NEED TO CLEAR MY HEAD.
ARE YOU SURE YOU WANT TO HIDE
IN THE AMMO STOCKROOM?
OH CRAP.
RUTH? RUTH!
SHE'S BARELY BREATHING!
BUGGER THIS FOR A GAME OF SOLDIERS.
CHAMBER, DON'T DO ANYTHING ST--
NAH. NAH.
SORRY, MATE. LITTLE PUNK WENT THROUGH US LIKE BUTTER...
...NO MORE KID GLOVES.
STOP, JONO, WAIT--

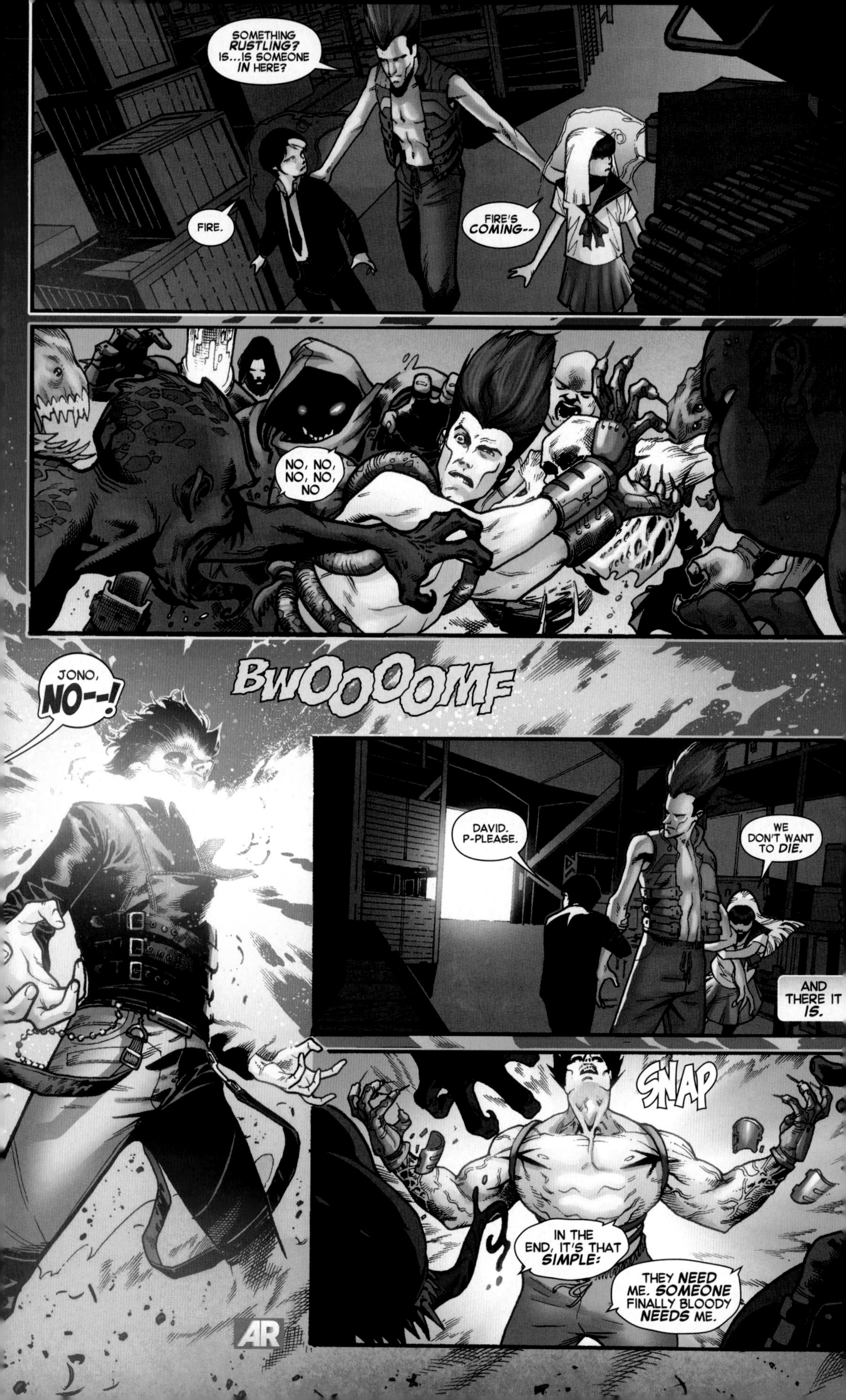
SOMETHING RUSTLING? IS...IS SOMEONE IN HERE?
FIRE.
FIRE'S COMING--
NO, NO, NO, NO, NO
JONO, NO--!
BWOOOOOMF
DAVID. P-PLEASE.
WE DON'T WANT TO DIE.
AND THERE IT IS.
SNAP
IN THE END, IT'S THAT SIMPLE:
THEY NEED ME. SOMEONE FINALLY BLOODY NEEDS ME.
AR

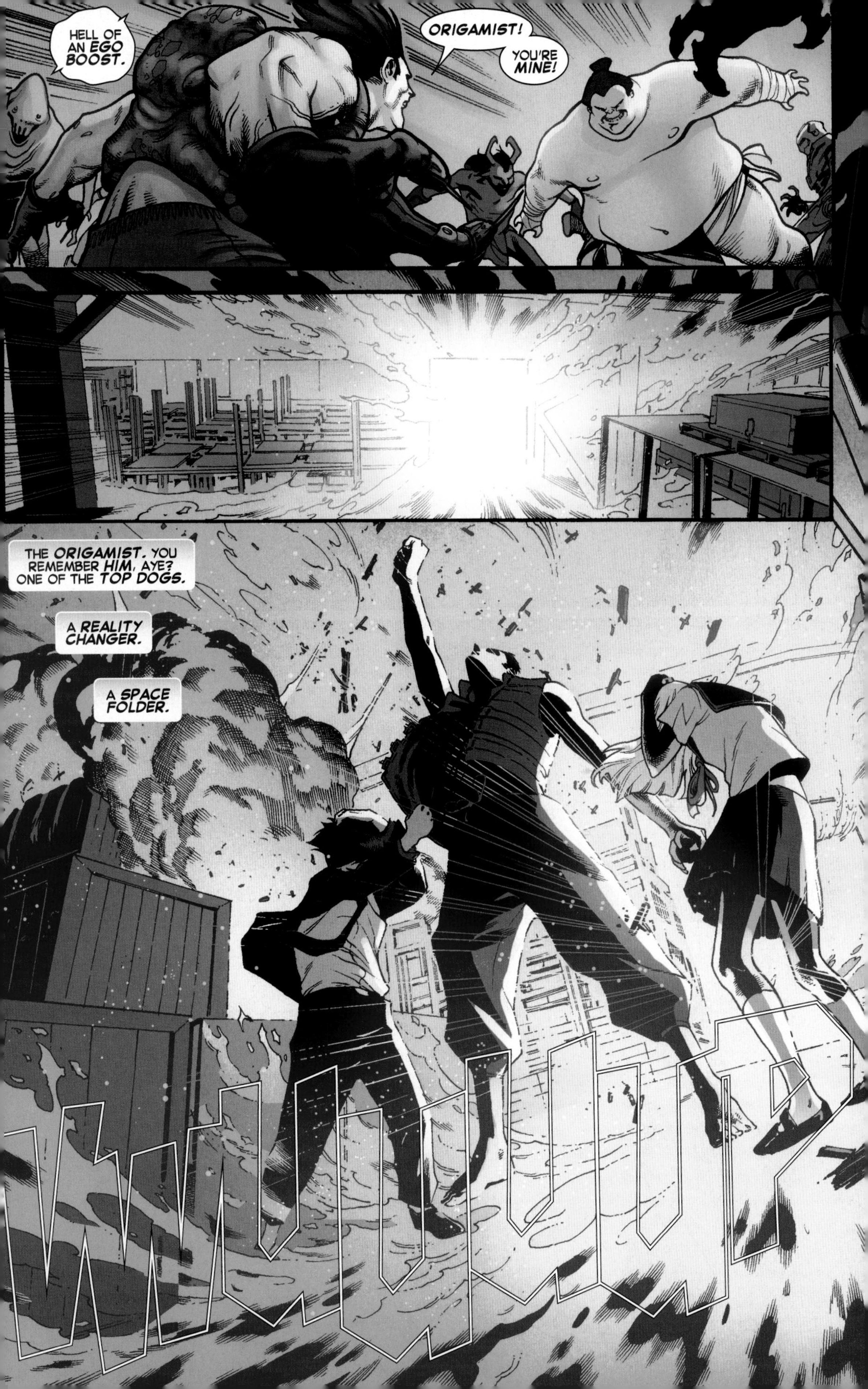
HELL OF AN EGO BOOST.
ORIGAMIST!
YOU'RE MINE!
THE ORIGAMIST. YOU REMEMBER HIM, AYE? ONE OF THE TOP DOGS.
A REALITY CHANGER.
A SPACE FOLDER.
WHUMP

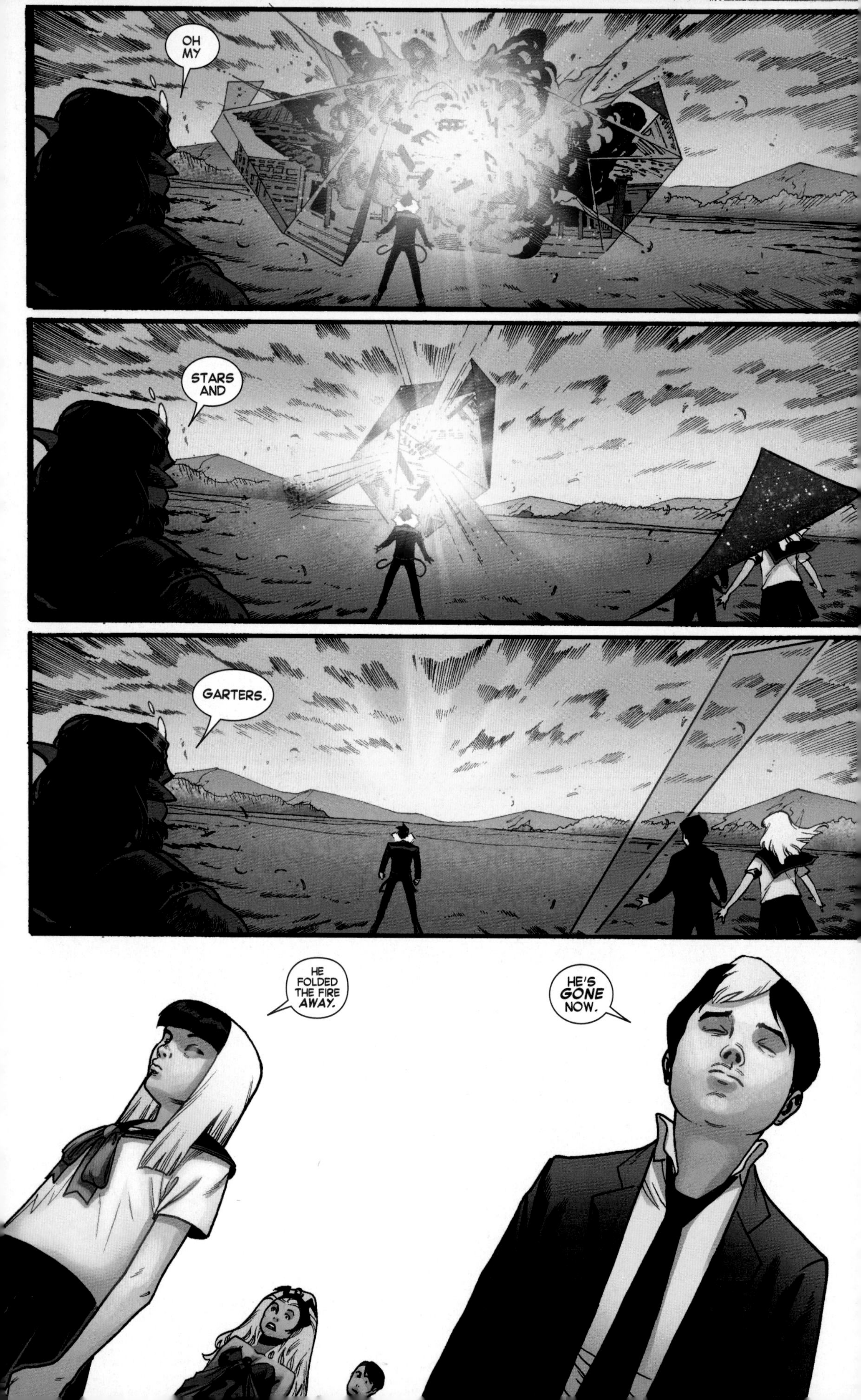
OH MY
STARS AND
GARTERS.
HE FOLDED THE FIRE AWAY.
HE'S GONE NOW.

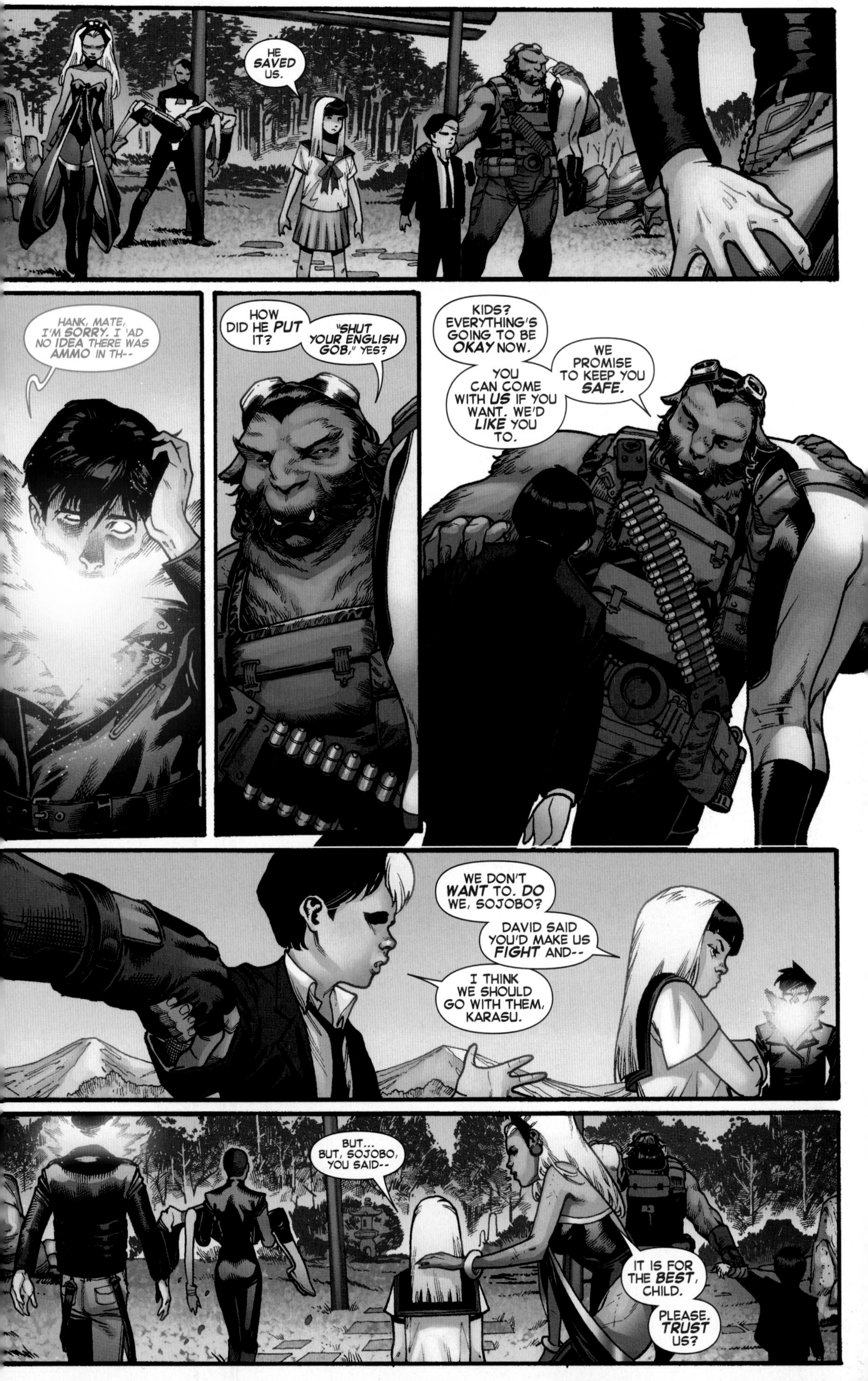
HE SAVED US.
HANK, MATE, I'M SORRY. I 'AD NO IDEA THERE WAS AMMO IN TH--
HOW DID HE PUT IT?
"SHUT YOUR ENGLISH GOB," YES?
KIDS? EVERYTHING'S GOING TO BE OKAY NOW.
YOU CAN COME WITH US IF YOU WANT. WE'D LIKE YOU TO.
WE PROMISE TO KEEP YOU SAFE.
WE DON'T WANT TO. DO WE, SOJOBO?
DAVID SAID YOU'D MAKE US FIGHT AND--
I THINK WE SHOULD GO WITH THEM, KARASU.
BUT... BUT, SOJOBO, YOU SAID--
IT IS FOR THE BEST, CHILD.
PLEASE. TRUST US?

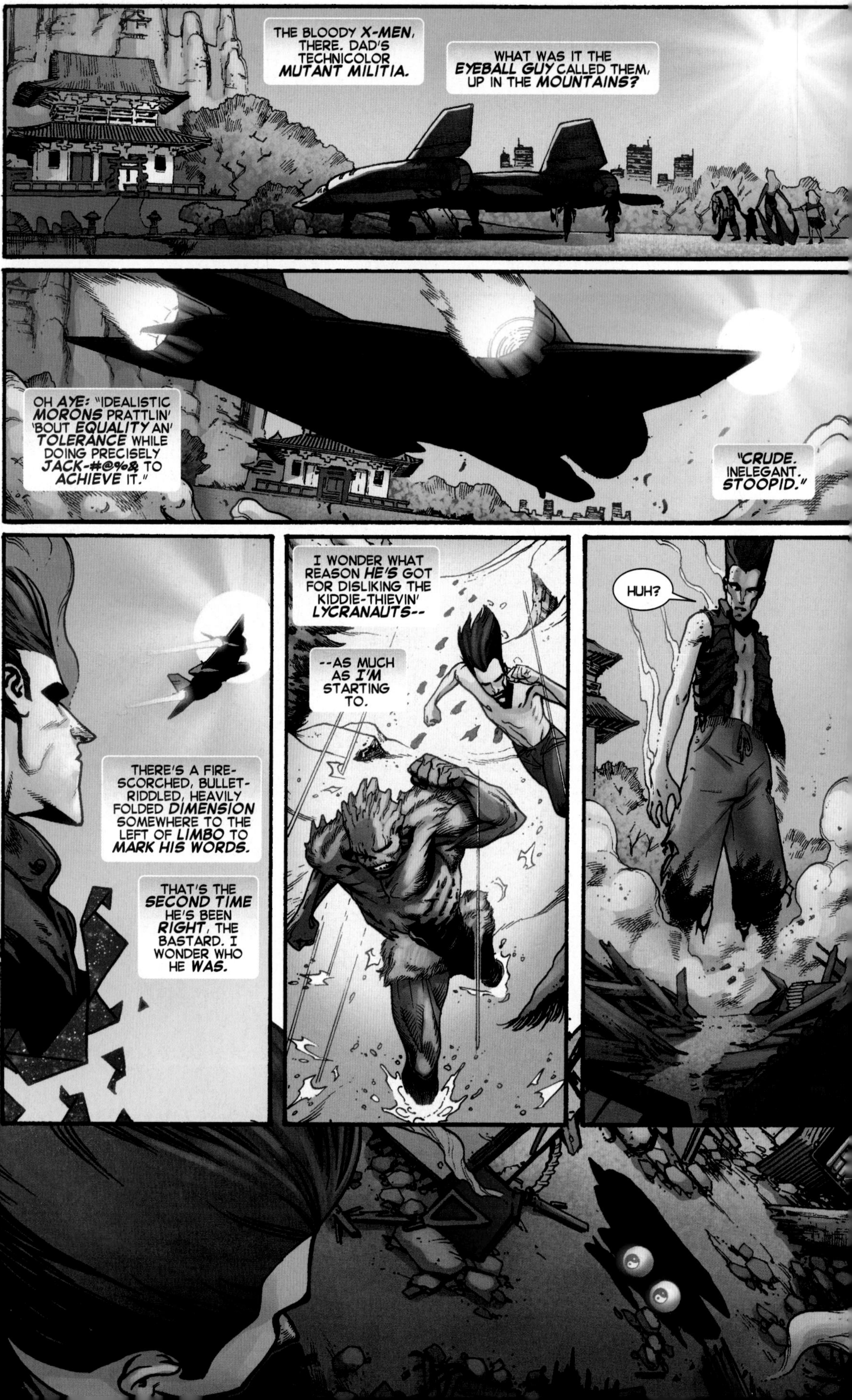

THE BLOODY X-MEN, THERE. DAD'S TECHNICOLOR MUTANT MILITIA.
WHAT WAS IT THE EYEBALL GUY CALLED THEM, UP IN THE MOUNTAINS?
OH AYE: "IDEALISTIC MORONS PRATTLIN' 'BOUT EQUALITY AN' TOLERANCE WHILE DOING PRECISELY JACK-#@%& TO ACHIEVE IT."
"CRUDE. INELEGANT. STOOPID."
THERE'S A FIRE-SCORCHED, BULLET-RIDDLED, HEAVILY FOLDED DIMENSION SOMEWHERE TO THE LEFT OF LIMBO TO MARK HIS WORDS.
THAT'S THE SECOND TIME HE'S BEEN RIGHT, THE BASTARD. I WONDER WHO HE WAS.
I WONDER WHAT REASON HE'S GOT FOR DISLIKING THE KIDDIE-THIEVIN' LYCRANAUTS--
--AS MUCH AS I'M STARTING TO.
HUH?

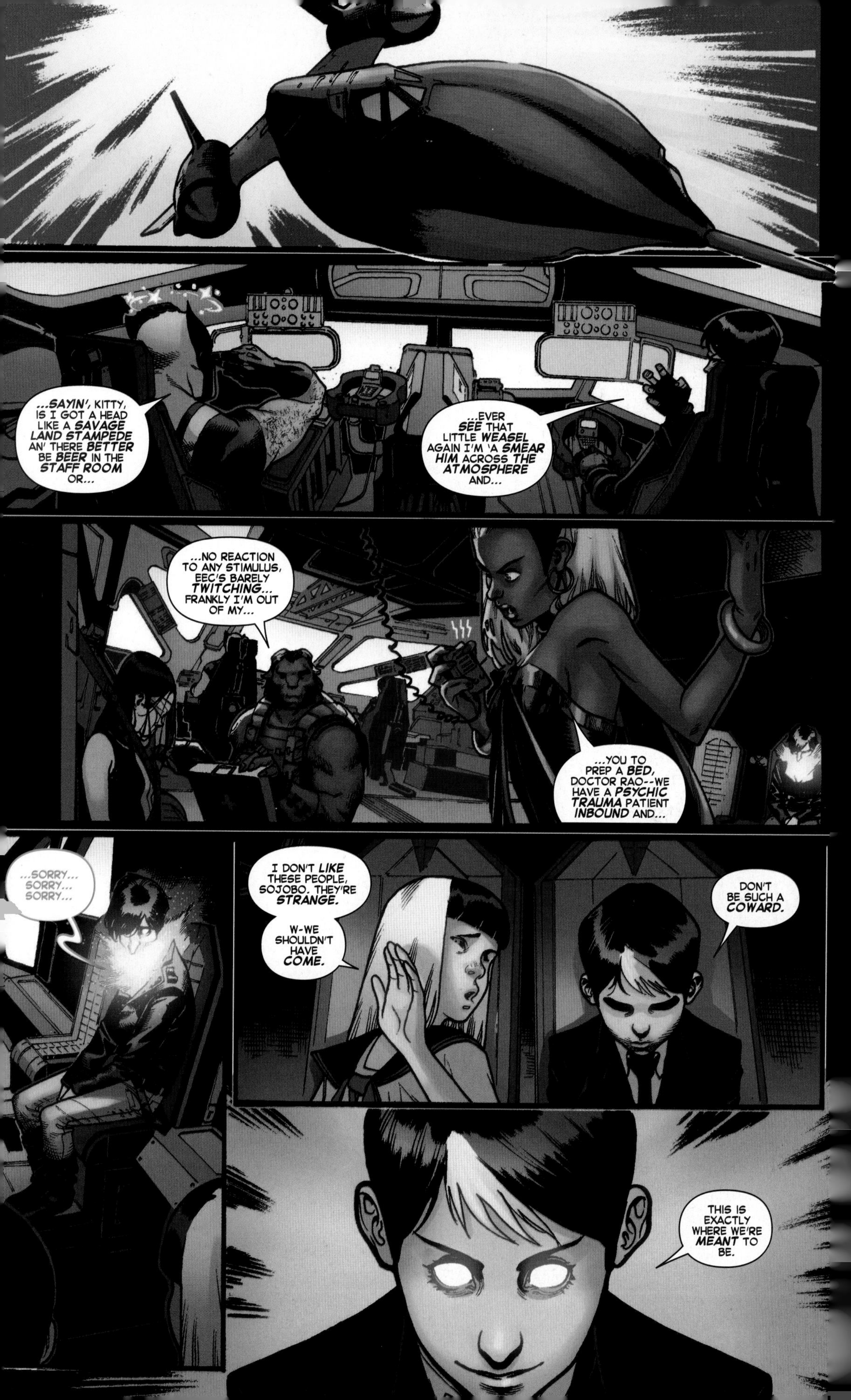
...SAYIN', KITTY, IS I GOT A HEAD LIKE A SAVAGE LAND STAMPEDE AN' THERE BETTER BE BEER IN THE STAFF ROOM OR...
...EVER SEE THAT LITTLE WEASEL AGAIN I'M 'A SMEAR HIM ACROSS THE ATMOSPHERE AND...
...NO REACTION TO ANY STIMULUS, EEC'S BARELY TWITCHING... FRANKLY I'M OUT OF MY...
...YOU TO PREP A BED, DOCTOR RAO--WE HAVE A PSYCHIC TRAUMA PATIENT INBOUND AND...
...SORRY... SORRY... SORRY...
I DON'T LIKE THESE PEOPLE, SOJOBO. THEY'RE STRANGE.
W-WE SHOULDN'T HAVE COME.
DON'T BE SUCH A COWARD.
THIS IS EXACTLY WHERE WE'RE MEANT TO BE.

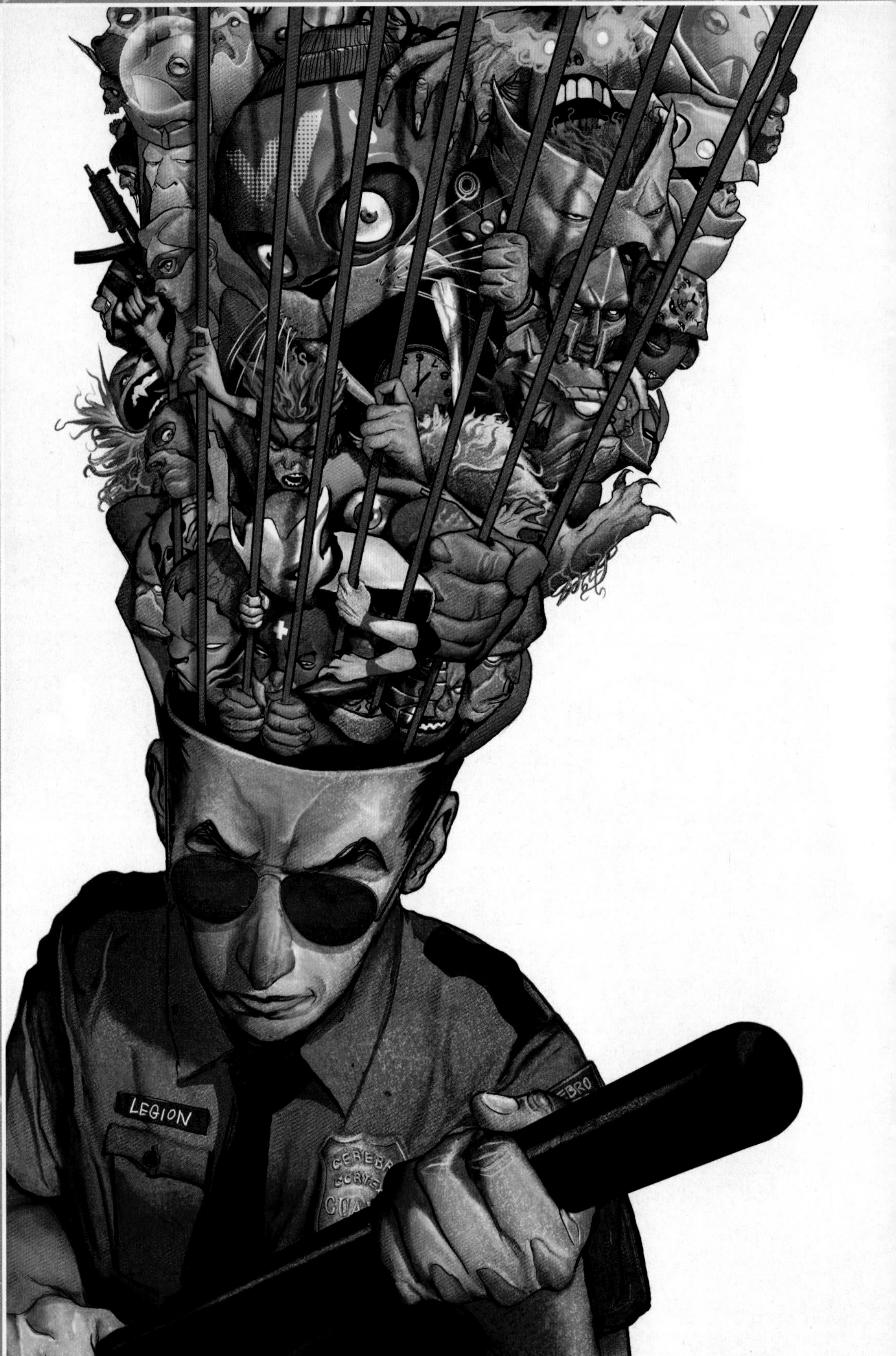

LEGION

FIVE

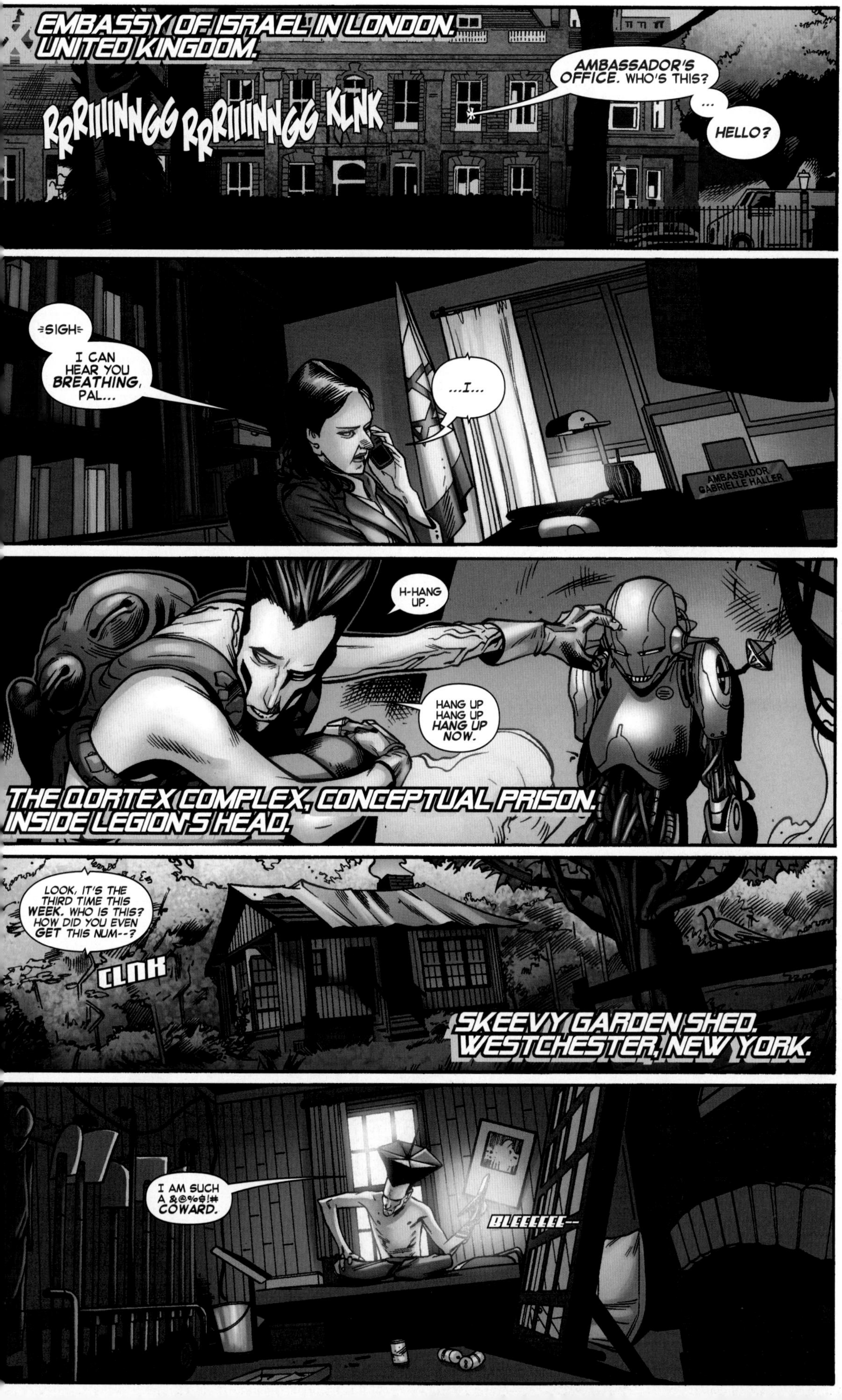
EMBASSY OF ISRAEL IN LONDON. UNITED KINGDOM.
RRRIIIINNGG RRRIIIINNGG KLNK
AMBASSADOR'S OFFICE. WHO'S THIS?
...
HELLO?
=SIGH=
I CAN HEAR YOU BREATHING, PAL...
...I...
AMBASSADOR GABRIELLE HALLER
H-HANG UP.
HANG UP HANG UP HANG UP NOW.
THE QORTEX COMPLEX, CONCEPTUAL PRISON. INSIDE LEGION'S HEAD.
LOOK, IT'S THE THIRD TIME THIS WEEK. WHO IS THIS? HOW DID YOU EVEN GET THIS NUM--?
CLNK
SKEEVY GARDEN SHED. WESTCHESTER, NEW YORK.
I AM SUCH A &@%$!# COWARD.
BLEEEEEE--

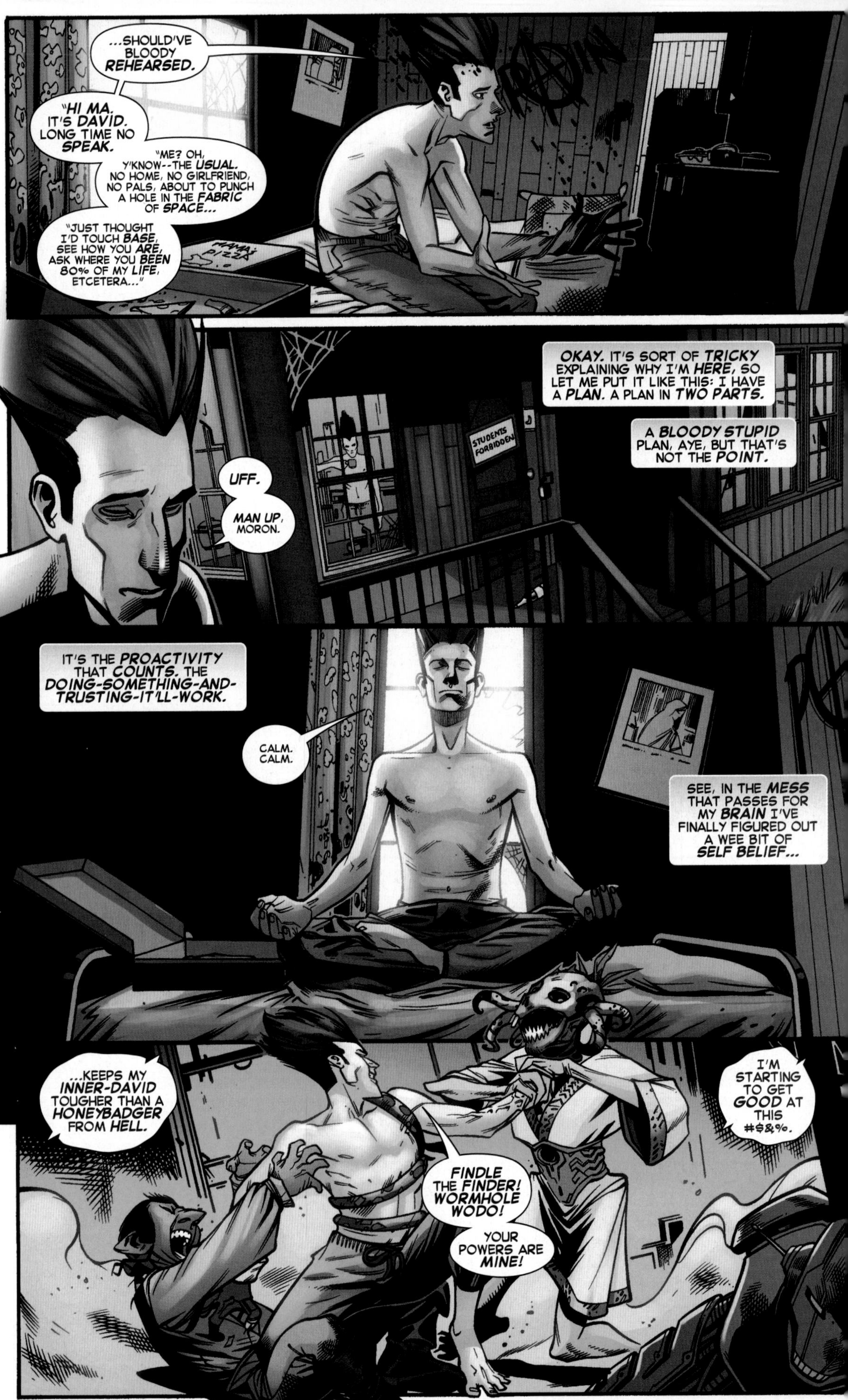
...SHOULD'VE BLOODY REHEARSED.
"HI MA. IT'S DAVID. LONG TIME NO SPEAK.
"ME? OH, Y'KNOW--THE USUAL. NO HOME, NO GIRLFRIEND, NO PALS, ABOUT TO PUNCH A HOLE IN THE FABRIC OF SPACE...
"JUST THOUGHT I'D TOUCH BASE, SEE HOW YOU ARE, ASK WHERE YOU BEEN 80% OF MY LIFE, ETCETERA..."
MAMA'S PIZZA
UFF.
MAN UP, MORON.
STUDENTS FORBIDDEN
OKAY. IT'S SORT OF TRICKY EXPLAINING WHY I'M HERE, SO LET ME PUT IT LIKE THIS: I HAVE A PLAN. A PLAN IN TWO PARTS.
A BLOODY STUPID PLAN, AYE, BUT THAT'S NOT THE POINT.
IT'S THE PROACTIVITY THAT COUNTS. THE DOING-SOMETHING-AND-TRUSTING-IT'LL-WORK.
CALM. CALM.
SEE, IN THE MESS THAT PASSES FOR MY BRAIN I'VE FINALLY FIGURED OUT A WEE BIT OF SELF BELIEF...
...KEEPS MY INNER-DAVID TOUGHER THAN A HONEYBADGER FROM HELL.
FINDLE THE FINDER! WORMHOLE WODO!
YOUR POWERS ARE MINE!
I'M STARTING TO GET GOOD AT THIS #$&%.

FOR *INSTANCE:* RIGHT NOW I'M LOCATING A BUNCH OF *DISGUSTING ALIEN MONSTERS* SEVERAL THOUSAND *LIGHT-YEARS* AWAY, AND TELEPORTING 'EM FIFTY YARDS *NORTH* OF HERE.

WHICH IS BASICALLY *IMPOSSIBLE,* TO ANYONE *WITHOUT* 200 OMEGA-LEVEL *SPLIT PERSONALITIES* IN THEIR *BRAIN.* YAY ME.

IT'S ALSO, I CONCEDE, A SOMEWHAT *INCONSIDERATE* THING TO *DO* TO THE FOLKS WHO LIVE *NEAR HERE.*

STILL: IT'S ONLY *PART ONE* OF THE PLAN. WE'LL COME BACK TO IT IN A *MINUTE,* WHEN THE *COSMIC WORMHOLES'VE* DONE THEIR *JOB.*

PART *TWO'S* THE *IMPORTANT BIT* ANYWAY.

PART *TWO'S* ALL ABOUT MY *DELIGHTFUL, TENTACLED BACKPACK BUDDY...*

ONE DAY I'LL *EAT YOUR LUNGS,* YOU BIG-HAIRED *BAAAAAAA*

...TYRANNIX THE *ABOMINOID.*

THANKS TO *HIM,* MINE'S THE POWER OF *TELEPATHY.* I'LL BE *NEEDING* THAT.

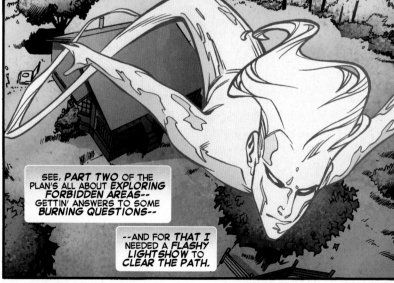

SEE, *PART TWO* OF THE PLAN'S ALL ABOUT *EXPLORING FORBIDDEN AREAS--* GETTIN' ANSWERS TO SOME *BURNING QUESTIONS--*

--AND FOR *THAT I* NEEDED A *FLASHY LIGHTSHOW* TO *CLEAR THE PATH.*

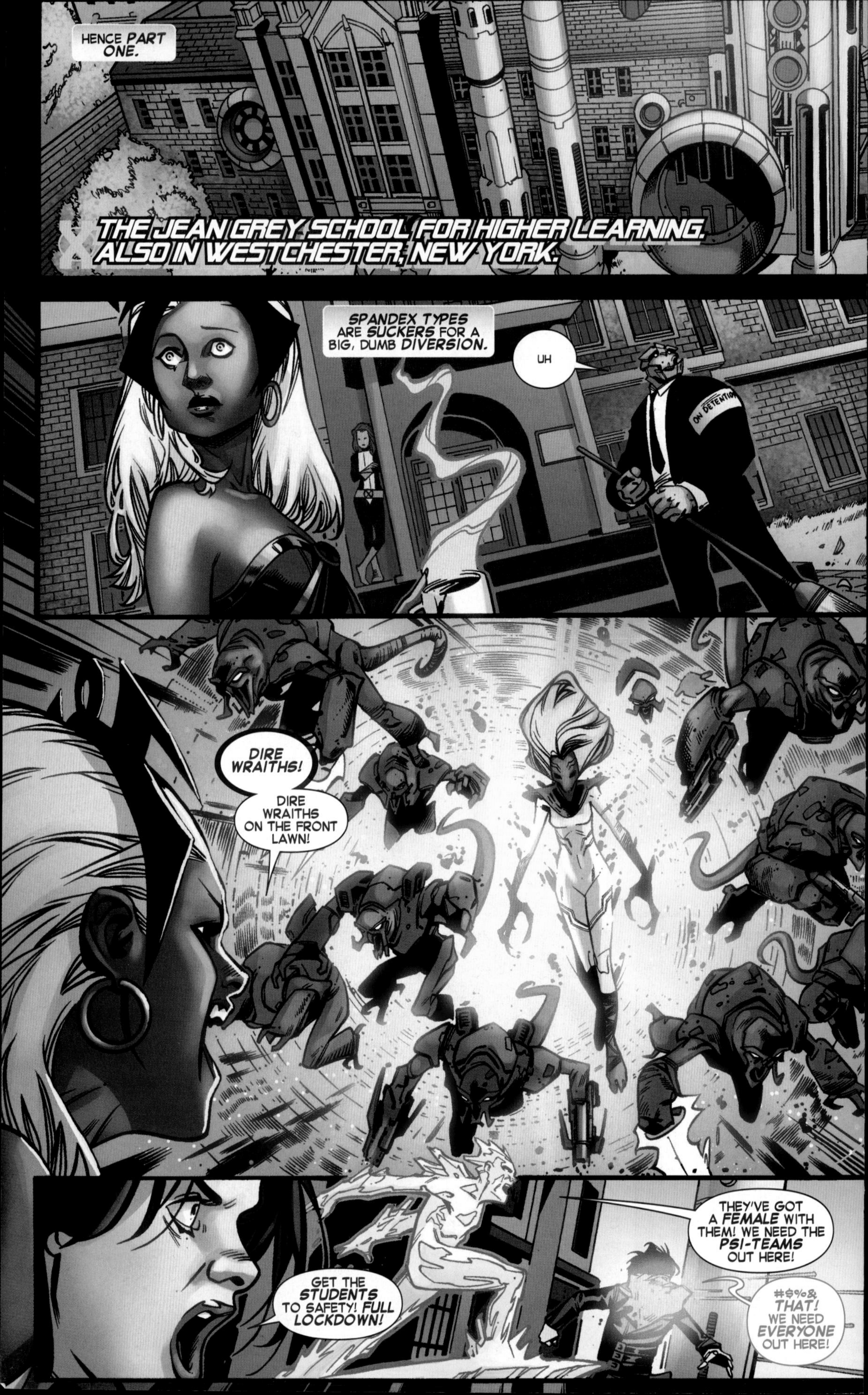

HENCE PART ONE.
THE JEAN GREY SCHOOL FOR HIGHER LEARNING. ALSO IN WESTCHESTER, NEW YORK.
SPANDEX TYPES ARE SUCKERS FOR A BIG, DUMB DIVERSION.
UH
ON DETENTION
DIRE WRAITHS!
DIRE WRAITHS ON THE FRONT LAWN!
THEY'VE GOT A FEMALE WITH THEM! WE NEED THE PSI-TEAMS OUT HERE!
GET THE STUDENTS TO SAFETY! FULL LOCKDOWN!
#$%& THAT! WE NEED EVERYONE OUT HERE!

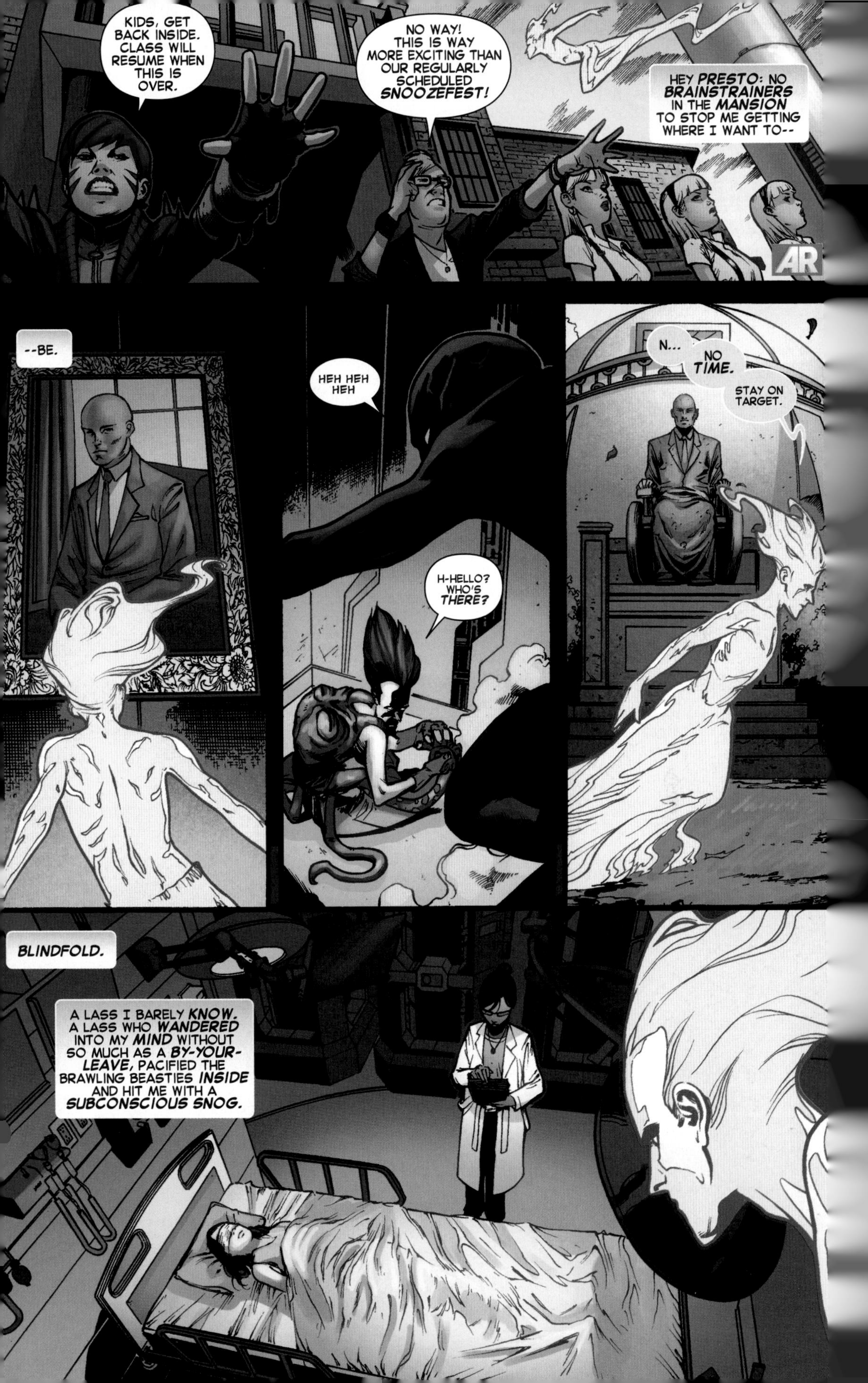
KIDS, GET BACK INSIDE. CLASS WILL RESUME WHEN THIS IS OVER.
NO WAY! THIS IS WAY MORE EXCITING THAN OUR REGULARLY SCHEDULED SNOOZEFEST!
HEY PRESTO: NO BRAINSTRAINERS IN THE MANSION TO STOP ME GETTING WHERE I WANT TO--
--BE.
HEH HEH HEH
H-HELLO? WHO'S THERE?
N...
NO TIME.
STAY ON TARGET.
BLINDFOLD.
A LASS I BARELY KNOW. A LASS WHO WANDERED INTO MY MIND WITHOUT SO MUCH AS A BY-YOUR-LEAVE, PACIFIED THE BRAWLING BEASTIES INSIDE AND HIT ME WITH A SUBCONSCIOUS SNOG.

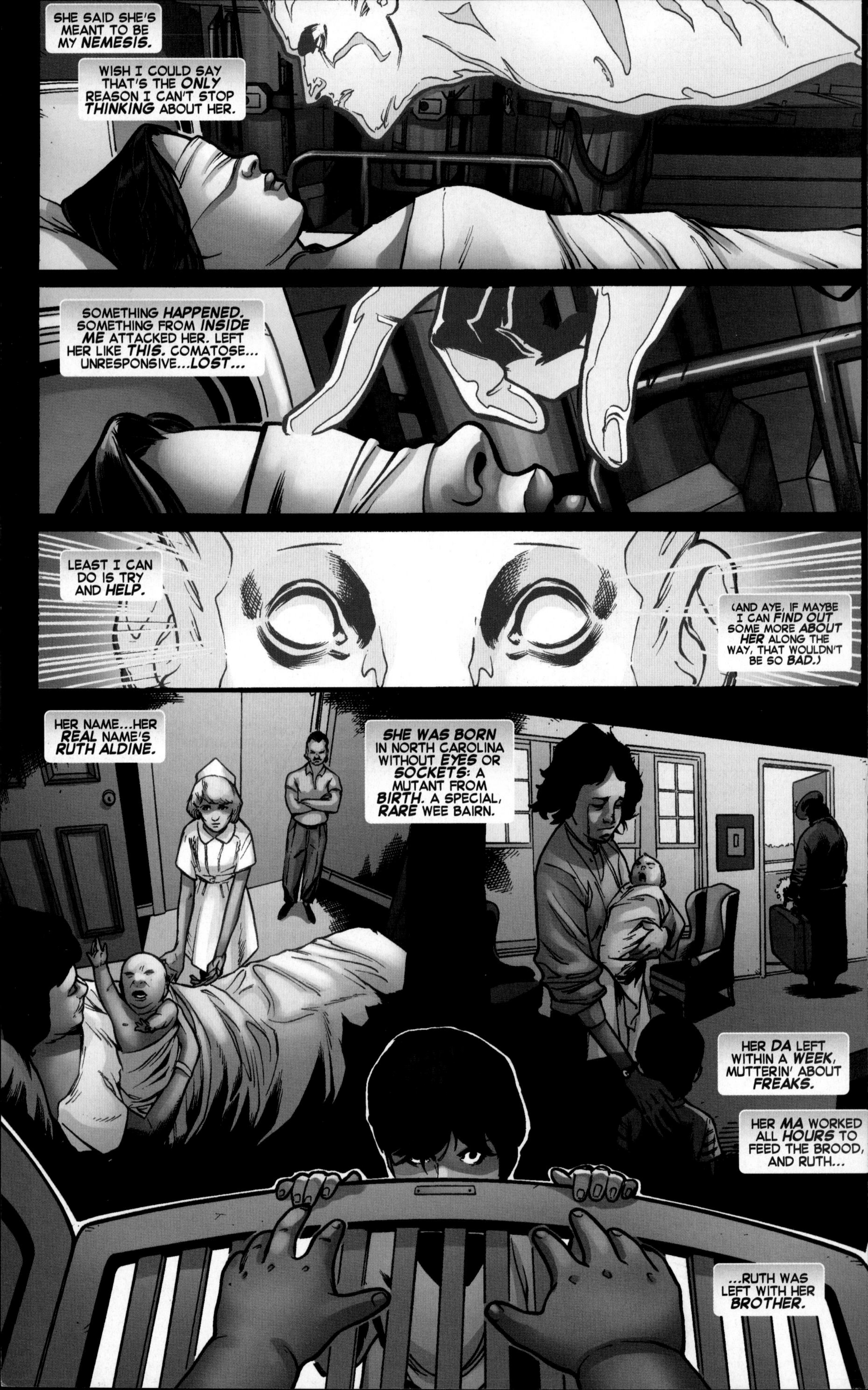
SHE SAID SHE'S MEANT TO BE MY NEMESIS.
WISH I COULD SAY THAT'S THE ONLY REASON I CAN'T STOP THINKING ABOUT HER.
SOMETHING HAPPENED. SOMETHING FROM INSIDE ME ATTACKED HER. LEFT HER LIKE THIS. COMATOSE... UNRESPONSIVE...LOST...
LEAST I CAN DO IS TRY AND HELP.
(AND AYE, IF MAYBE I CAN FIND OUT SOME MORE ABOUT HER ALONG THE WAY, THAT WOULDN'T BE SO BAD.)
HER NAME...HER REAL NAME'S RUTH ALDINE.
SHE WAS BORN IN NORTH CAROLINA WITHOUT EYES OR SOCKETS: A MUTANT FROM BIRTH. A SPECIAL, RARE WEE BAIRN.
HER DA LEFT WITHIN A WEEK, MUTTERIN' ABOUT FREAKS.
HER MA WORKED ALL HOURS TO FEED THE BROOD, AND RUTH...
...RUTH WAS LEFT WITH HER BROTHER.

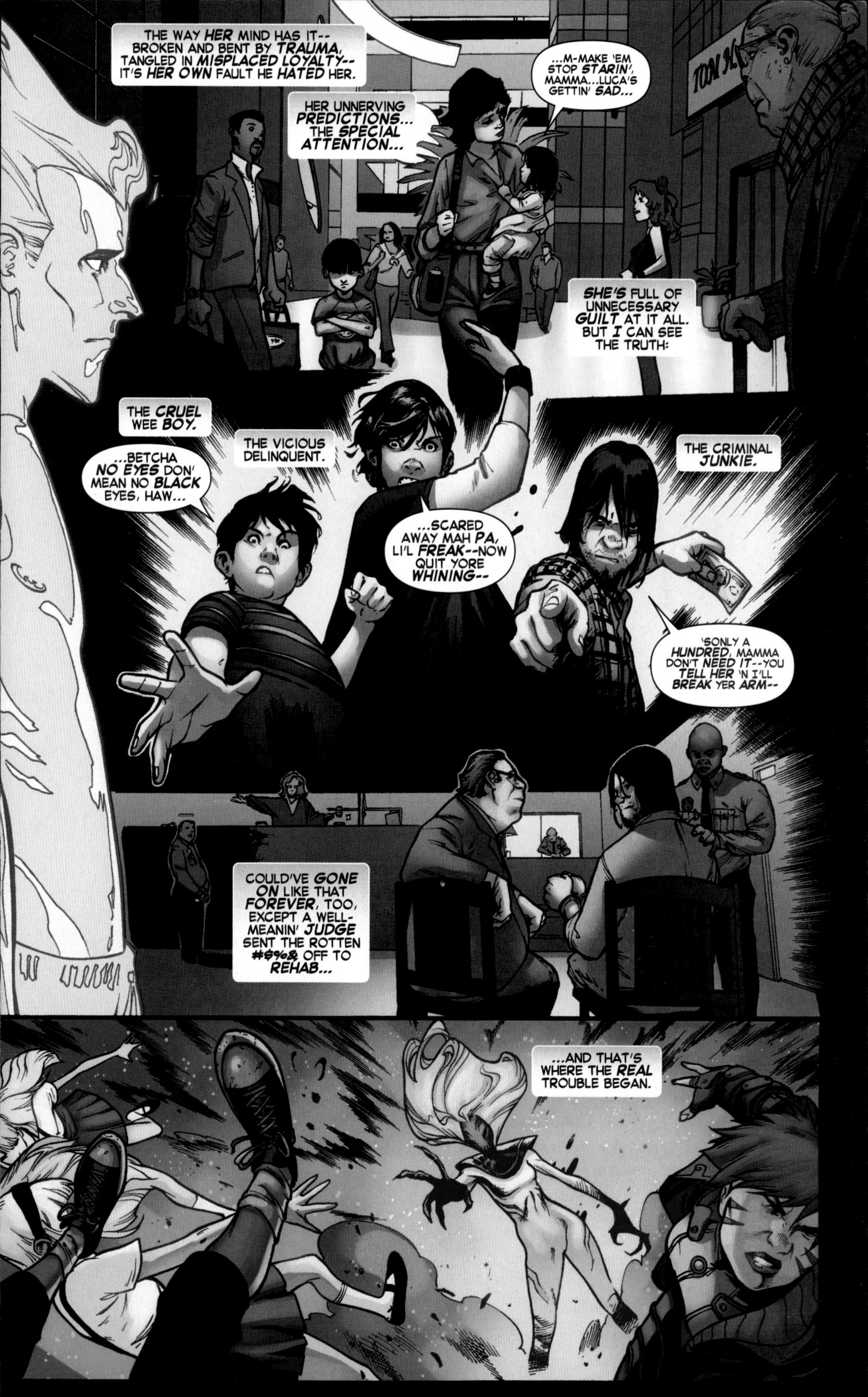
THE WAY HER MIND HAS IT-- BROKEN AND BENT BY TRAUMA, TANGLED IN MISPLACED LOYALTY-- IT'S HER OWN FAULT HE HATED HER.
...M-MAKE 'EM STOP STARIN', MAMMA...LUCA'S GETTIN' SAD...
HER UNNERVING PREDICTIONS... THE SPECIAL ATTENTION...
SHE'S FULL OF UNNECESSARY GUILT AT IT ALL. BUT I CAN SEE THE TRUTH:
THE CRUEL WEE BOY.
...BETCHA NO EYES DON' MEAN NO BLACK EYES, HAW...
THE VICIOUS DELINQUENT.
...SCARED AWAY MAH PA, LI'L FREAK--NOW QUIT YORE WHINING--
THE CRIMINAL JUNKIE.
'SONLY A HUNDRED, MAMMA DON'T NEED IT--YOU TELL HER 'N I'LL BREAK YER ARM--
COULD'VE GONE ON LIKE THAT FOREVER, TOO, EXCEPT A WELL-MEANIN' JUDGE SENT THE ROTTEN #$%& OFF TO REHAB...
...AND THAT'S WHERE THE REAL TROUBLE BEGAN.

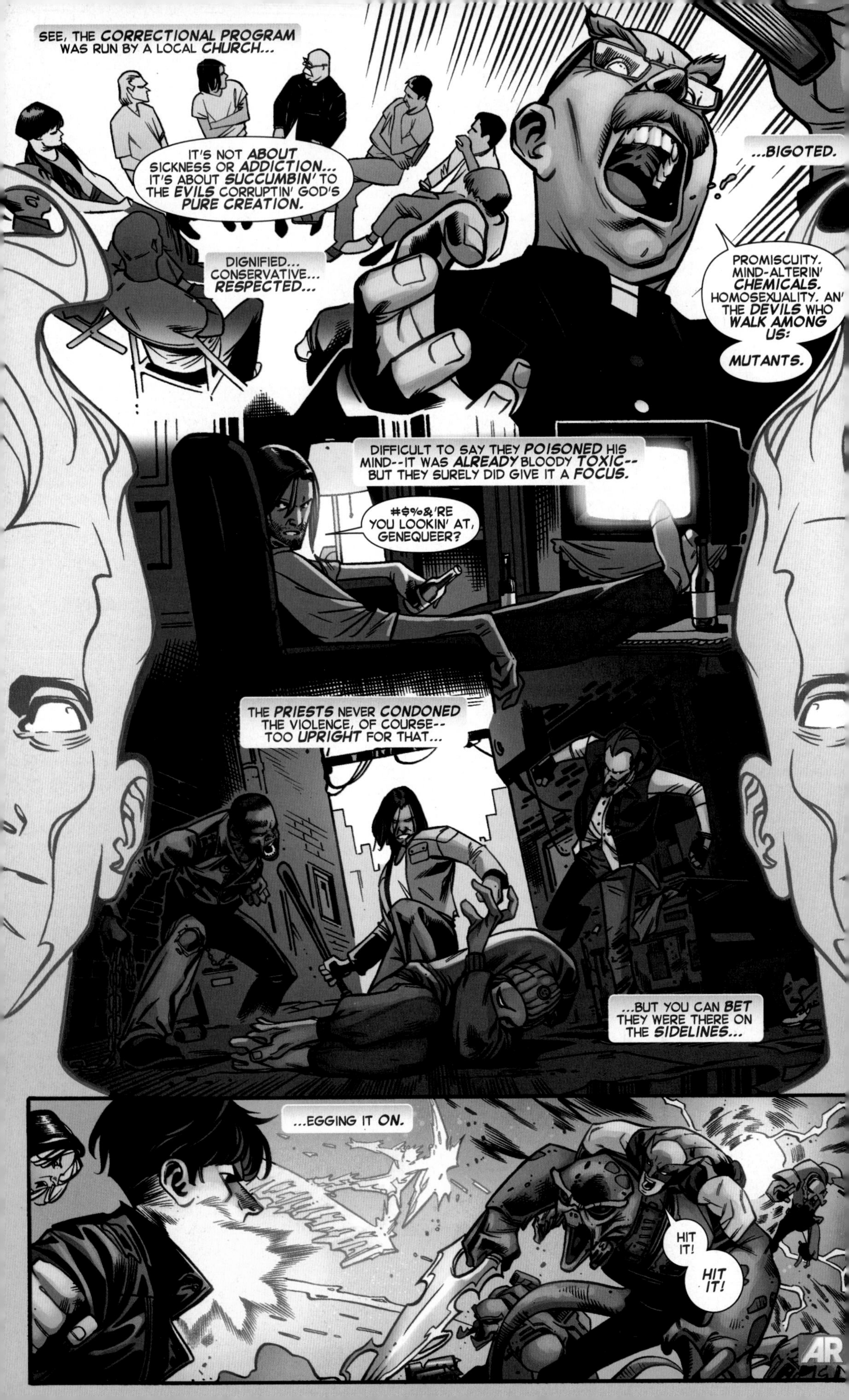

SEE, THE CORRECTIONAL PROGRAM WAS RUN BY A LOCAL CHURCH...
IT'S NOT ABOUT SICKNESS OR ADDICTION... IT'S ABOUT SUCCUMBIN' TO THE EVILS CORRUPTIN' GOD'S PURE CREATION.
DIGNIFIED... CONSERVATIVE... RESPECTED...
...BIGOTED.
PROMISCUITY. MIND-ALTERIN' CHEMICALS. HOMOSEXUALITY. AN' THE DEVILS WHO WALK AMONG US:
MUTANTS.
DIFFICULT TO SAY THEY POISONED HIS MIND--IT WAS ALREADY BLOODY TOXIC--BUT THEY SURELY DID GIVE IT A FOCUS.
#$%&'RE YOU LOOKIN' AT, GENEQUEER?
THE PRIESTS NEVER CONDONED THE VIOLENCE, OF COURSE--TOO UPRIGHT FOR THAT...
...BUT YOU CAN BET THEY WERE THERE ON THE SIDELINES...
...EGGING IT ON.
HIT IT!
HIT IT!
AR

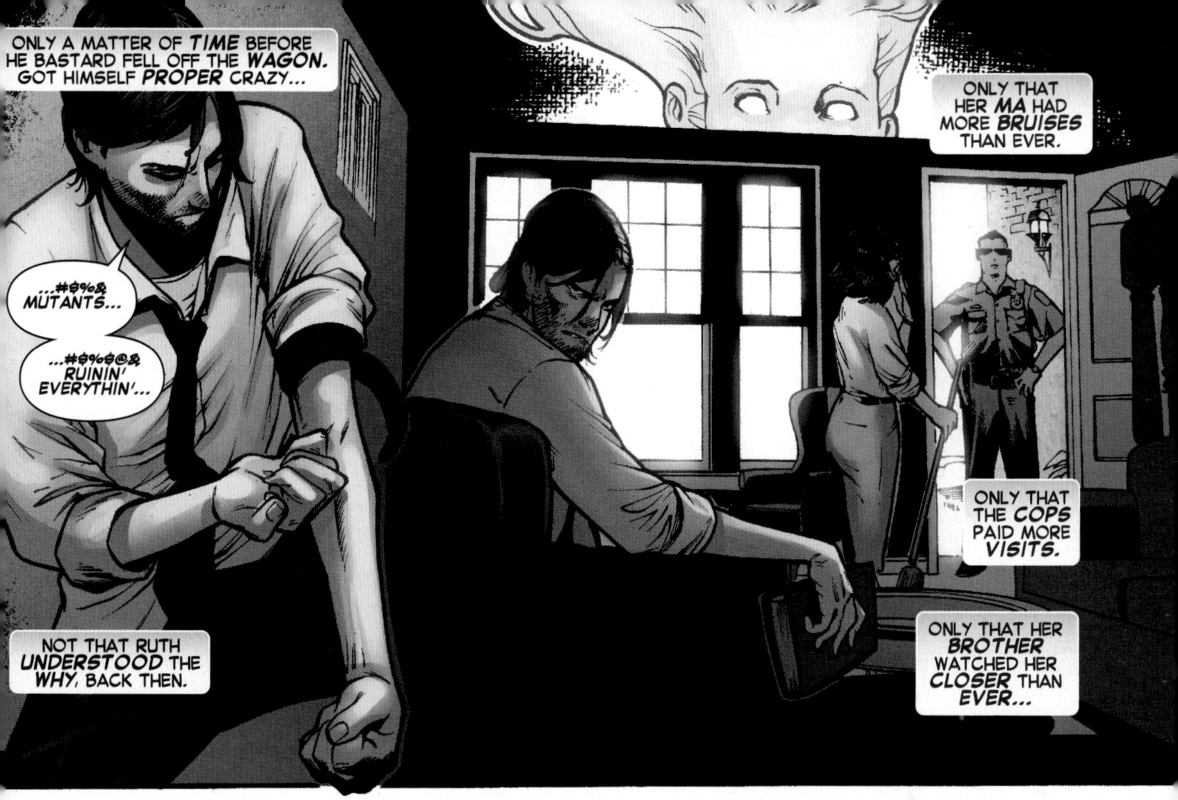
ONLY A MATTER OF *TIME* BEFORE HE BASTARD FELL OFF THE *WAGON.* GOT HIMSELF *PROPER* CRAZY...
...#$%& MUTANTS...
...#$%$@& RUININ' EVERYTHIN'...
NOT THAT RUTH *UNDERSTOOD* THE *WHY,* BACK THEN.
ONLY THAT HER *MA* HAD MORE *BRUISES* THAN EVER.
ONLY THAT THE *COPS* PAID MORE *VISITS.*
ONLY THAT HER *BROTHER* WATCHED HER *CLOSER* THAN *EVER...*

'TIL THE DAY LUCA WENT AS *QUIET* AS *SIN,* AND SLIPPED OUT TO THE *WOODSHED,* AND...AND...

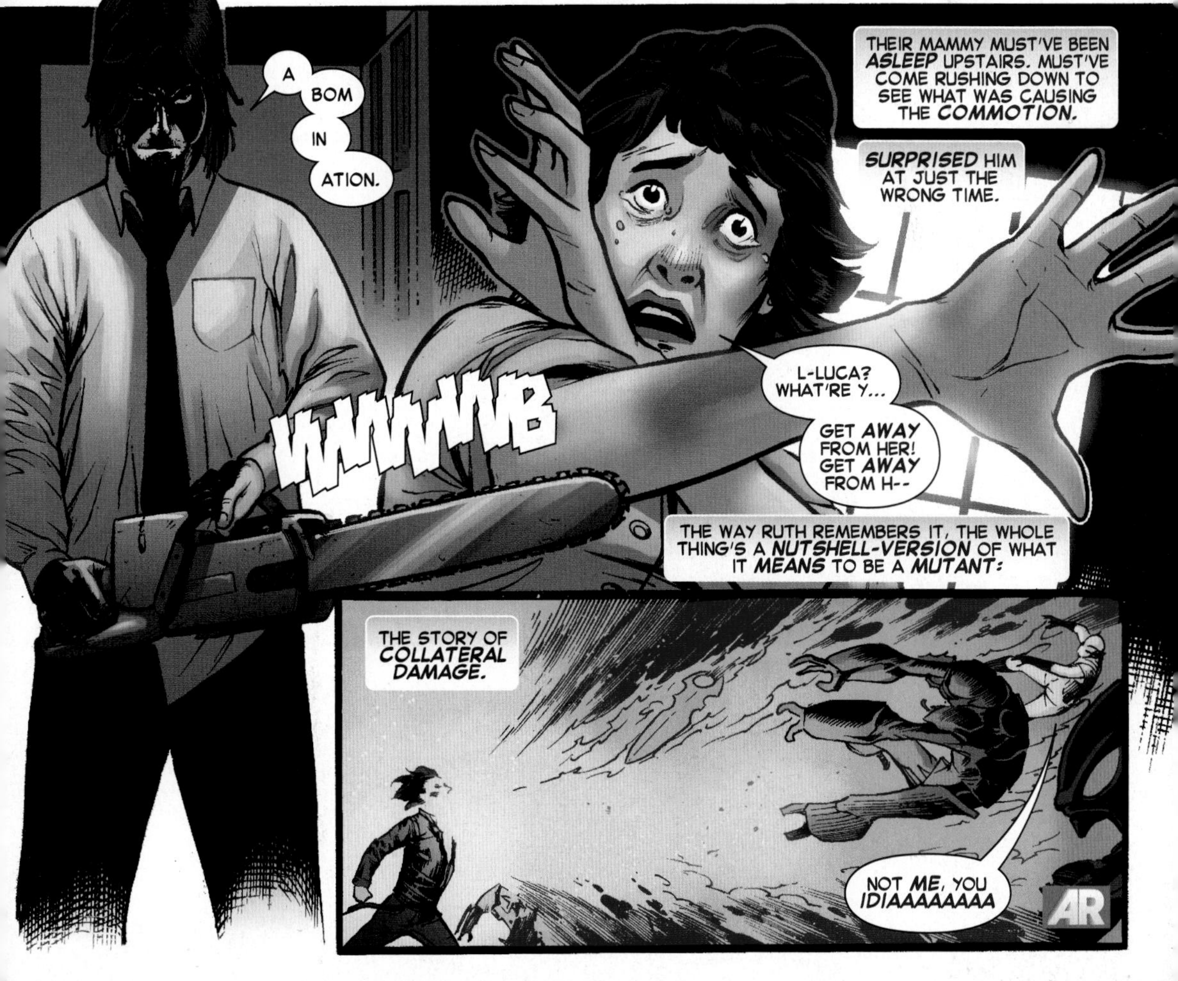
A BOM IN ATION.
THEIR MAMMY MUST'VE BEEN *ASLEEP* UPSTAIRS. MUST'VE COME RUSHING DOWN TO SEE WHAT WAS CAUSING THE *COMMOTION.*
SURPRISED HIM AT JUST THE WRONG TIME.
WWWWWB
L-LUCA? WHAT'RE Y...
GET *AWAY* FROM HER! GET *AWAY* FROM H--
THE WAY RUTH REMEMBERS IT, THE WHOLE THING'S A *NUTSHELL-VERSION* OF WHAT IT *MEANS* TO BE A *MUTANT:*
THE STORY OF *COLLATERAL DAMAGE.*
NOT *ME,* YOU *IDIAAAAAAAA*
AR

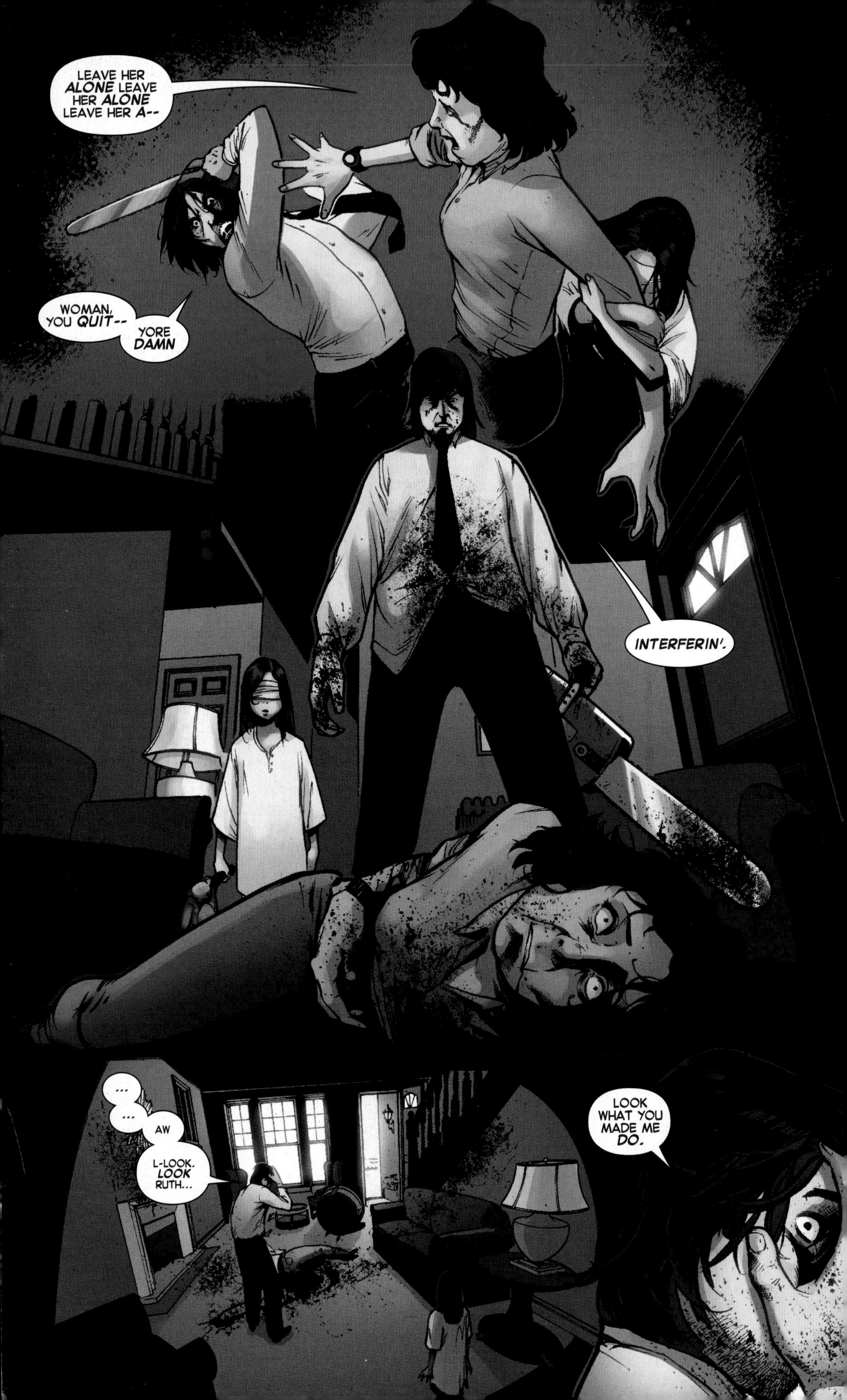
LEAVE HER ALONE LEAVE HER ALONE LEAVE HER A--
WOMAN, YOU QUIT--
YORE DAMN
INTERFERIN'.
...
...
AW
L-LOOK. LOOK RUTH...
LOOK WHAT YOU MADE ME DO.

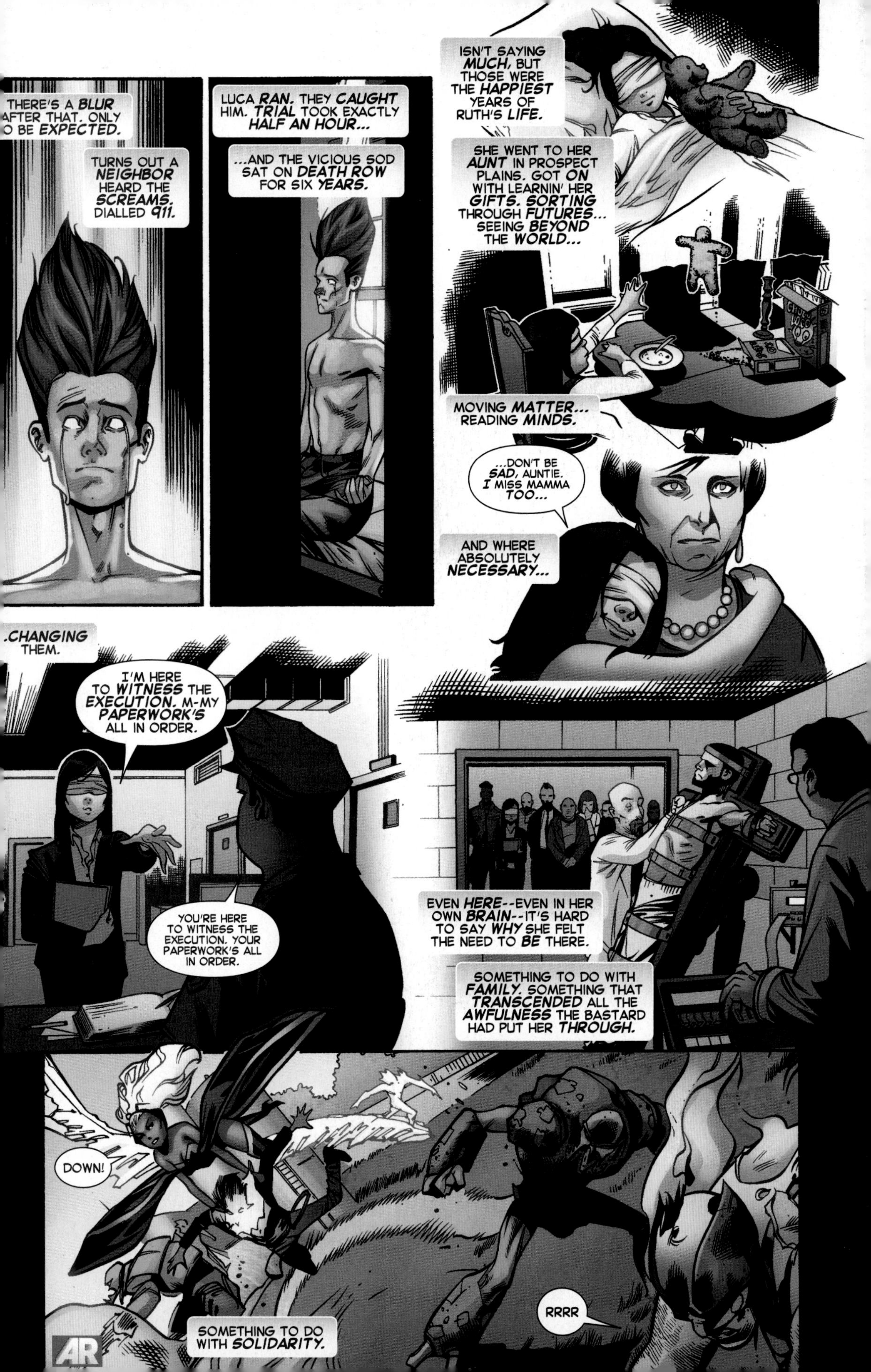
THERE'S A BLUR AFTER THAT. ONLY O BE EXPECTED.
TURNS OUT A NEIGHBOR HEARD THE SCREAMS. DIALLED 911.
LUCA RAN. THEY CAUGHT HIM. TRIAL TOOK EXACTLY HALF AN HOUR...
...AND THE VICIOUS SOD SAT ON DEATH ROW FOR SIX YEARS.
ISN'T SAYING MUCH, BUT THOSE WERE THE HAPPIEST YEARS OF RUTH'S LIFE.
SHE WENT TO HER AUNT IN PROSPECT PLAINS. GOT ON WITH LEARNIN' HER GIFTS. SORTING THROUGH FUTURES... SEEING BEYOND THE WORLD...
MOVING MATTER... READING MINDS.
...DON'T BE SAD, AUNTIE. I MISS MAMMA TOO...
AND WHERE ABSOLUTELY NECESSARY...
.CHANGING THEM.
I'M HERE TO WITNESS THE EXECUTION. M-MY PAPERWORK'S ALL IN ORDER.
YOU'RE HERE TO WITNESS THE EXECUTION. YOUR PAPERWORK'S ALL IN ORDER.
EVEN HERE--EVEN IN HER OWN BRAIN--IT'S HARD TO SAY WHY SHE FELT THE NEED TO BE THERE.
SOMETHING TO DO WITH FAMILY. SOMETHING THAT TRANSCENDED ALL THE AWFULNESS THE BASTARD HAD PUT HER THROUGH.
DOWN!
RRRR
SOMETHING TO DO WITH SOLIDARITY.
AR

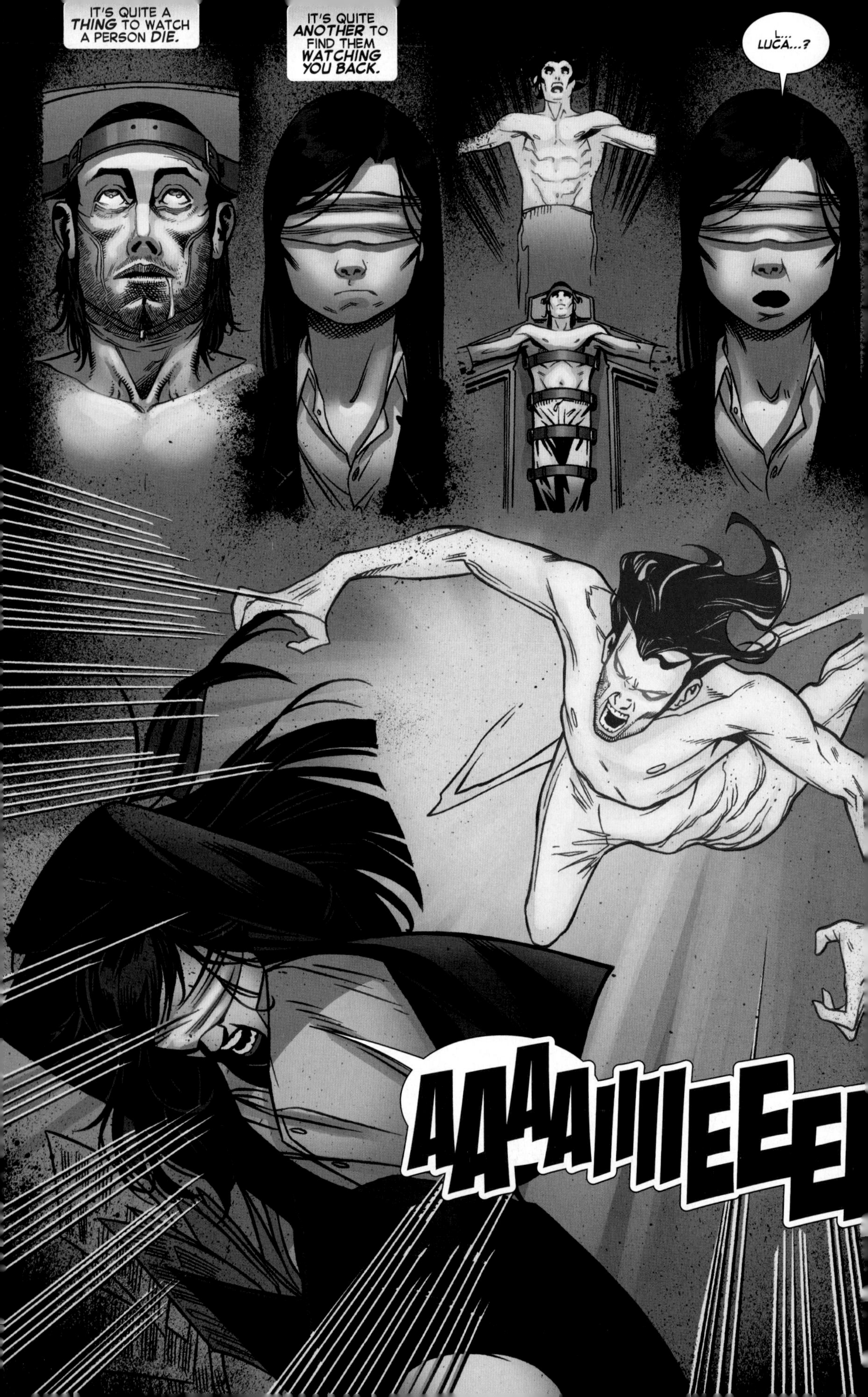
IT'S QUITE A THING TO WATCH A PERSON DIE.
IT'S QUITE ANOTHER TO FIND THEM WATCHING YOU BACK.
L... LUCA...?
AAAAIIIIEEEE

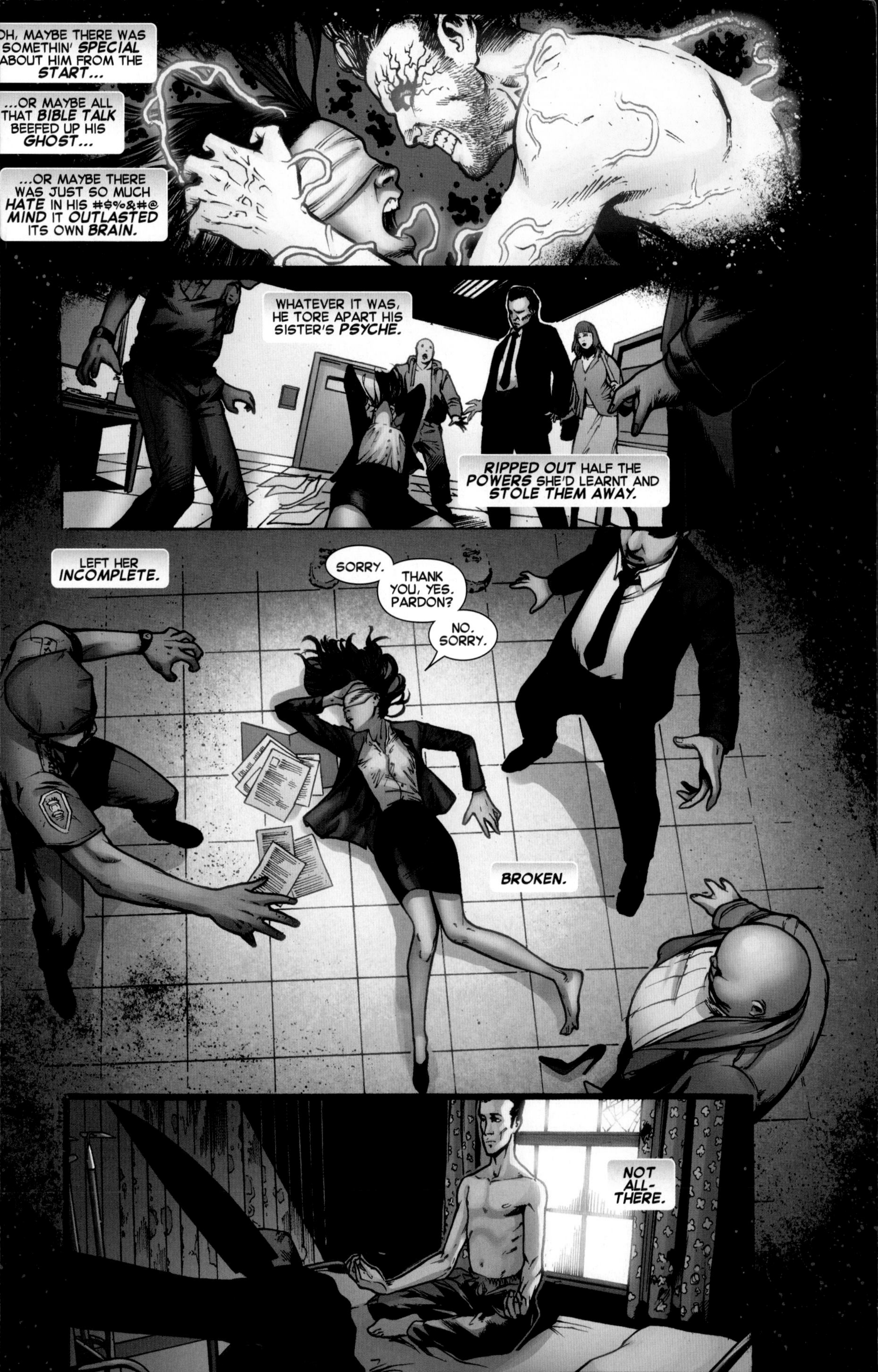

OH, MAYBE THERE WAS SOMETHIN' SPECIAL ABOUT HIM FROM THE START...
...OR MAYBE ALL THAT BIBLE TALK BEEFED UP HIS GHOST...
...OR MAYBE THERE WAS JUST SO MUCH HATE IN HIS #$%&#@ MIND IT OUTLASTED ITS OWN BRAIN.
WHATEVER IT WAS, HE TORE APART HIS SISTER'S PSYCHE.
RIPPED OUT HALF THE POWERS SHE'D LEARNT AND STOLE THEM AWAY.
LEFT HER INCOMPLETE.
SORRY.
THANK YOU, YES. PARDON?
NO. SORRY.
BROKEN.
NOT ALL-THERE.

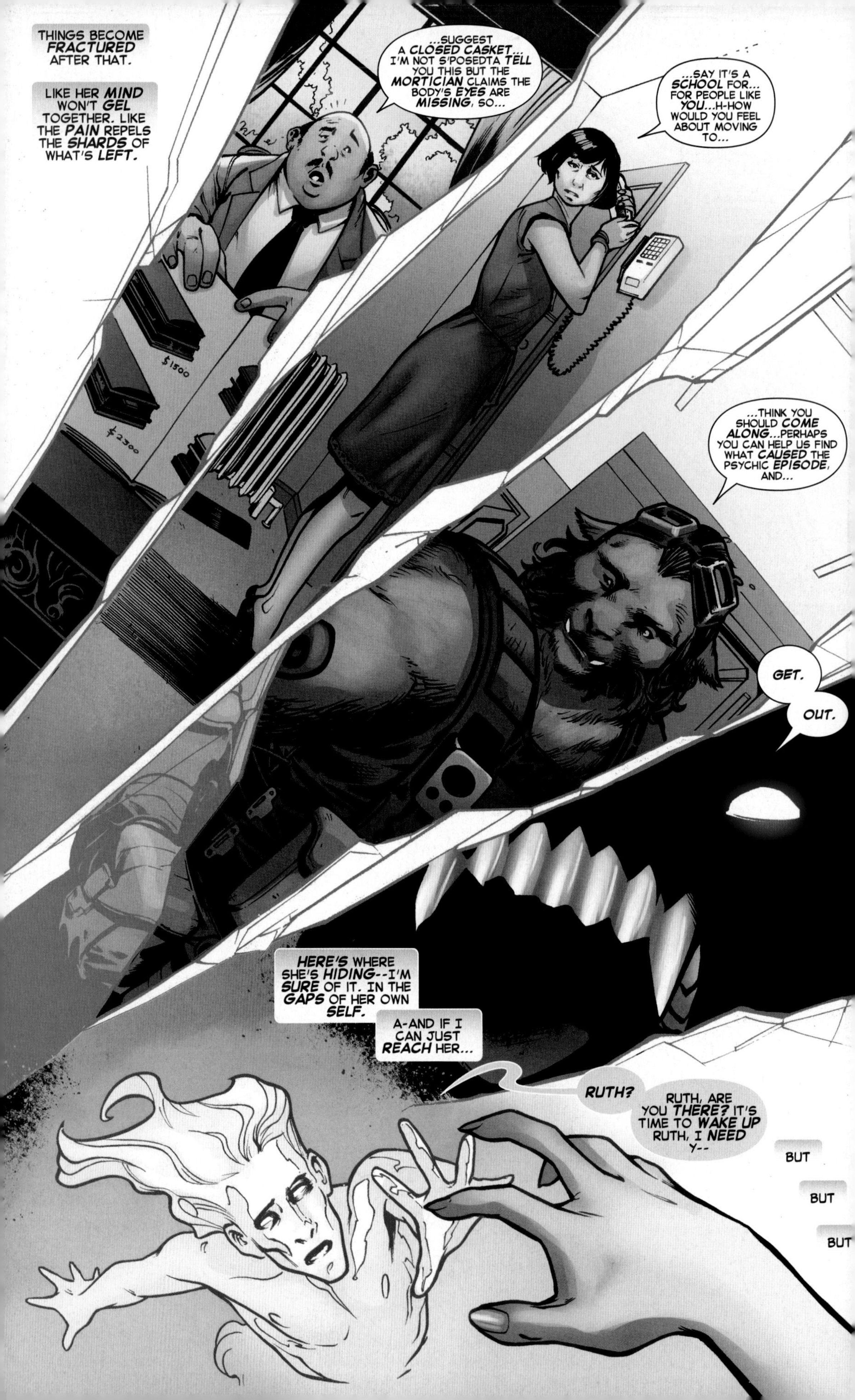
THINGS BECOME FRACTURED AFTER THAT.
LIKE HER MIND WON'T GEL TOGETHER. LIKE THE PAIN REPELS THE SHARDS OF WHAT'S LEFT.
...SUGGEST A CLOSED CASKET... I'M NOT S'POSEDTA TELL YOU THIS BUT THE MORTICIAN CLAIMS THE BODY'S EYES ARE MISSING, SO...
...SAY IT'S A SCHOOL FOR... FOR PEOPLE LIKE YOU...H-HOW WOULD YOU FEEL ABOUT MOVING TO...
$1500
$2300
...THINK YOU SHOULD COME ALONG...PERHAPS YOU CAN HELP US FIND WHAT CAUSED THE PSYCHIC EPISODE, AND...
GET.
OUT.
HERE'S WHERE SHE'S HIDING--I'M SURE OF IT. IN THE GAPS OF HER OWN SELF.
A-AND IF I CAN JUST REACH HER...
RUTH?
RUTH, ARE YOU THERE? IT'S TIME TO WAKE UP RUTH, I NEED Y--
BUT
BUT
BUT

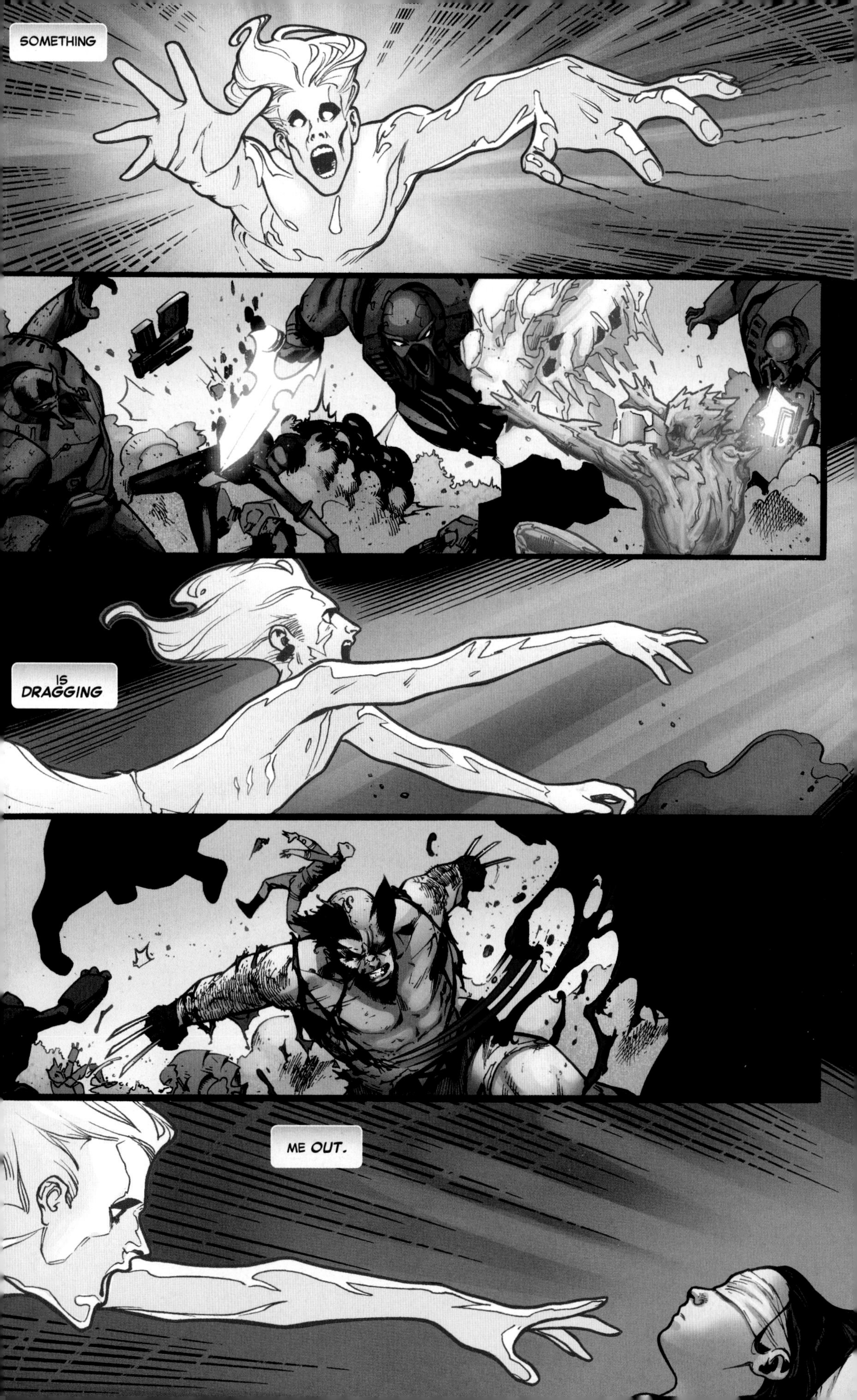
SOMETHING
IS DRAGGING
ME OUT.

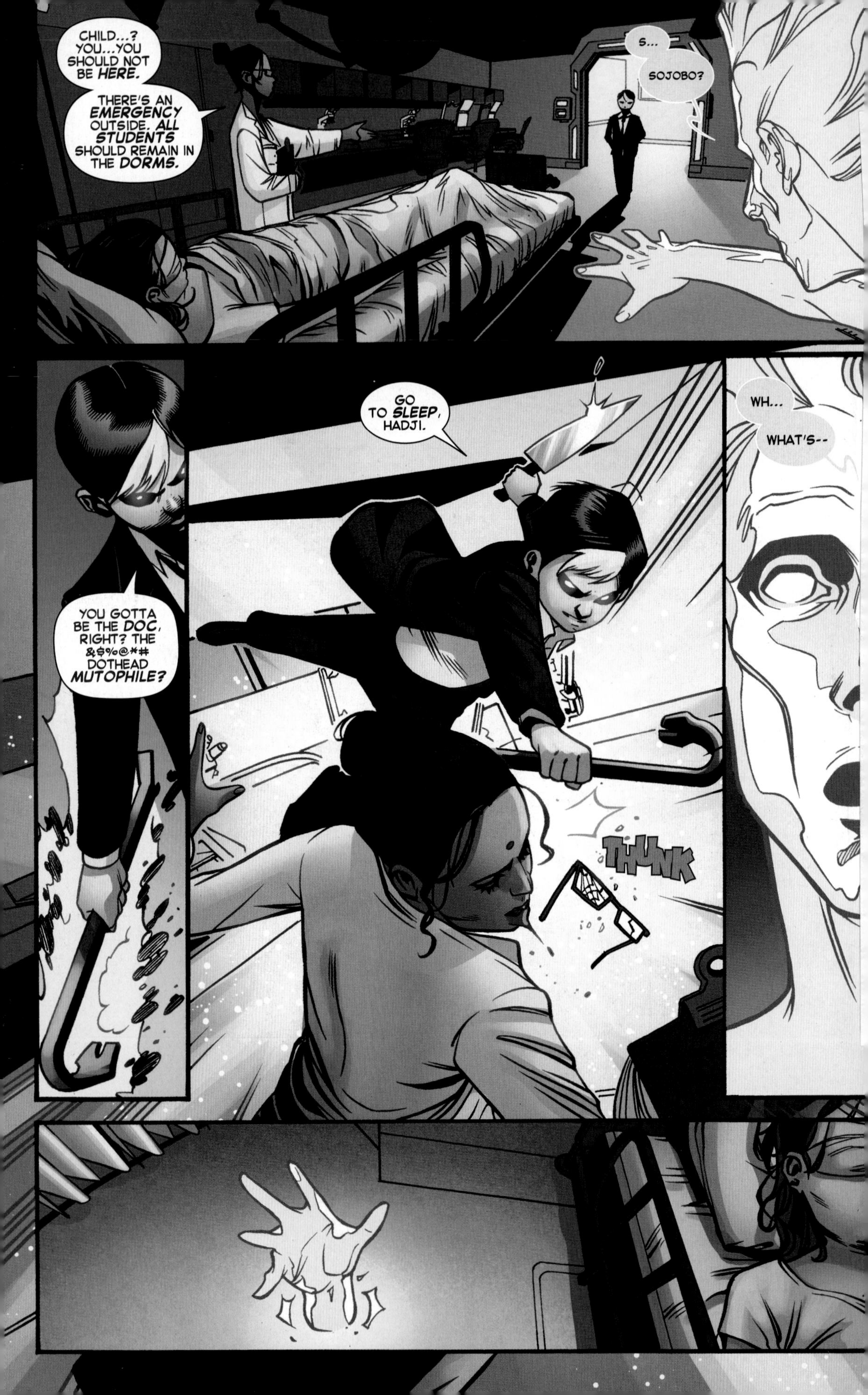
CHILD...? YOU...YOU SHOULD NOT BE HERE.
THERE'S AN EMERGENCY OUTSIDE. ALL STUDENTS SHOULD REMAIN IN THE DORMS.
S...
SOJOBO?
GO TO SLEEP, HADJI.
YOU GOTTA BE THE DOC, RIGHT? THE &$%@*# DOTHEAD MUTOPHILE?
WH...
WHAT'S--
THUNK

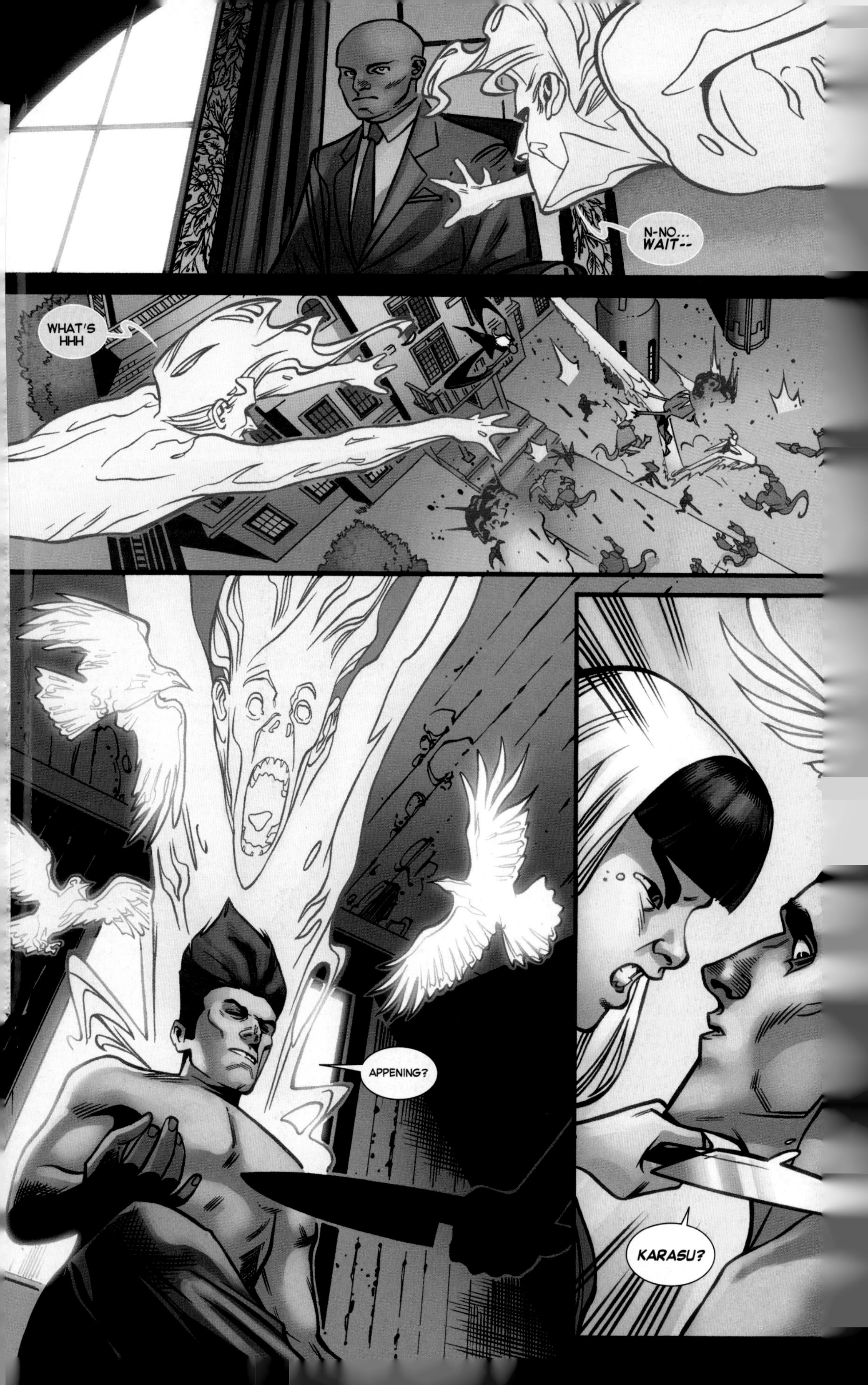
N-NO... WAIT--
WHAT'S HHH
APPENING?
KARASU?

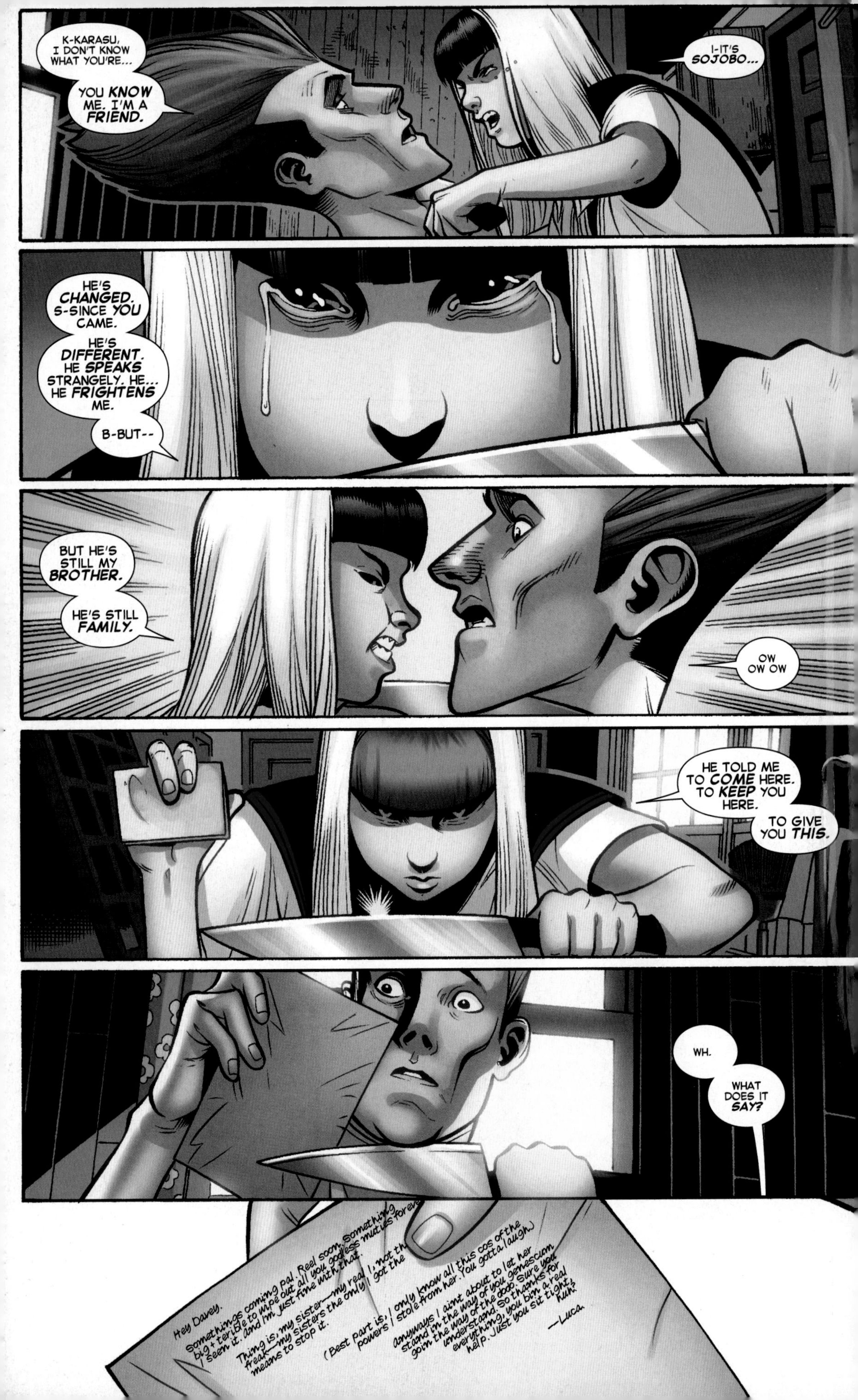
K-KARASU, I DON'T KNOW WHAT YOU'RE...
YOU KNOW ME. I'M A FRIEND.
I-IT'S SOJOBO...
HE'S CHANGED. S-SINCE YOU CAME.
HE'S DIFFERENT. HE SPEAKS STRANGELY. HE... HE FRIGHTENS ME.
B-BUT--
BUT HE'S STILL MY BROTHER.
HE'S STILL FAMILY.
OW OW OW
HE TOLD ME TO COME HERE. TO KEEP YOU HERE.
TO GIVE YOU THIS.
WH.
WHAT DOES IT SAY?
Hey Davey.
Somethings coming pal. Reel soon. Something big + terible to wipe out all you godless muties forev
I seen it. And I'm just fine with that.
Thing is, my sister—my real I, not th
freak—my sisters the only I got the means to stop it.
(Best part is, I only know all this cos of the powers I stole from her. You gotta laugh.)
Anyways I aint about to let her stand in the way of you genescum goin the way of the dodo. Sure you understand. So thanks for everything, you bin a real help. Just you sit tight, huh?
—Luca.

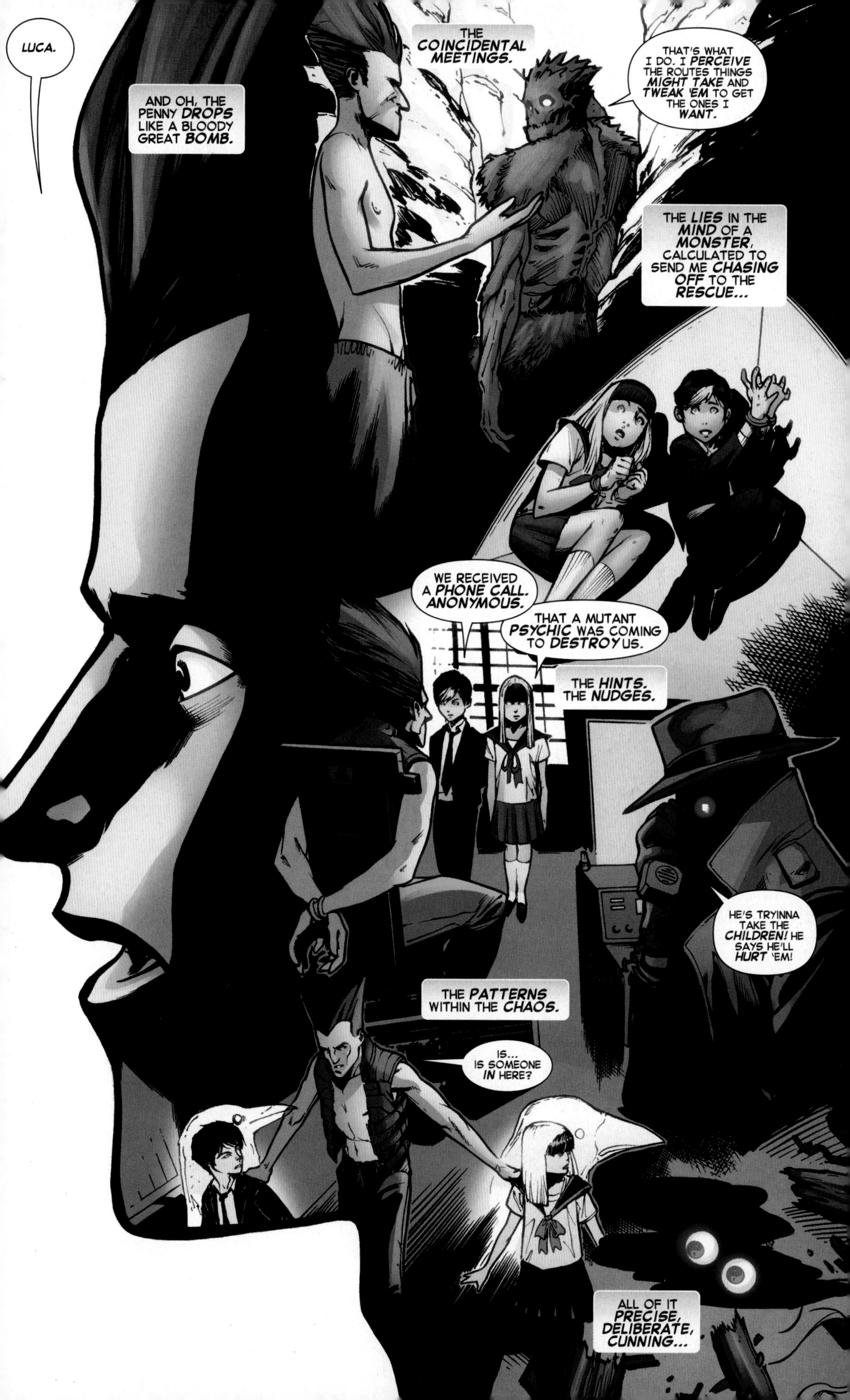
LUCA.
AND OH, THE PENNY DROPS LIKE A BLOODY GREAT BOMB.
THE COINCIDENTAL MEETINGS.
THAT'S WHAT I DO. I PERCEIVE THE ROUTES THINGS MIGHT TAKE AND TWEAK 'EM TO GET THE ONES I WANT.
THE LIES IN THE MIND OF A MONSTER, CALCULATED TO SEND ME CHASING OFF TO THE RESCUE...
WE RECEIVED A PHONE CALL. ANONYMOUS.
THAT A MUTANT PSYCHIC WAS COMING TO DESTROY US.
THE HINTS. THE NUDGES.
HE'S TRYINNA TAKE THE CHILDREN! HE SAYS HE'LL HURT 'EM!
THE PATTERNS WITHIN THE CHAOS.
IS... IS SOMEONE IN HERE?
ALL OF IT PRECISE, DELIBERATE, CUNNING...

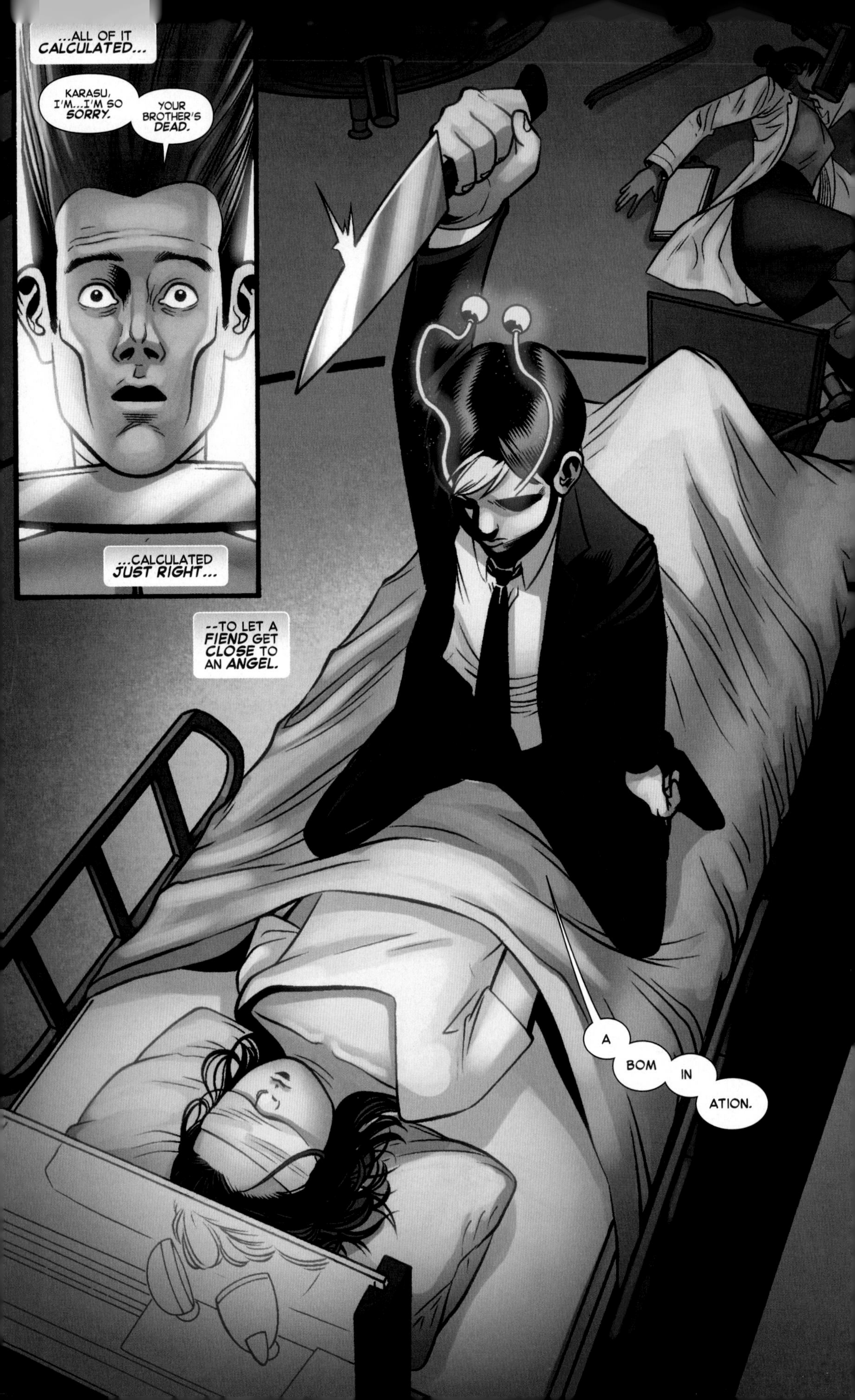
...ALL OF IT CALCULATED...
KARASU, I'M...I'M SO SORRY.
YOUR BROTHER'S DEAD.
...CALCULATED JUST RIGHT...
--TO LET A FIEND GET CLOSE TO AN ANGEL.
A BOM IN ATION.

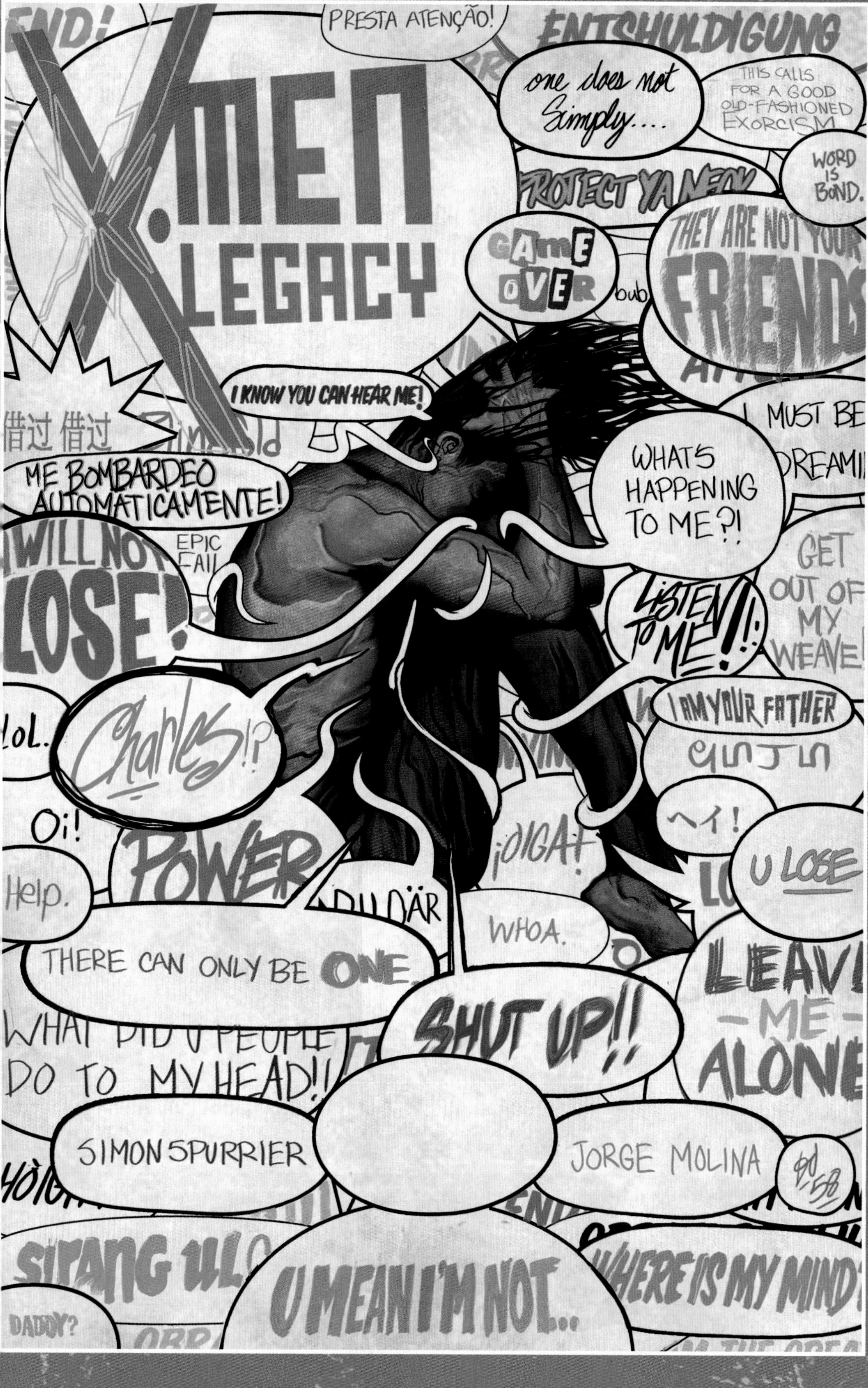

X-MEN LEGACY
PRESTA ATENÇÃO!
ENTSHULDIGUNG
one does not Simply....
THIS CALLS FOR A GOOD OLD-FASHIONED EXORCISM
PROTECT YA NECK
WORD IS BOND.
GAME OVER
bub
THEY ARE NOT YOUR FRIENDS
I KNOW YOU CAN HEAR ME!
借过 借过
I MUST BE DREAMI
ME BOMBARDEO AUTOMATICAMENTE!
WHAT'S HAPPENING TO ME?!
I WILL NOT LOSE!
EPIC FAIL
GET OUT OF MY WEAVE!
LISTEN TO ME!!
LOL.
Charles!?
I AM YOUR FATHER
ヘイ!
Oi!
POWER
¡OIGA!
U LOSE
Help.
WHOA.
THERE CAN ONLY BE ONE.
SHUT UP!!
LEAVE -ME- ALONE
WHAT DID U PEOPLE DO TO MY HEAD!!
SIMON SPURRIER
JORGE MOLINA
U MEAN I'M NOT...
WHERE IS MY MIND?
DADDY?

SIX

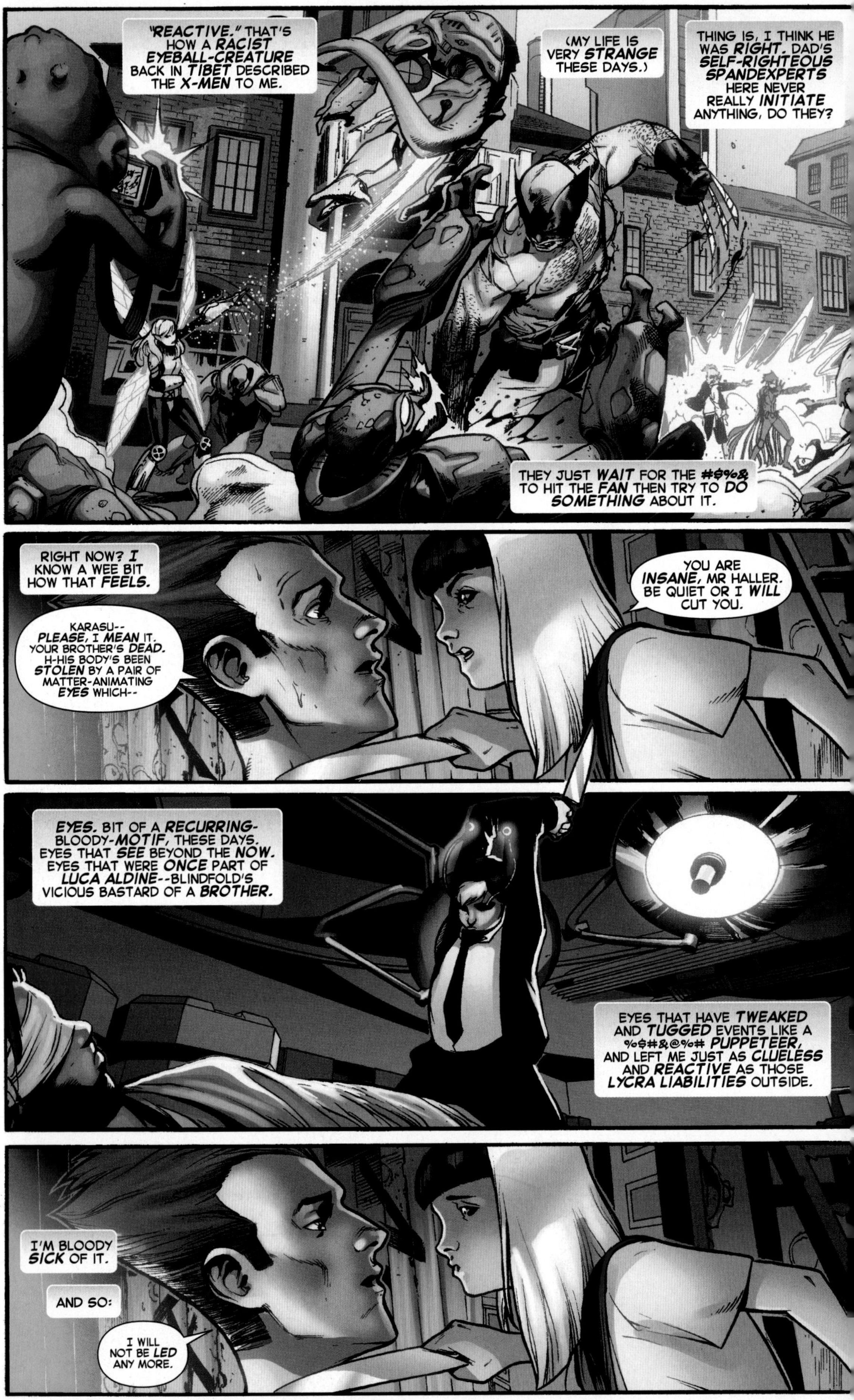
"REACTIVE." THAT'S HOW A RACIST EYEBALL-CREATURE BACK IN TIBET DESCRIBED THE X-MEN TO ME.
(MY LIFE IS VERY STRANGE THESE DAYS.)
THING IS, I THINK HE WAS RIGHT. DAD'S SELF-RIGHTEOUS SPANDEXPERTS HERE NEVER REALLY INITIATE ANYTHING, DO THEY?
THEY JUST WAIT FOR THE #$%& TO HIT THE FAN THEN TRY TO DO SOMETHING ABOUT IT.
RIGHT NOW? I KNOW A WEE BIT HOW THAT FEELS.
KARASU-- PLEASE, I MEAN IT. YOUR BROTHER'S DEAD. H-HIS BODY'S BEEN STOLEN BY A PAIR OF MATTER-ANIMATING EYES WHICH--
YOU ARE INSANE, MR HALLER. BE QUIET OR I WILL CUT YOU.
EYES. BIT OF A RECURRING-BLOODY-MOTIF, THESE DAYS. EYES THAT SEE BEYOND THE NOW. EYES THAT WERE ONCE PART OF LUCA ALDINE--BLINDFOLD'S VICIOUS BASTARD OF A BROTHER.
EYES THAT HAVE TWEAKED AND TUGGED EVENTS LIKE A %$#&@%# PUPPETEER, AND LEFT ME JUST AS CLUELESS AND REACTIVE AS THOSE LYCRA LIABILITIES OUTSIDE.
I'M BLOODY SICK OF IT.
AND SO:
I WILL NOT BE LED ANY MORE.

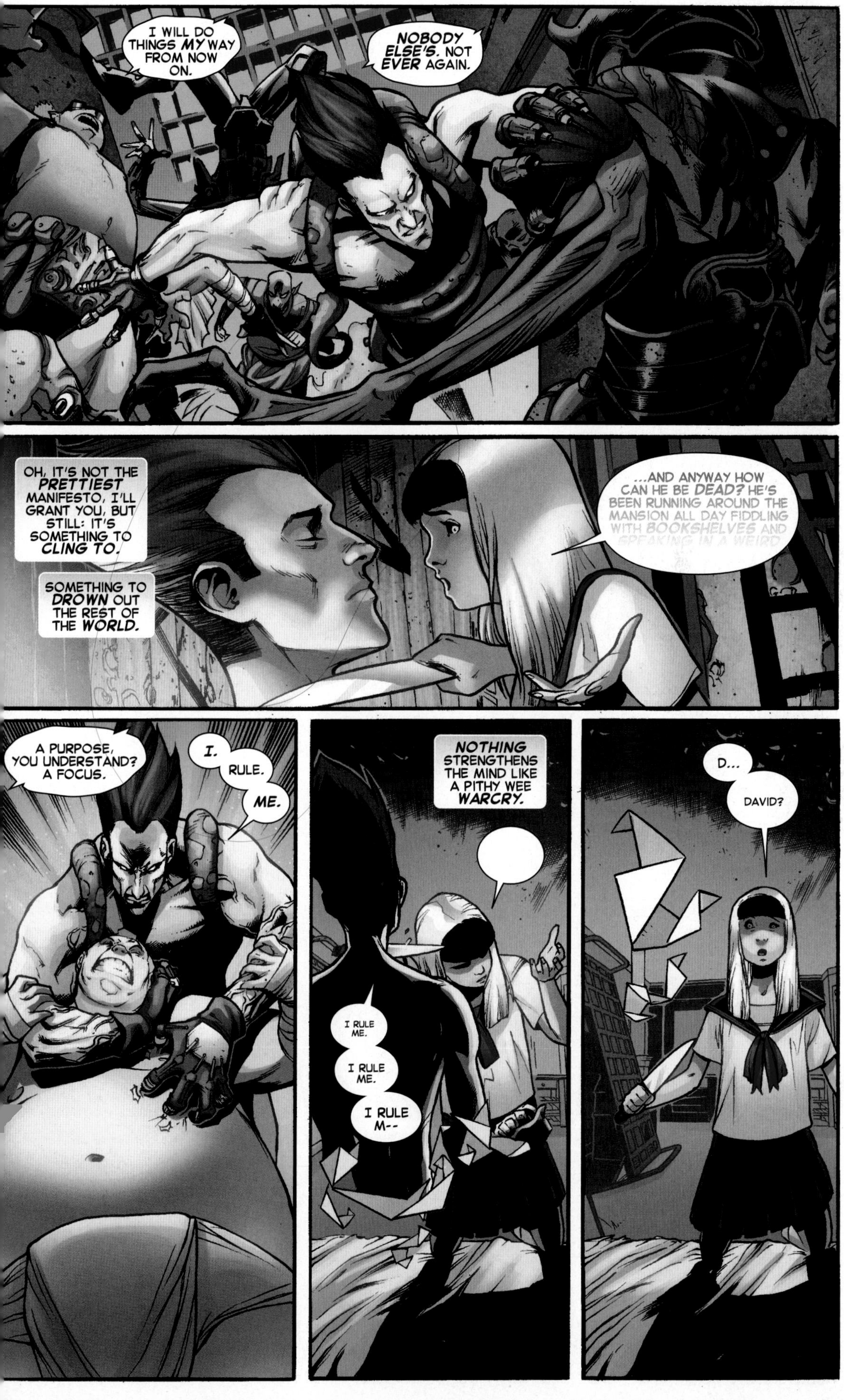
I WILL DO THINGS MY WAY FROM NOW ON.
NOBODY ELSE'S. NOT EVER AGAIN.
OH, IT'S NOT THE PRETTIEST MANIFESTO, I'LL GRANT YOU, BUT STILL: IT'S SOMETHING TO CLING TO.
SOMETHING TO DROWN OUT THE REST OF THE WORLD.
...AND ANYWAY HOW CAN HE BE DEAD? HE'S BEEN RUNNING AROUND THE MANSION ALL DAY FIDDLING WITH BOOKSHELVES AND SPEAKING IN A WEIRD
A PURPOSE, YOU UNDERSTAND? A FOCUS.
I.
RULE.
ME.
NOTHING STRENGTHENS THE MIND LIKE A PITHY WEE WARCRY.
I RULE ME.
I RULE ME.
I RULE M--
D...
DAVID?

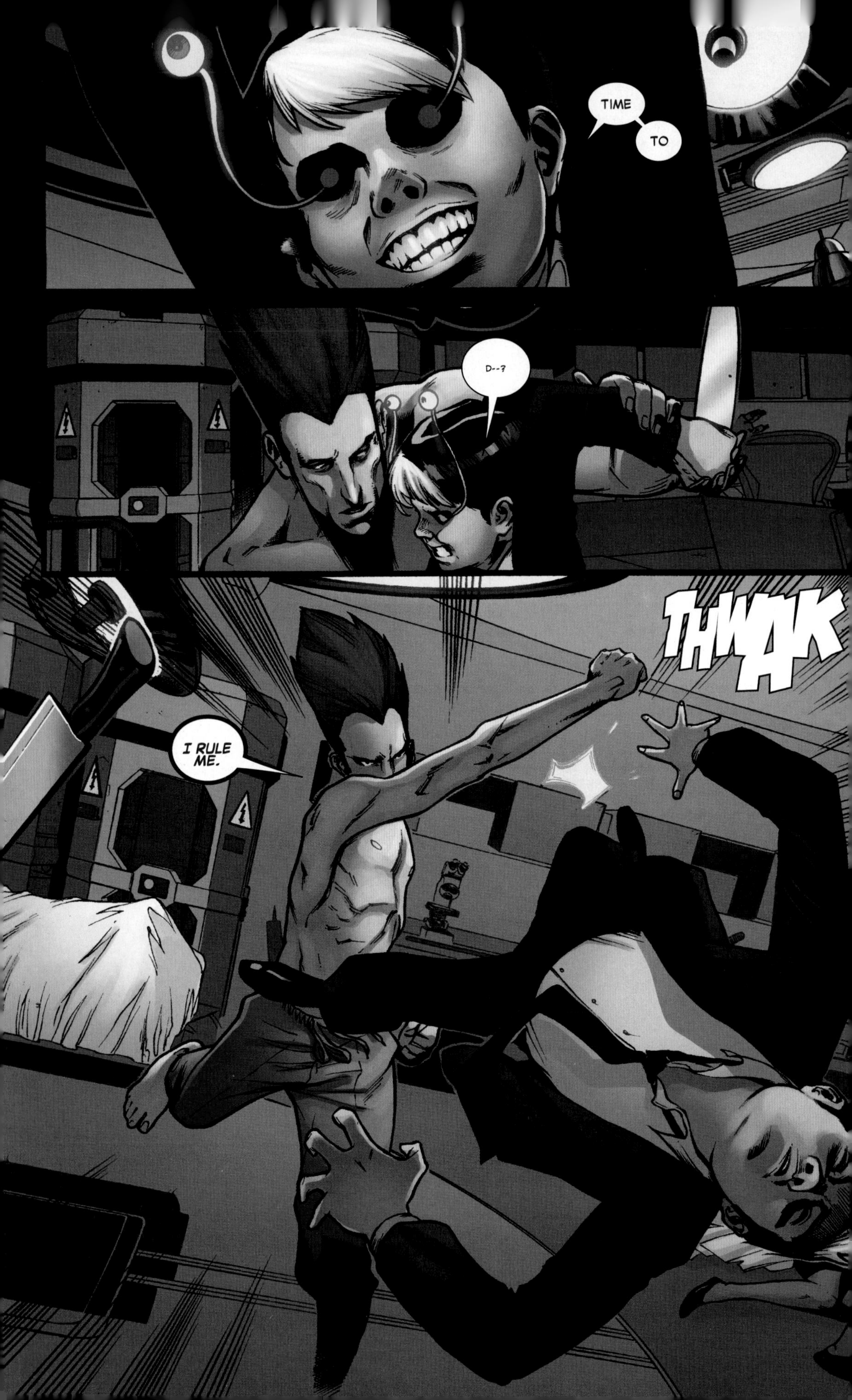

TIME
TO
D--?
THWAK
I RULE ME.

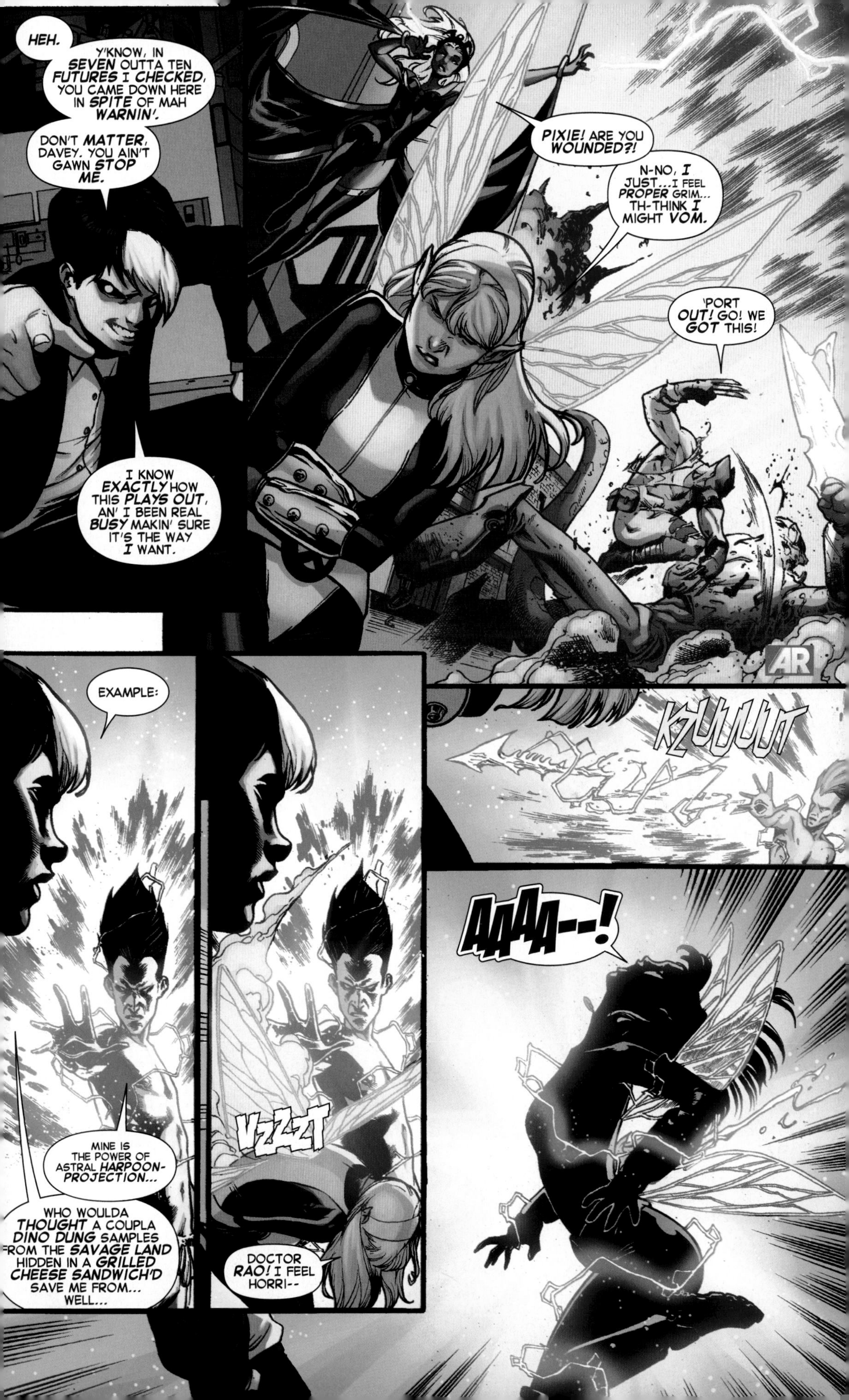
HEH.
Y'KNOW, IN SEVEN OUTTA TEN FUTURES I CHECKED, YOU CAME DOWN HERE IN SPITE OF MAH WARNIN'.
DON'T MATTER, DAVEY. YOU AIN'T GAWN STOP ME.
PIXIE! ARE YOU WOUNDED?!
N-NO, I JUST...I FEEL PROPER GRIM... TH-THINK I MIGHT VOM.
'PORT OUT! GO! WE GOT THIS!
I KNOW EXACTLY HOW THIS PLAYS OUT, AN' I BEEN REAL BUSY MAKIN' SURE IT'S THE WAY I WANT.
EXAMPLE:
MINE IS THE POWER OF ASTRAL HARPOON-PROJECTION...
WHO WOULDA THOUGHT A COUPLA DINO DUNG SAMPLES FROM THE SAVAGE LAND HIDDEN IN A GRILLED CHEESE SANDWICH'D SAVE ME FROM... WELL...
VZZZT
DOCTOR RAO! I FEEL HORRI--
KZUUUUT
AAAA--!

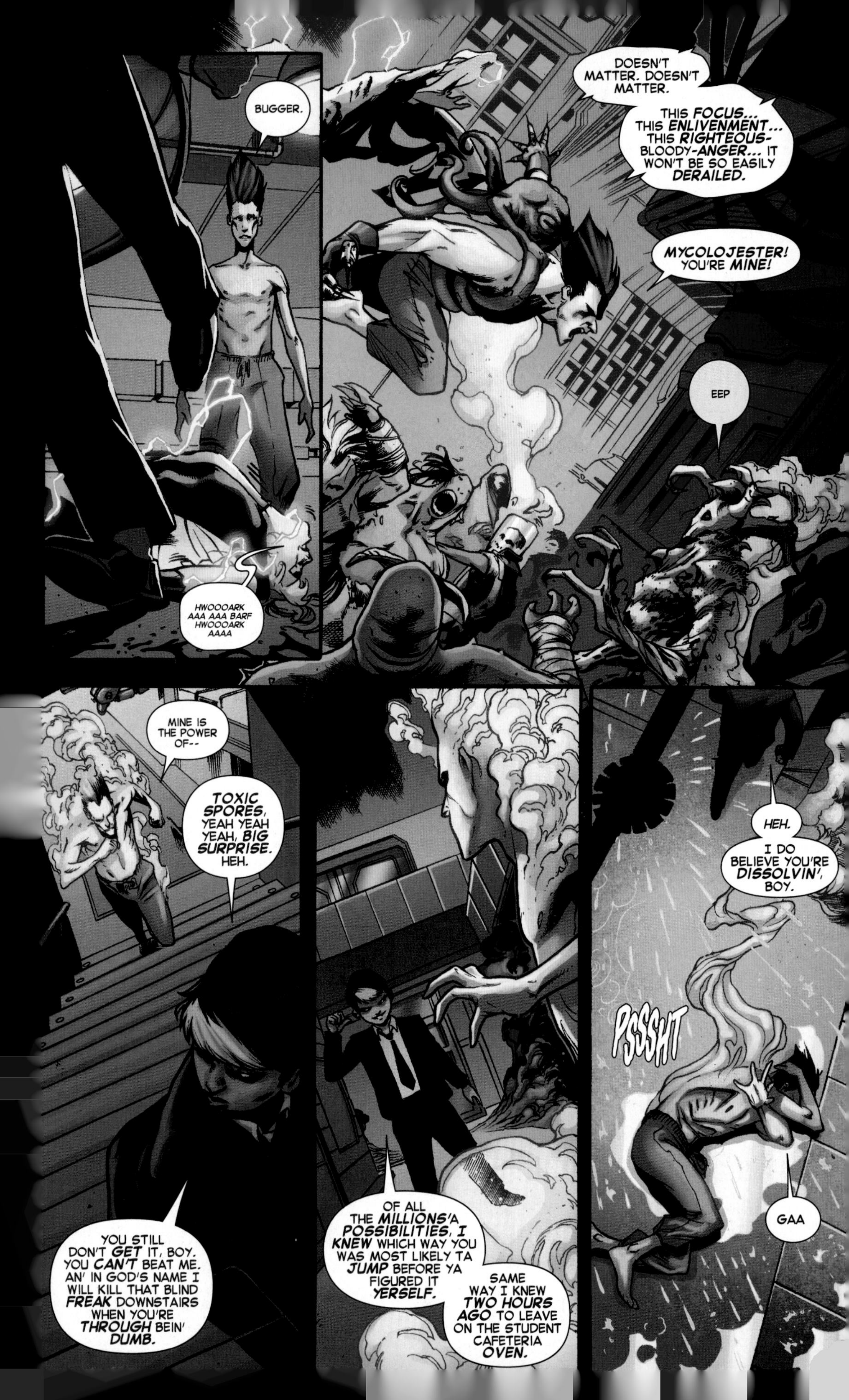
BUGGER.
HWOOOARK AAA AAA BARF HWOOOARK AAAA
DOESN'T MATTER. DOESN'T MATTER.
THIS FOCUS... THIS ENLIVENMENT... THIS RIGHTEOUS-BLOODY-ANGER... IT WON'T BE SO EASILY DERAILED.
MYCOLOJESTER! YOU'RE MINE!
EEP
MINE IS THE POWER OF--
TOXIC SPORES, YEAH YEAH YEAH, BIG SURPRISE. HEH.
YOU STILL DON'T GET IT, BOY. YOU CAN'T BEAT ME. AN' IN GOD'S NAME I WILL KILL THAT BLIND FREAK DOWNSTAIRS WHEN YOU'RE THROUGH BEIN' DUMB.
OF ALL THE MILLIONS'A POSSIBILITIES, I KNEW WHICH WAY YOU WAS MOST LIKELY TA JUMP BEFORE YA FIGURED IT YERSELF.
SAME WAY I KNEW TWO HOURS AGO TO LEAVE ON THE STUDENT CAFETERIA OVEN.
HEH.
I DO BELIEVE YOU'RE DISSOLVIN', BOY.
PSSSHT
GAA

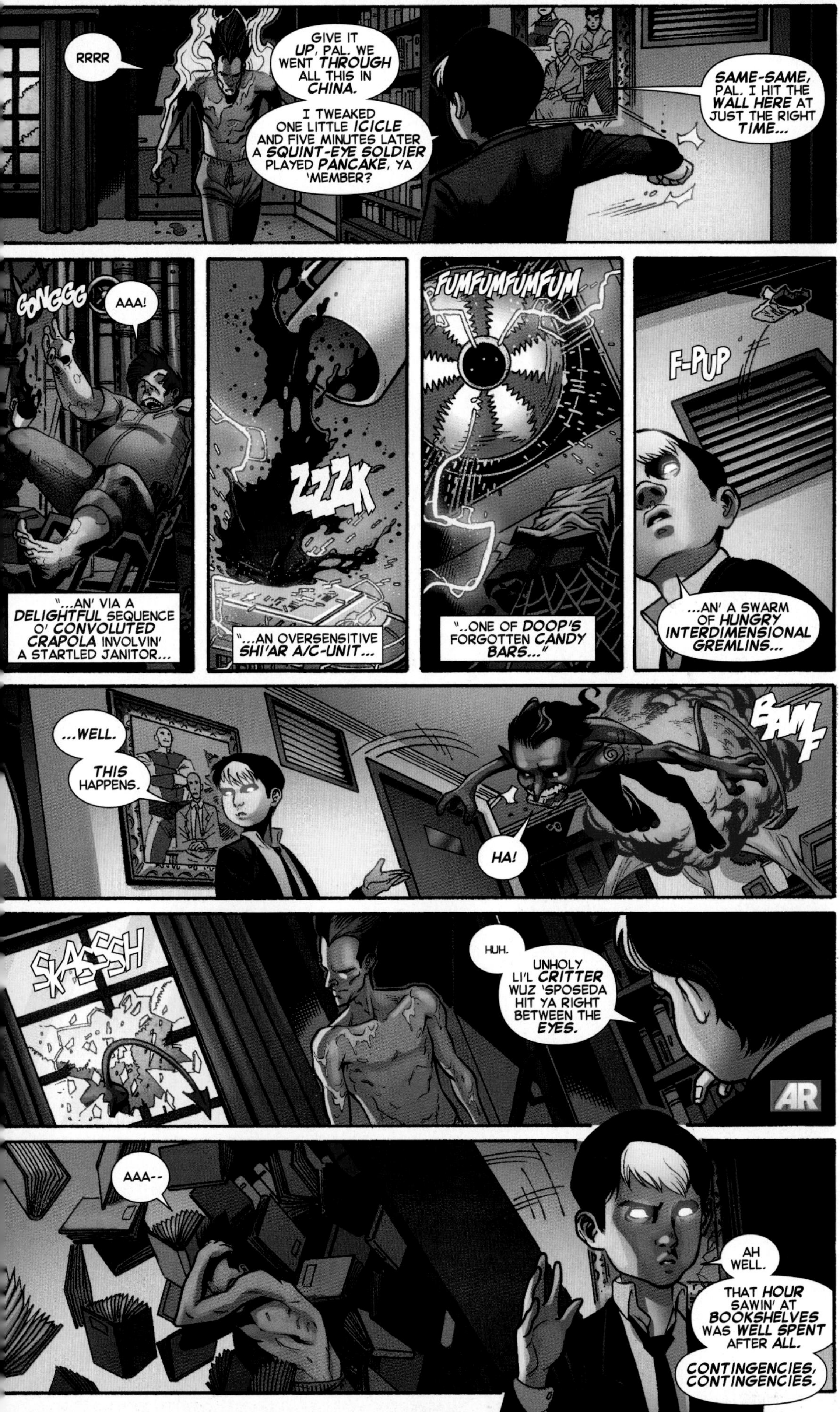
RRRR
GIVE IT UP, PAL. WE WENT THROUGH ALL THIS IN CHINA.
I TWEAKED ONE LITTLE ICICLE AND FIVE MINUTES LATER A SQUINT-EYE SOLDIER PLAYED PANCAKE, YA 'MEMBER?
SAME-SAME, PAL. I HIT THE WALL HERE AT JUST THE RIGHT TIME...
GONGGG
AAA!
"...AN' VIA A DELIGHTFUL SEQUENCE O' CONVOLUTED CRAPOLA INVOLVIN' A STARTLED JANITOR...
ZZZK
"...AN OVERSENSITIVE SHI'AR A/C-UNIT...
FUMFUMFUMFUM
"..ONE OF DOOP'S FORGOTTEN CANDY BARS..."
F-PUP
...AN' A SWARM OF HUNGRY INTERDIMENSIONAL GREMLINS...
...WELL.
THIS HAPPENS.
BAMF
HA!
SKASSH
HUH.
UNHOLY LI'L CRITTER WUZ 'SPOSEDA HIT YA RIGHT BETWEEN THE EYES.
AR
AAA--
AH WELL.
THAT HOUR SAWIN' AT BOOKSHELVES WAS WELL SPENT AFTER ALL.
CONTINGENCIES, CONTINGENCIES.

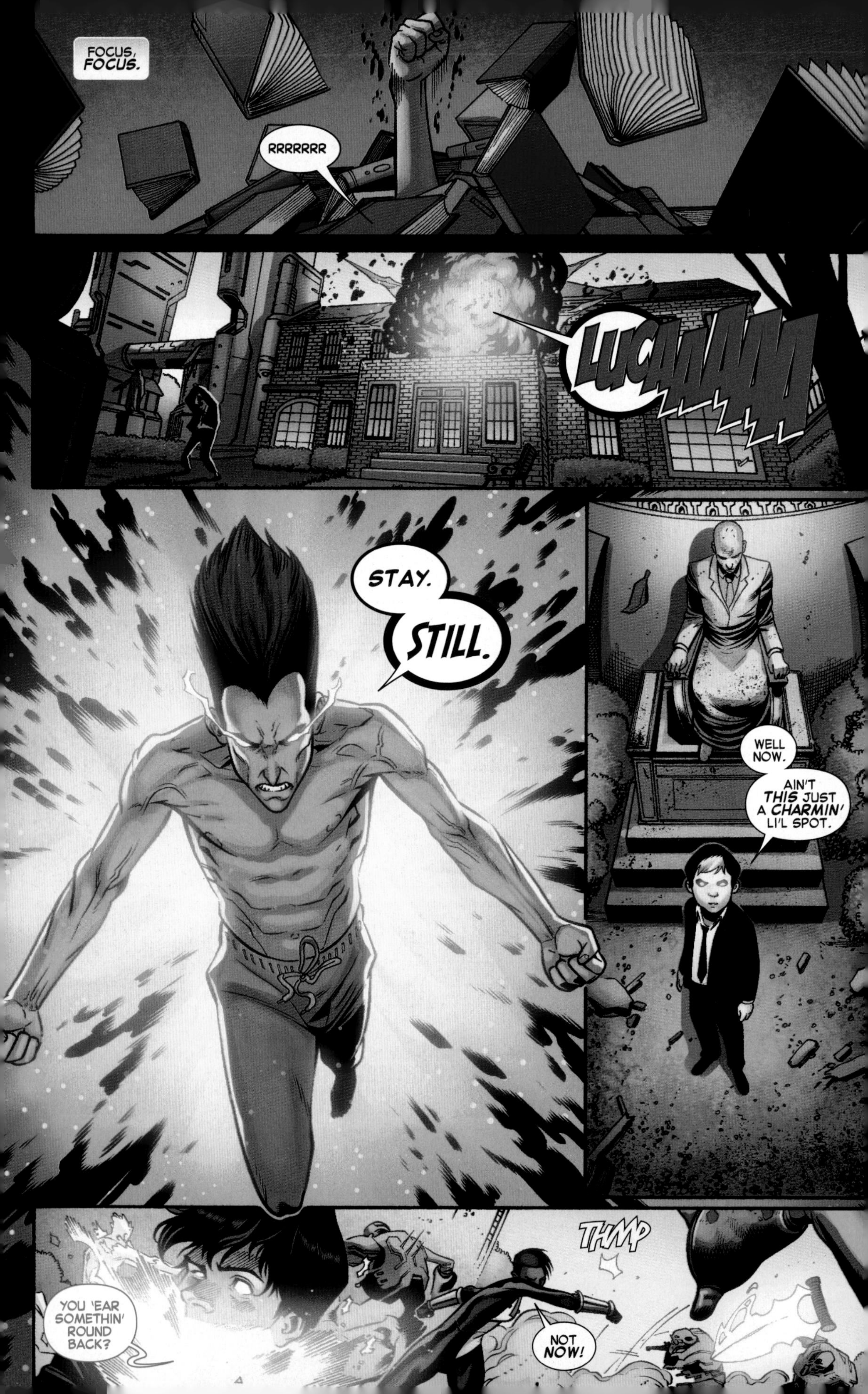
FOCUS, FOCUS.
RRRRRRR
LUCAAAAA
STAY.
STILL.
WELL NOW.
AIN'T THIS JUST A CHARMIN' LI'L SPOT.
THMP
YOU 'EAR SOMETHIN' ROUND BACK?
NOT NOW!

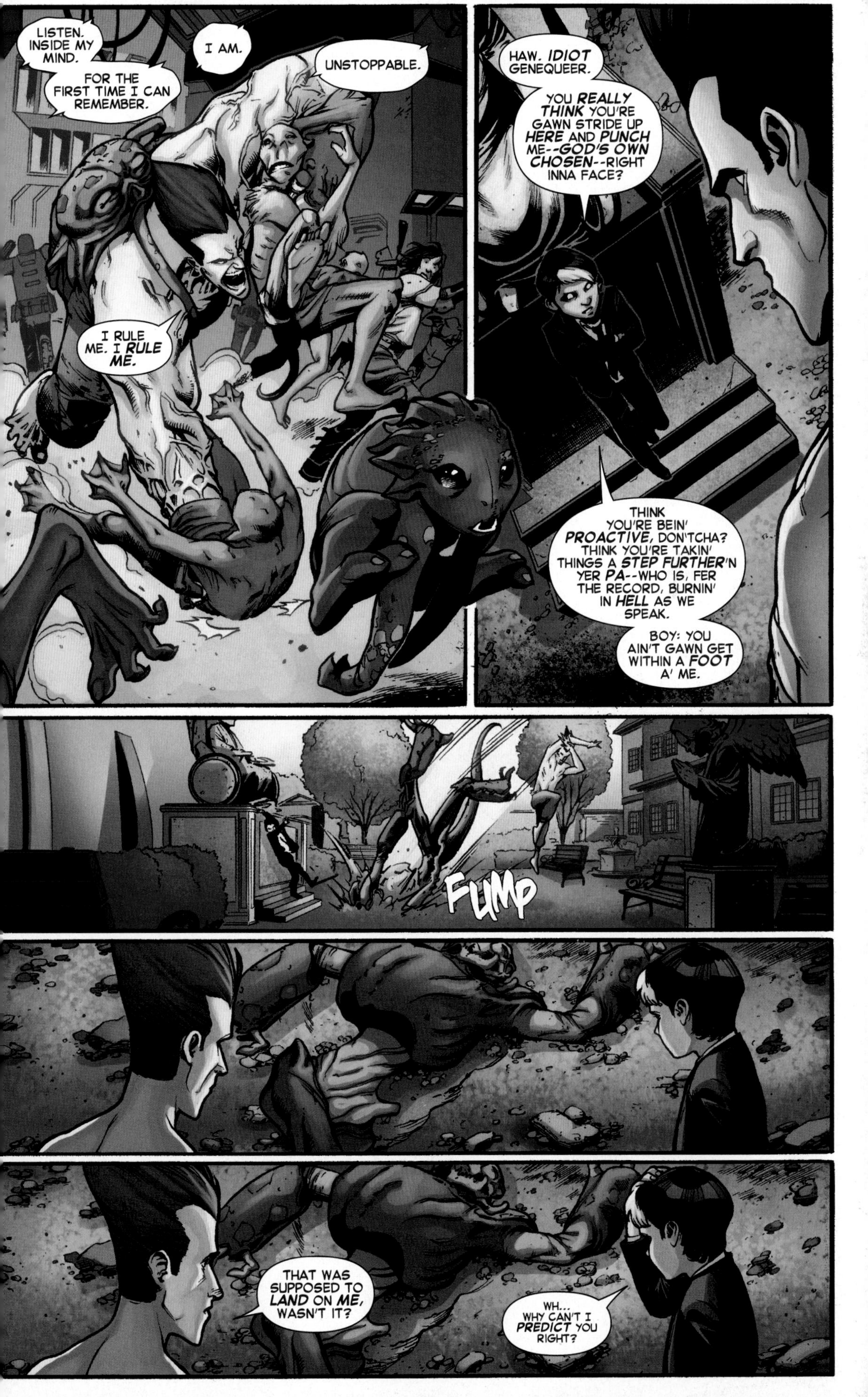

LISTEN. INSIDE MY MIND.
FOR THE FIRST TIME I CAN REMEMBER.
I AM.
UNSTOPPABLE.
I RULE ME. I *RULE ME.*
HAW. *IDIOT* GENEQUEER.
YOU *REALLY THINK* YOU'RE GAWN STRIDE UP *HERE* AND *PUNCH* ME--*GOD'S OWN CHOSEN*--RIGHT INNA FACE?
THINK YOU'RE BEIN' *PROACTIVE*, DON'TCHA? THINK YOU'RE TAKIN' THINGS A *STEP FURTHER*'N YER *PA*--WHO IS, FER THE RECORD, BURNIN' IN *HELL* AS WE SPEAK.
BOY: YOU AIN'T GAWN GET WITHIN A *FOOT* A' ME.
FUMP
THAT WAS SUPPOSED TO *LAND* ON *ME*, WASN'T IT?
WH... WHY CAN'T I *PREDICT* YOU RIGHT?

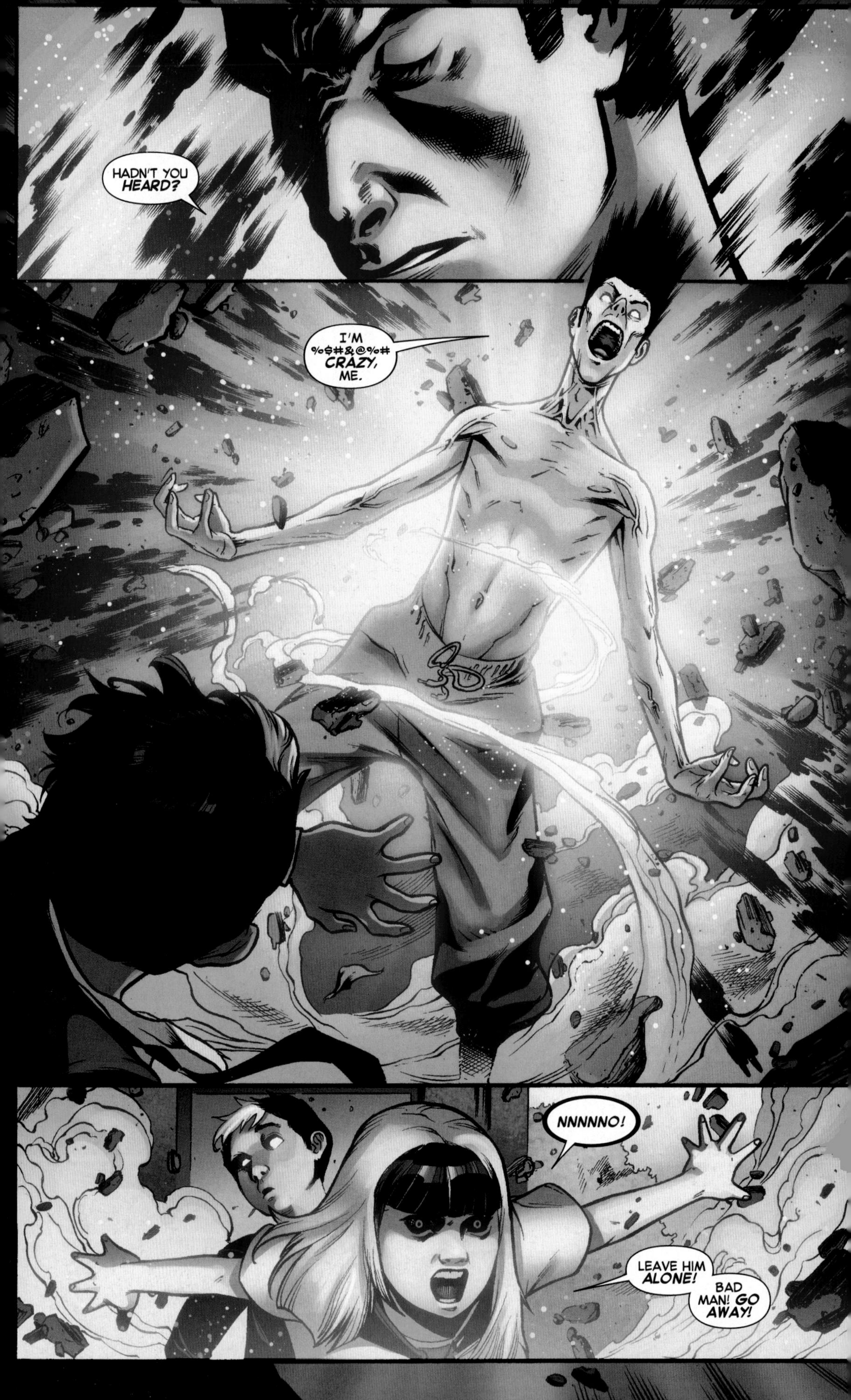
HADN'T YOU HEARD?
I'M %$#&@%# CRAZY, ME.
NNNNNO!
LEAVE HIM ALONE!
BAD MAN! GO AWAY!

...KARASU...YOU DON'T UNDERSTAND WHAT'S HAPPENING HERE. I'M ASKING YOU TO STEP ASIDE.

...

...BUT.

...BUT IF SHE DOESN'T?

I CAN CLICK MY FINGERS AND TURN HER TO ETHER IN THE SPLIT SECOND IT TAKES TO ANNIHILATE THE FIEND.

I CAN STRIKE ROUND HER WITH PARABOLIC BALEFIRE. I CAN BECOME A LIVING MELODY AND RAPTURE BEYOND HER EARS, OR ERASE HER FROM HISTORY WITH A SINGLE THOUGHT.

I HAVE ALL THE POWER IN THE WORLD AND A JUST CAUSE. WHAT DOES ONE SCARED WEE CHILD COUNT AGAINST THAT?

HA.

LOOK AT YOU. ALL SWOLLEN WITH SELF-RIGHTEOUS-NESS.

DOING YOUR BEST NOT TO THINK. TRICKING YOURSELF WITH A CONFIDENCE YOU NEITHER DESERVE NOR BELIEVE. "I RULE ME, I RULE ME..." PITIFUL.

TELL ME, BOY: WHEN DID YOU LAST SPARE A THOUGHT FOR YOUR FATHER?

WH...

HE'D BE ASHAMED OF YOU.

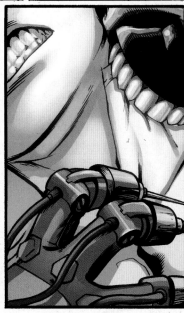

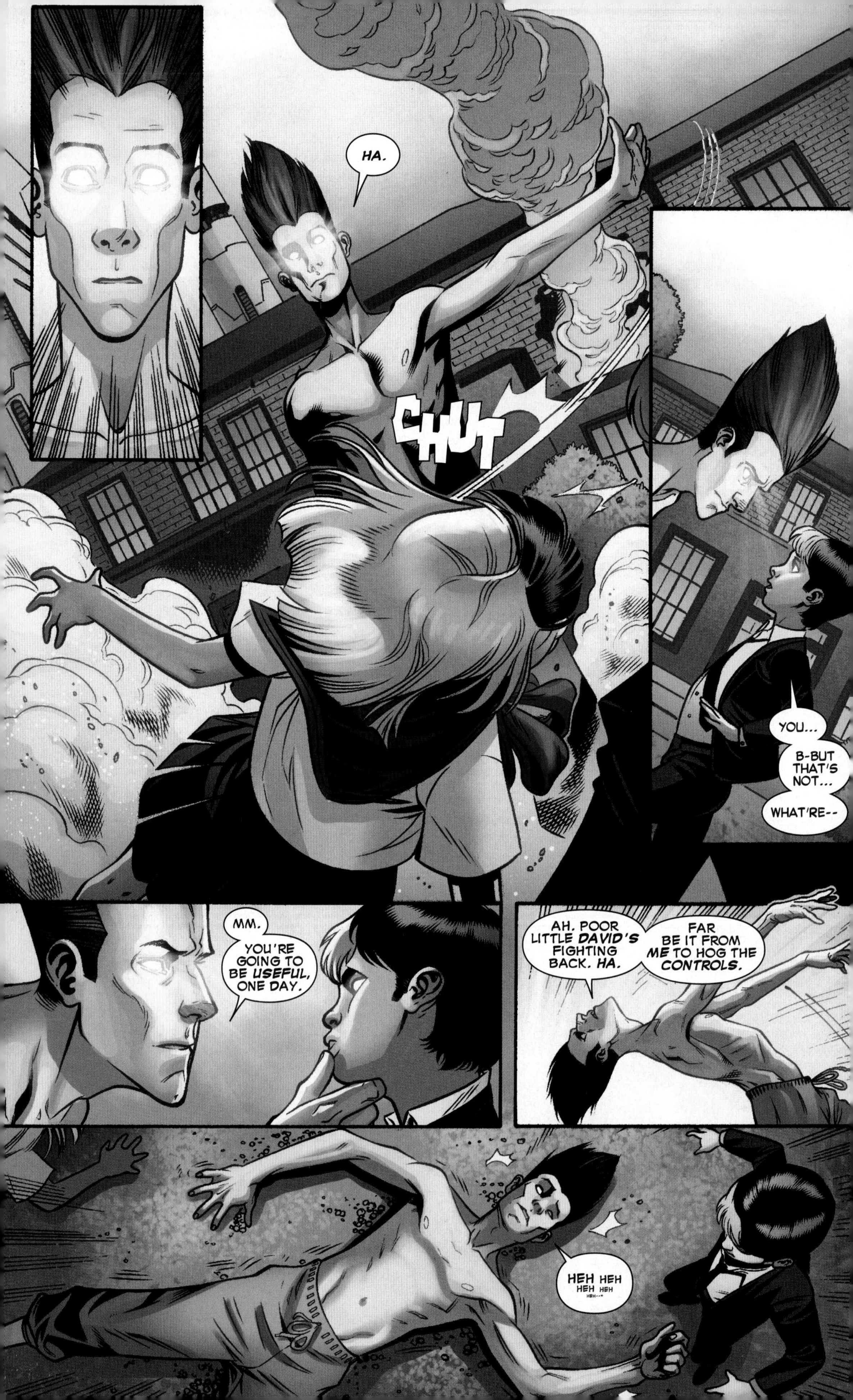
HA.
CHUT
YOU...
B-BUT THAT'S NOT...
WHAT'RE--
MM.
YOU'RE GOING TO BE USEFUL, ONE DAY.
AH. POOR LITTLE DAVID'S FIGHTING BACK. HA.
FAR BE IT FROM ME TO HOG THE CONTROLS.
HEH HEH HEH HEH HEH--

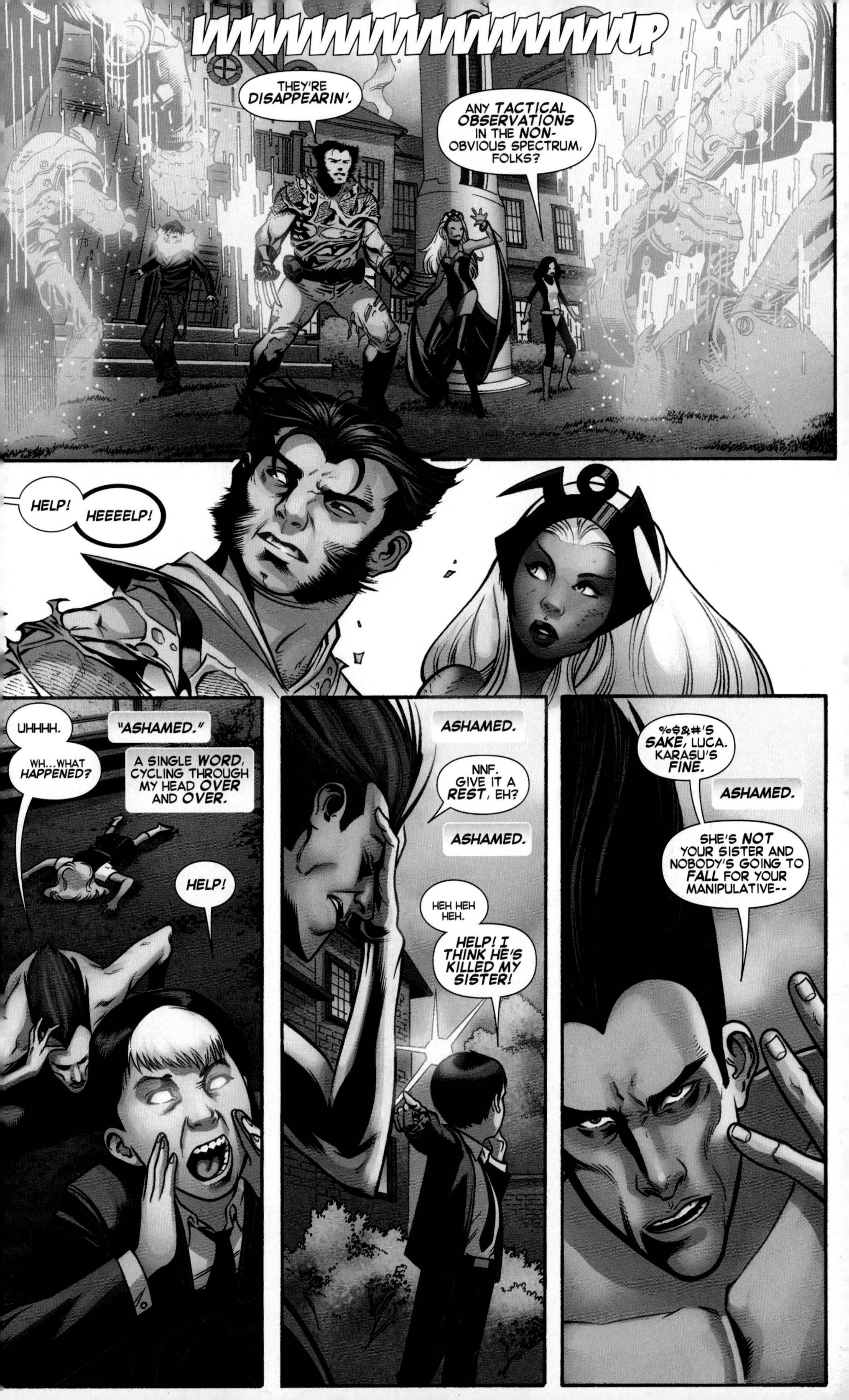
VVVVVVVVVVVVVVVVVVVVUP
THEY'RE DISAPPEARIN'.
ANY TACTICAL OBSERVATIONS IN THE NON-OBVIOUS SPECTRUM, FOLKS?
HELP!
HEEEEELP!
UHHHH.
WH...WHAT HAPPENED?
"ASHAMED."
A SINGLE WORD, CYCLING THROUGH MY HEAD OVER AND OVER.
HELP!
ASHAMED.
NNF. GIVE IT A REST, EH?
ASHAMED.
HEH HEH HEH.
HELP! I THINK HE'S KILLED MY SISTER!
%$&#'S SAKE, LUCA. KARASU'S FINE.
ASHAMED.
SHE'S NOT YOUR SISTER AND NOBODY'S GOING TO FALL FOR YOUR MANIPULATIVE--

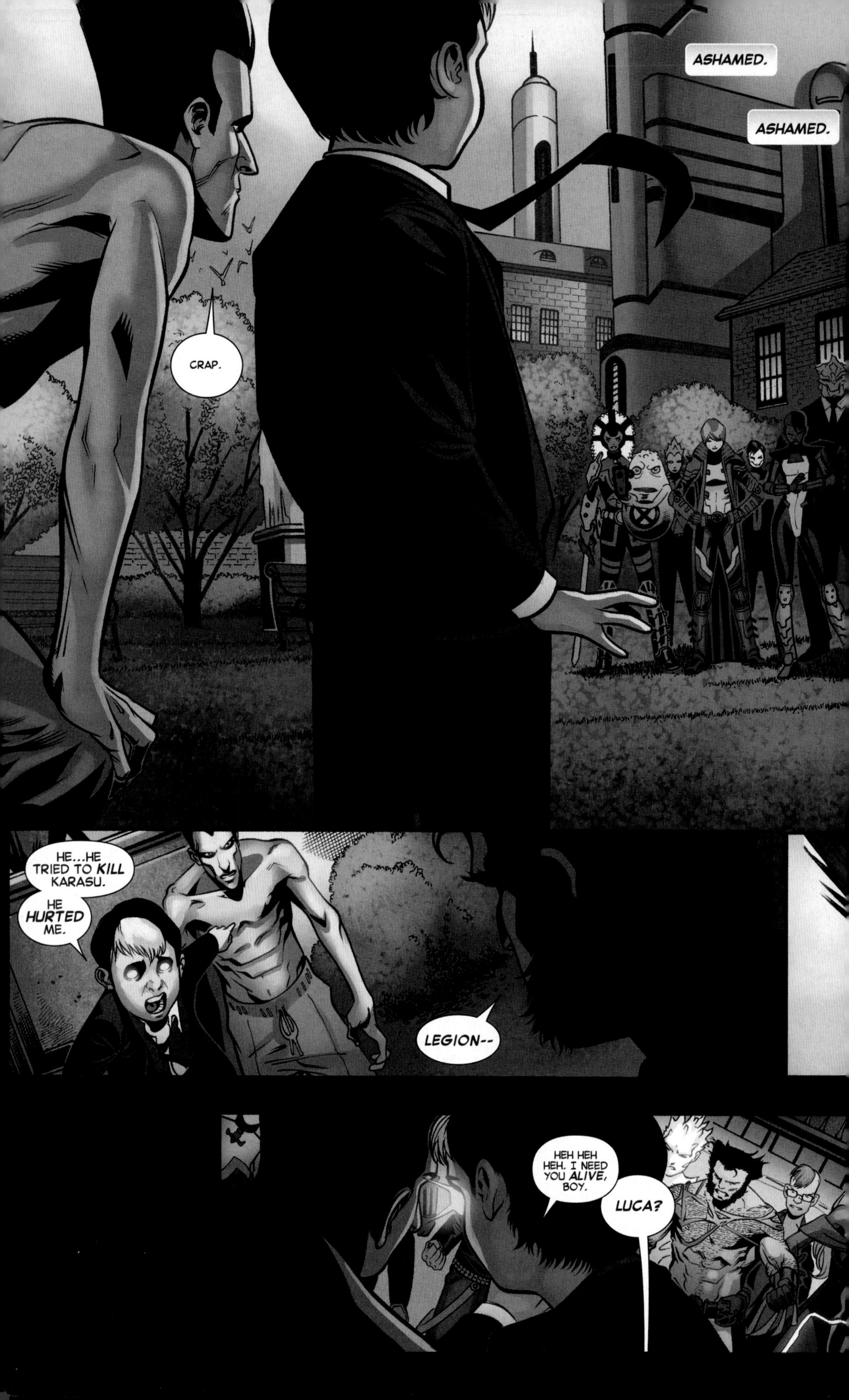
ASHAMED.
ASHAMED.
CRAP.
HE...HE TRIED TO KILL KARASU.
HE HURTED ME.
LEGION--
HEH HEH HEH. I NEED YOU ALIVE, BOY.
LUCA?

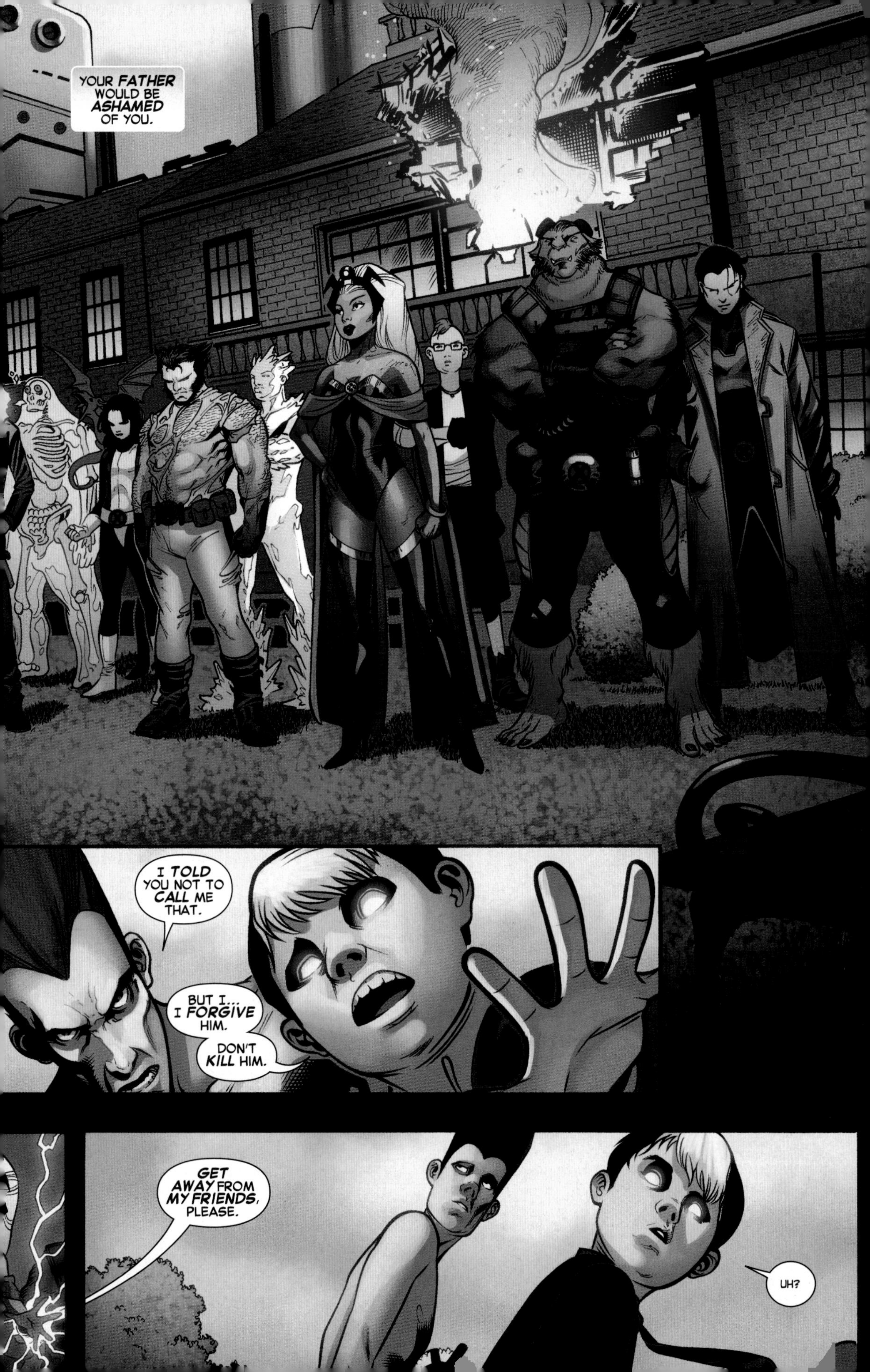
YOUR FATHER WOULD BE ASHAMED OF YOU.
I TOLD YOU NOT TO CALL ME THAT.
BUT I... I FORGIVE HIM.
DON'T KILL HIM.
GET AWAY FROM MY FRIENDS, PLEASE.
UH?

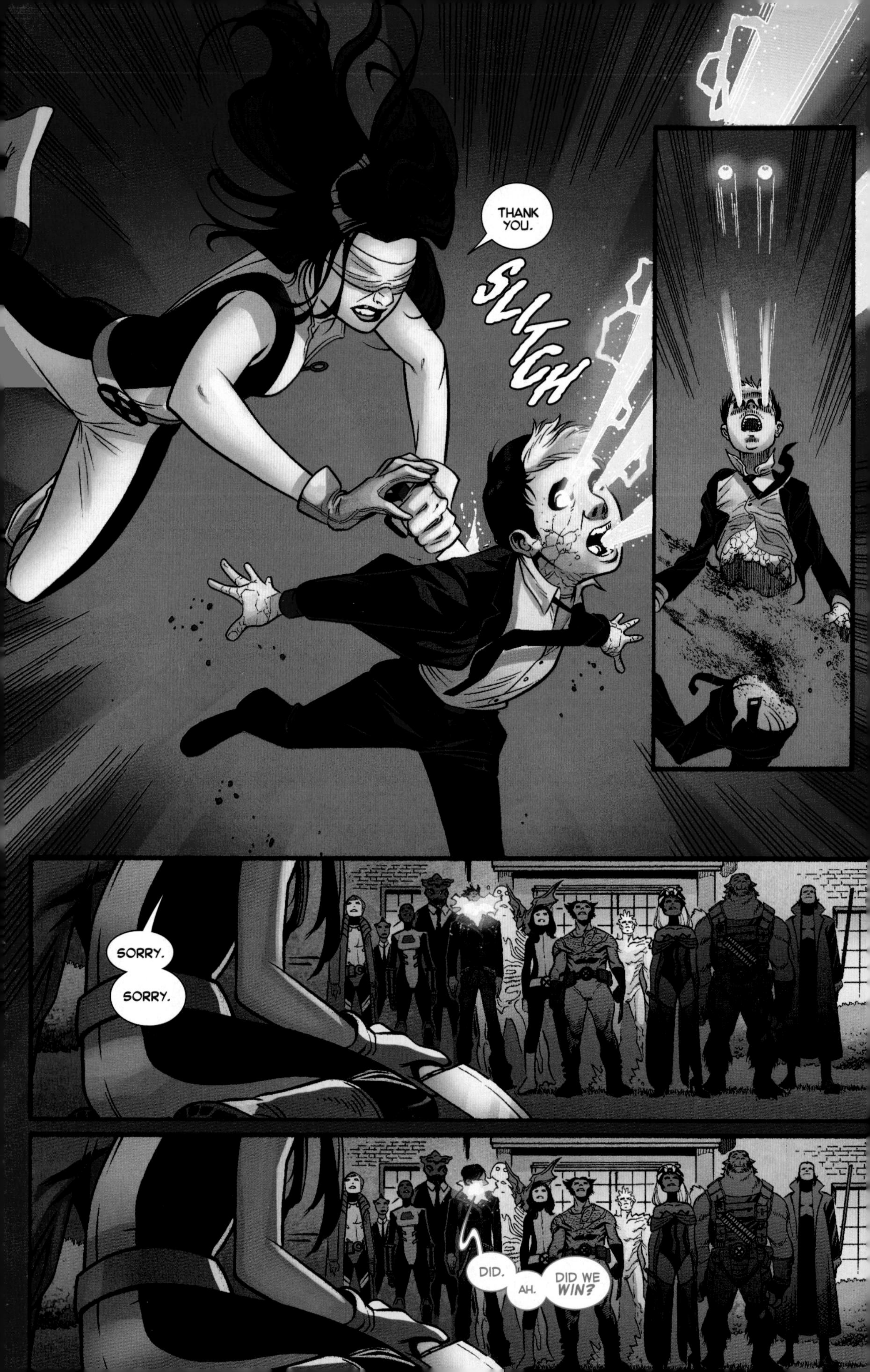
THANK YOU.
SLITCH
SORRY.
SORRY.
DID.
AH.
DID WE WIN?

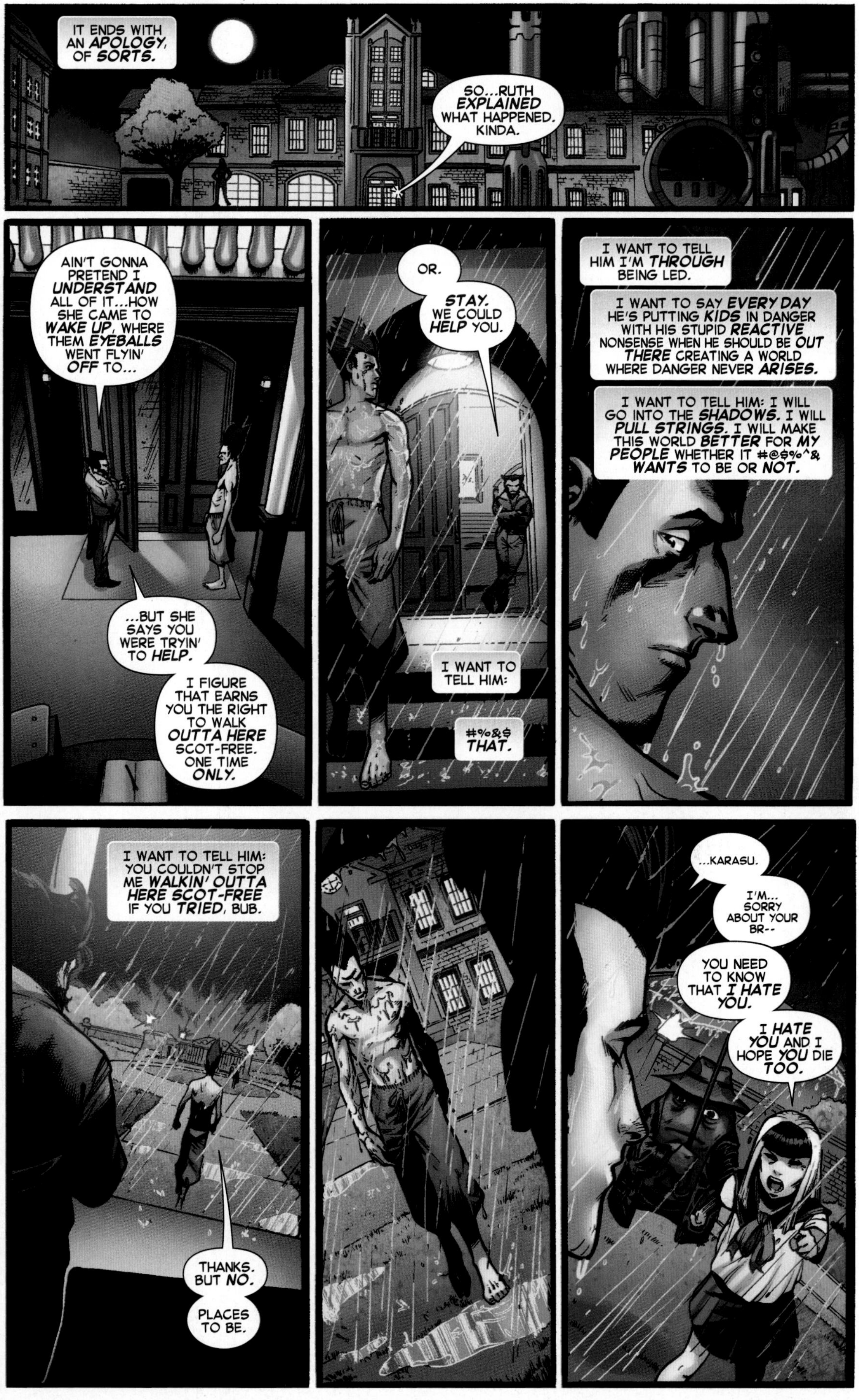

IT ENDS WITH AN APOLOGY, OF SORTS.
SO...RUTH EXPLAINED WHAT HAPPENED. KINDA.
AIN'T GONNA PRETEND I UNDERSTAND ALL OF IT...HOW SHE CAME TO WAKE UP, WHERE THEM EYEBALLS WENT FLYIN' OFF TO...
...BUT SHE SAYS YOU WERE TRYIN' TO HELP.
I FIGURE THAT EARNS YOU THE RIGHT TO WALK OUTTA HERE SCOT-FREE. ONE TIME ONLY.
OR.
STAY. WE COULD HELP YOU.
I WANT TO TELL HIM:
#%&$ THAT.
I WANT TO TELL HIM I'M THROUGH BEING LED.
I WANT TO SAY EVERY DAY HE'S PUTTING KIDS IN DANGER WITH HIS STUPID REACTIVE NONSENSE WHEN HE SHOULD BE OUT THERE CREATING A WORLD WHERE DANGER NEVER ARISES.
I WANT TO TELL HIM: I WILL GO INTO THE SHADOWS. I WILL PULL STRINGS. I WILL MAKE THIS WORLD BETTER FOR MY PEOPLE WHETHER IT #@$%^& WANTS TO BE OR NOT.
I WANT TO TELL HIM: YOU COULDN'T STOP ME WALKIN' OUTTA HERE SCOT-FREE IF YOU TRIED, BUB.
THANKS. BUT NO.
PLACES TO BE.
...KARASU.
I'M... SORRY ABOUT YOUR BR--
YOU NEED TO KNOW THAT I HATE YOU.
I HATE YOU AND I HOPE YOU DIE TOO.

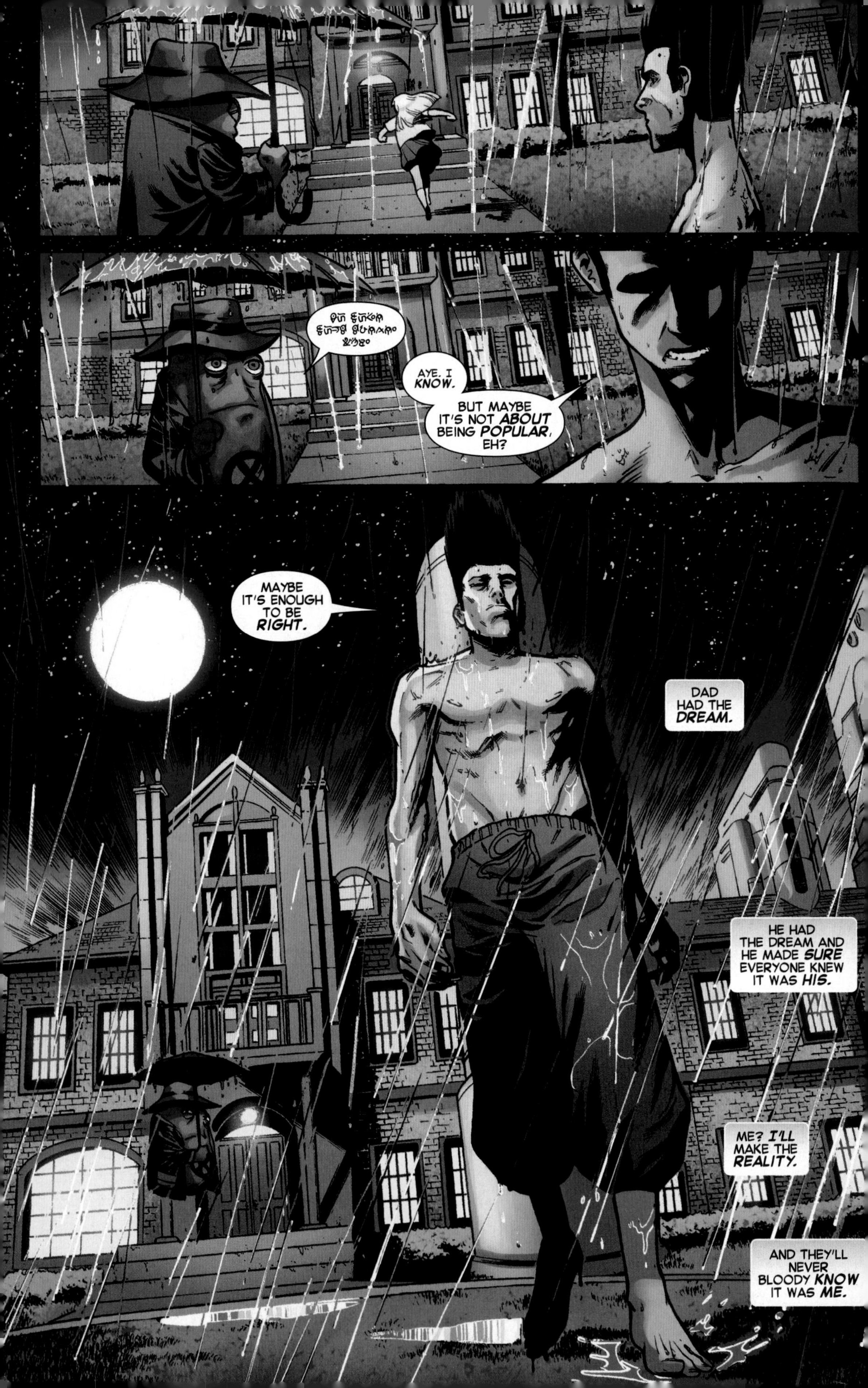
AYE. I KNOW.
BUT MAYBE IT'S NOT ABOUT BEING POPULAR, EH?
MAYBE IT'S ENOUGH TO BE RIGHT.
DAD HAD THE DREAM.
HE HAD THE DREAM AND HE MADE SURE EVERYONE KNEW IT WAS HIS.
ME? I'LL MAKE THE REALITY.
AND THEY'LL NEVER BLOODY KNOW IT WAS ME.

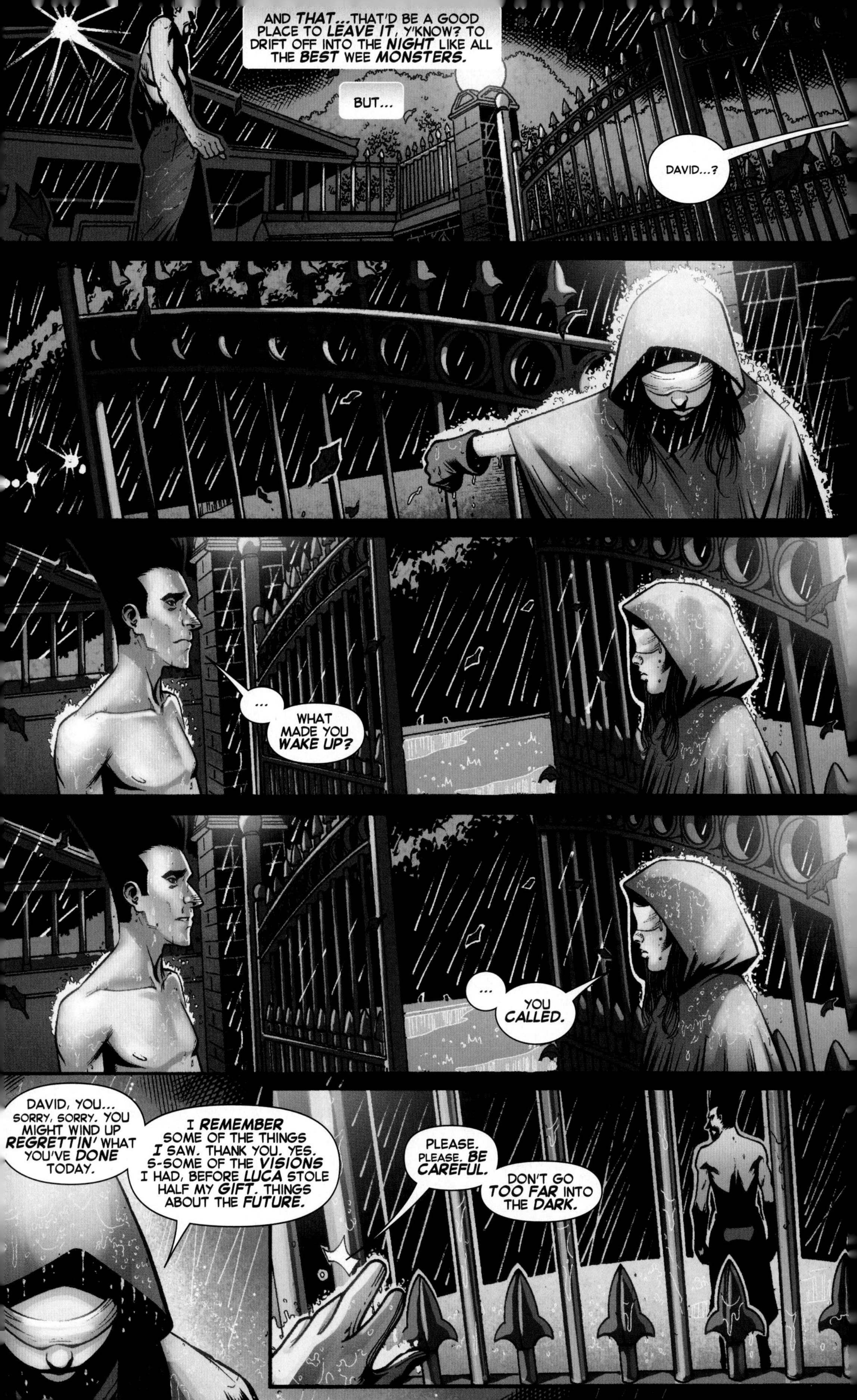

AND THAT...THAT'D BE A GOOD PLACE TO LEAVE IT, Y'KNOW? TO DRIFT OFF INTO THE NIGHT LIKE ALL THE BEST WEE MONSTERS.
BUT...
DAVID...?
...
WHAT MADE YOU WAKE UP?
...
YOU CALLED.
DAVID, YOU... SORRY, SORRY. YOU MIGHT WIND UP REGRETTIN' WHAT YOU'VE DONE TODAY.
I REMEMBER SOME OF THE THINGS I SAW. THANK YOU. YES. S-SOME OF THE VISIONS I HAD, BEFORE LUCA STOLE HALF MY GIFT. THINGS ABOUT THE FUTURE.
PLEASE. PLEASE. BE CAREFUL.
DON'T GO TOO FAR INTO THE DARK.

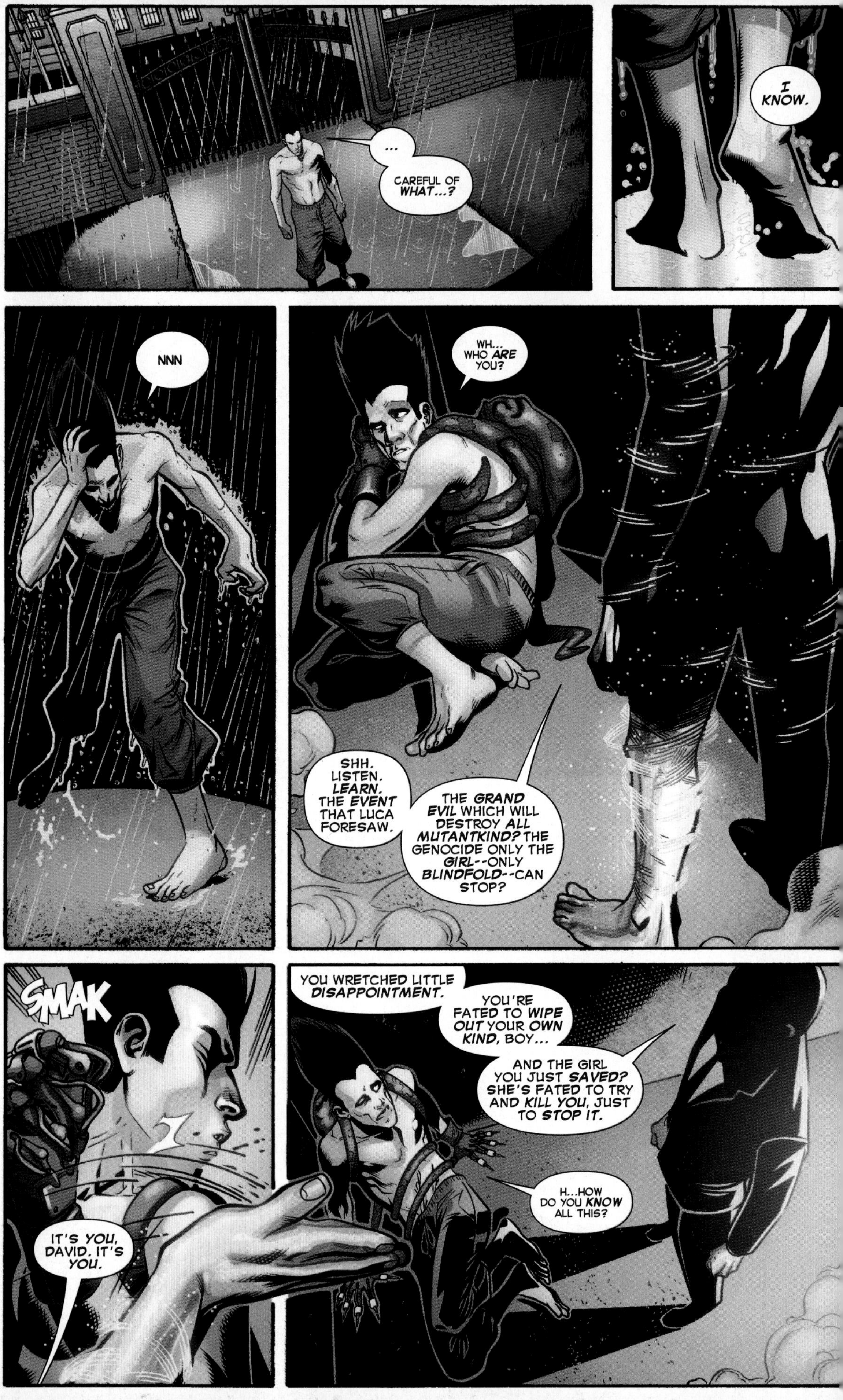
...
CAREFUL OF WHAT...?
I KNOW.
NNN
WH... WHO ARE YOU?
SHH. LISTEN. LEARN. THE EVENT THAT LUCA FORESAW.
THE GRAND EVIL WHICH WILL DESTROY ALL MUTANTKIND? THE GENOCIDE ONLY THE GIRL--ONLY BLINDFOLD--CAN STOP?
SMAK
IT'S YOU, DAVID. IT'S YOU.
YOU WRETCHED LITTLE DISAPPOINTMENT.
YOU'RE FATED TO WIPE OUT YOUR OWN KIND, BOY...
AND THE GIRL YOU JUST SAVED? SHE'S FATED TO TRY AND KILL YOU, JUST TO STOP IT.
H...HOW DO YOU KNOW ALL THIS?

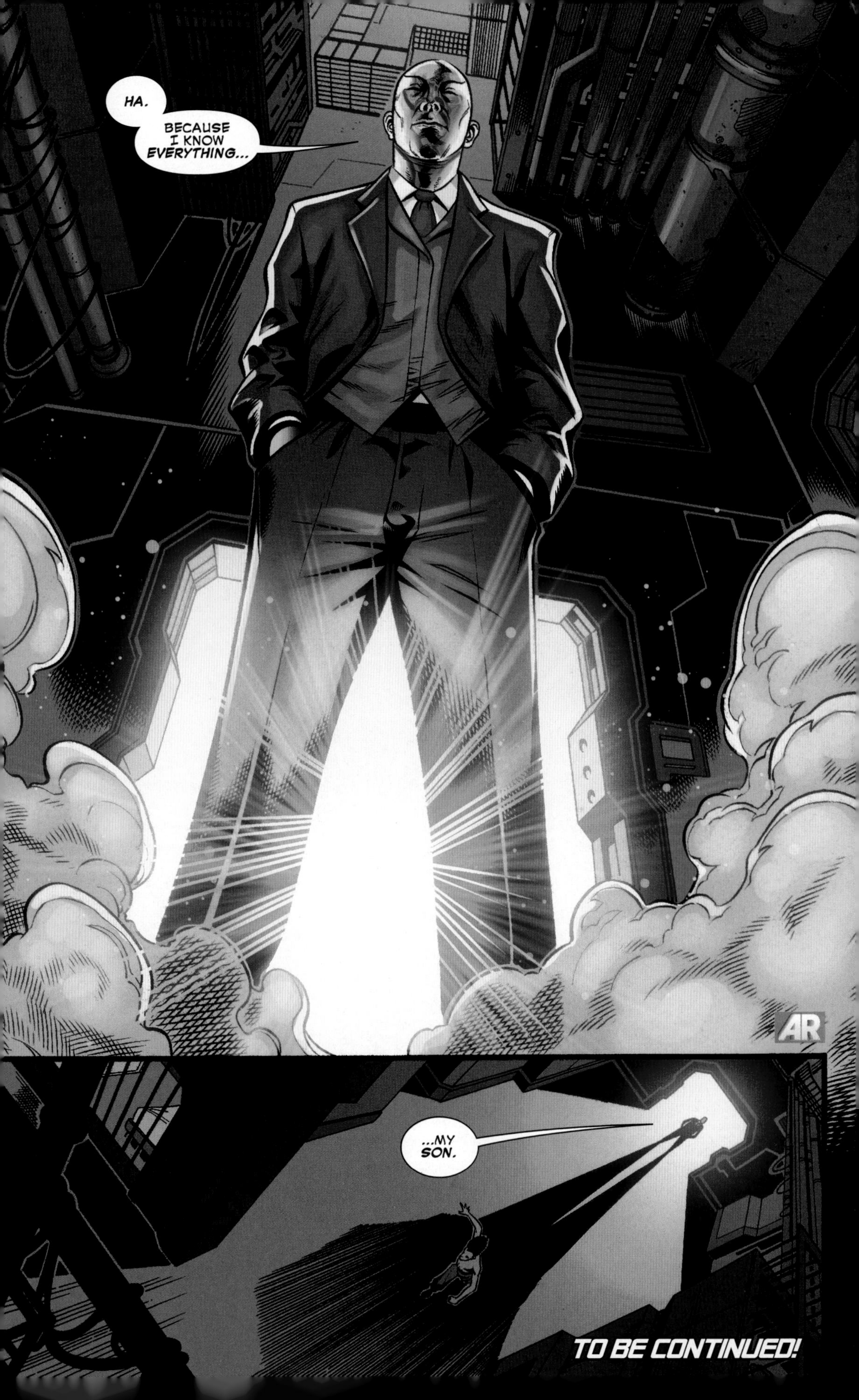
HA.
BECAUSE I KNOW EVERYTHING...
...MY SON.
TO BE CONTINUED!

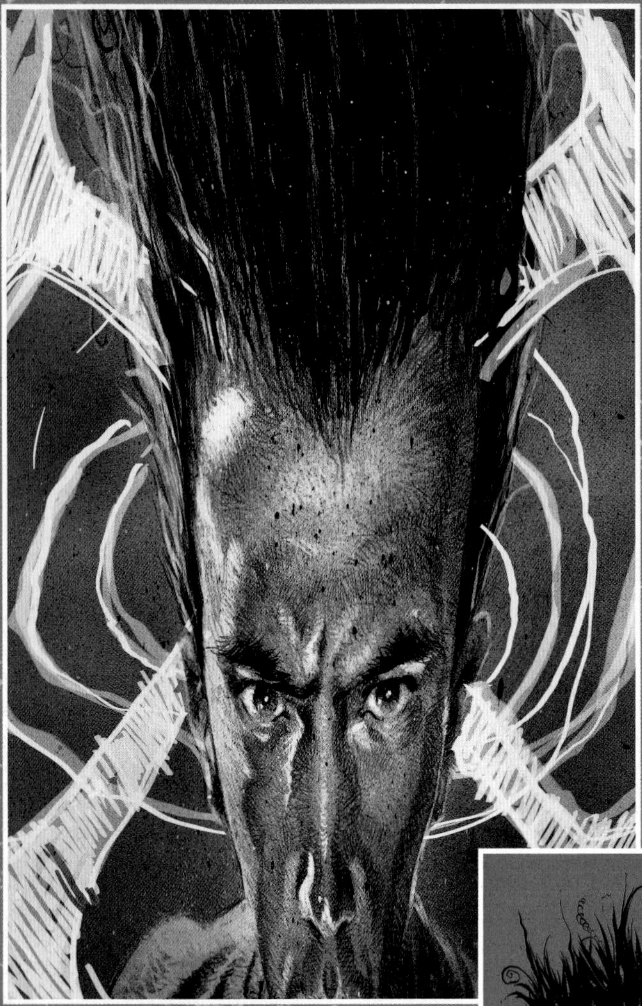

#1 variant
by Kaare Andrews

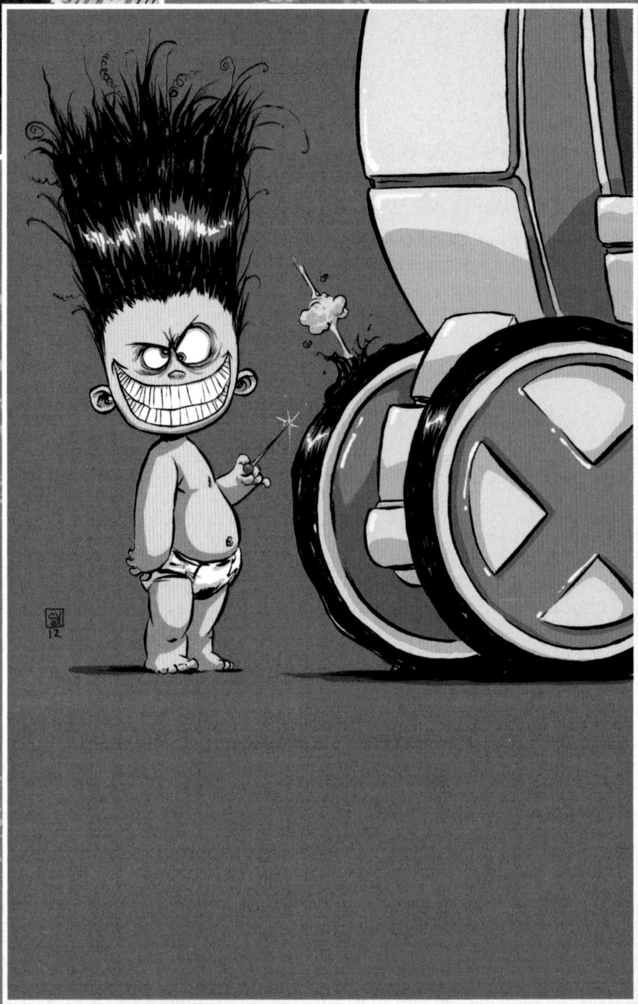

#1 variant
by Skottie Young

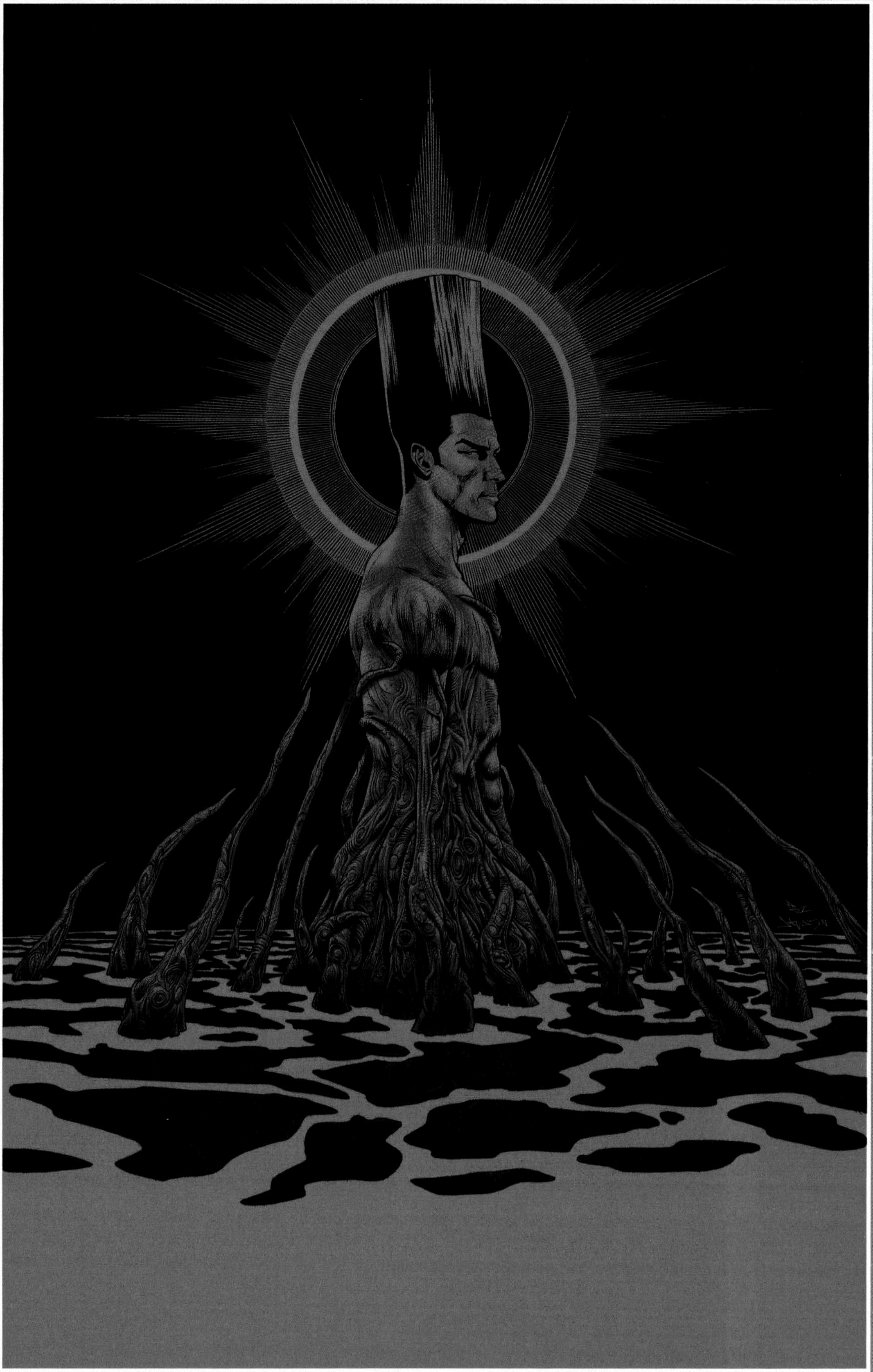

#2 variant by Paul Davidson

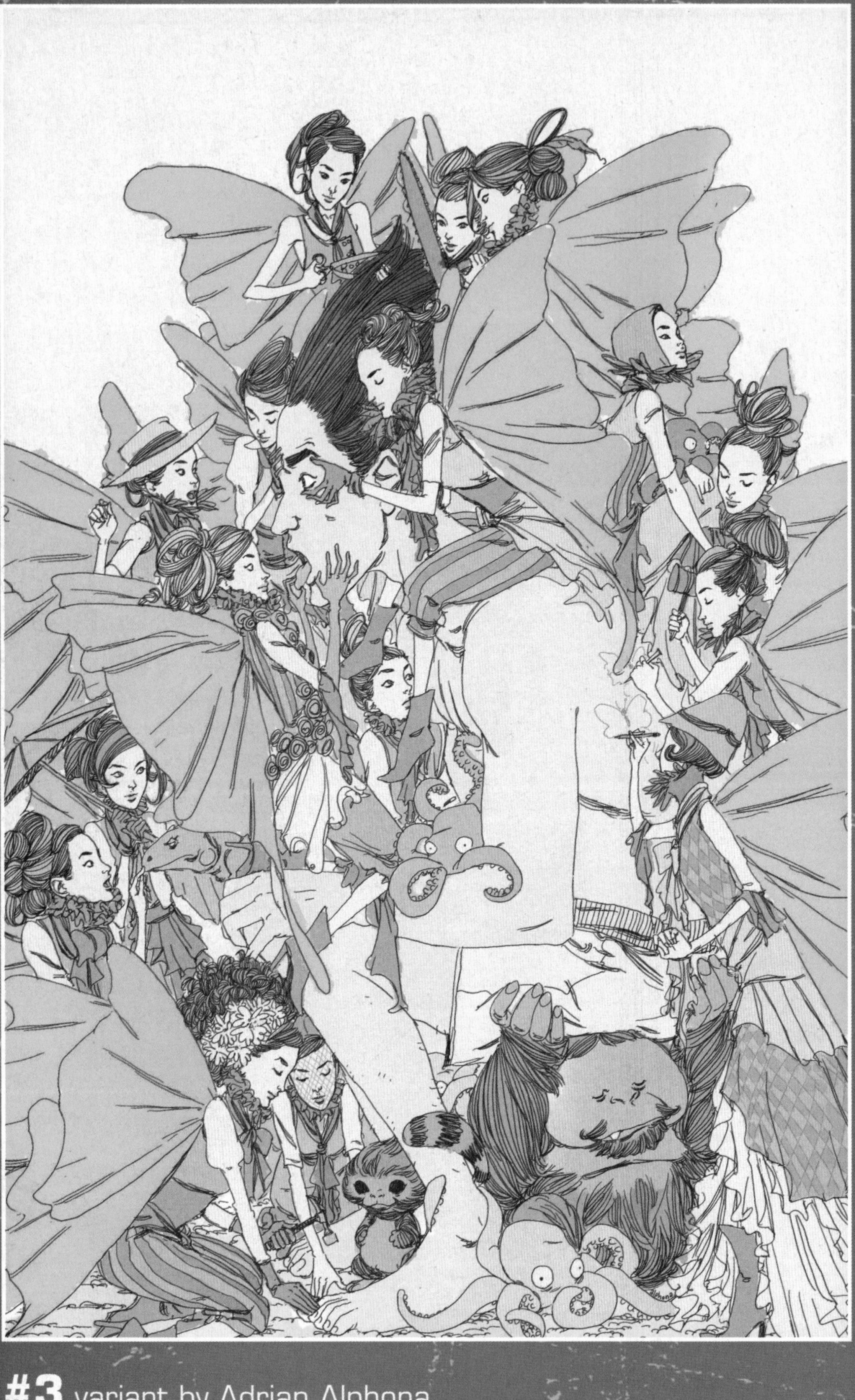

#3 variant by Adrian Alphona

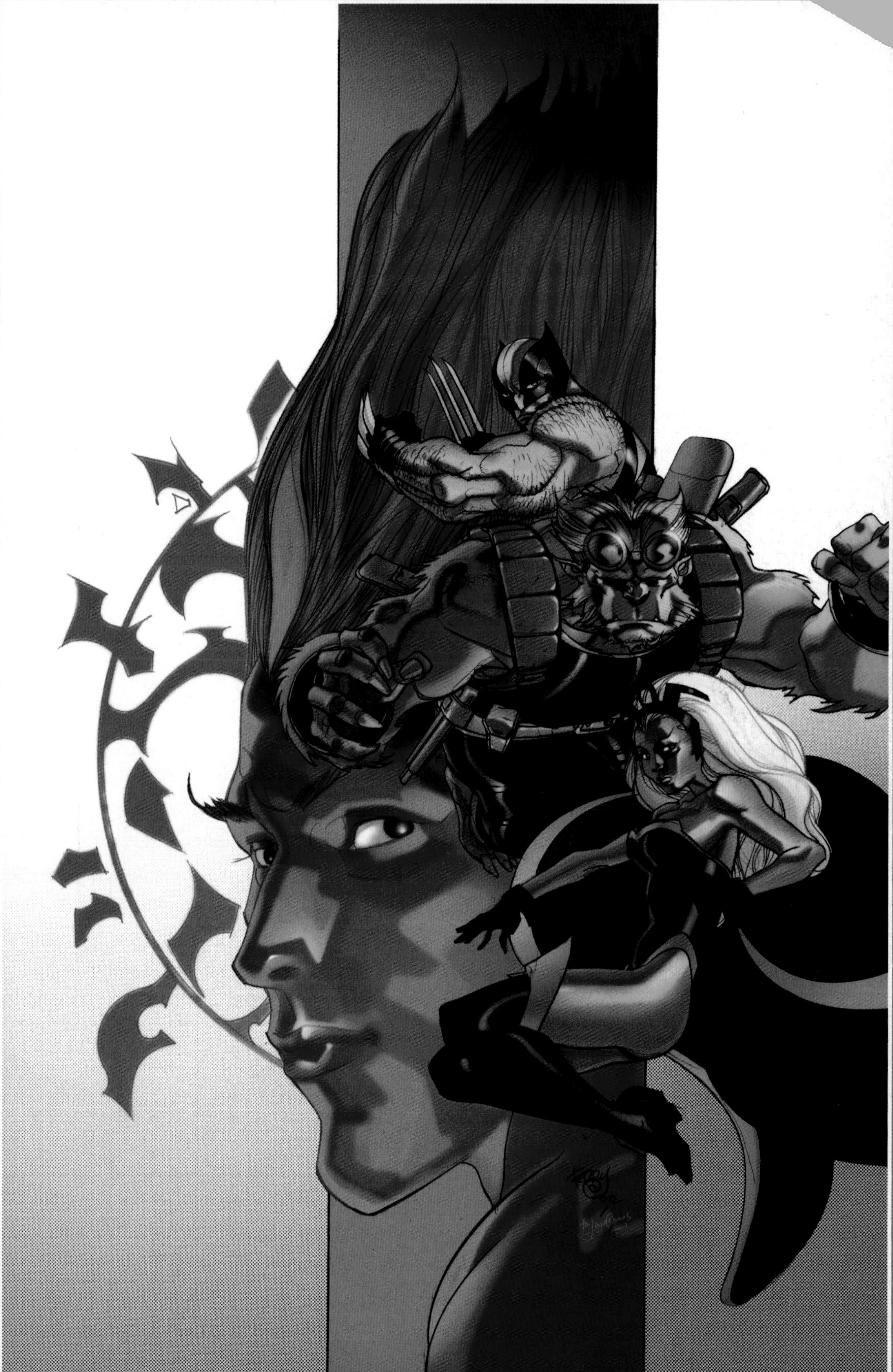

#4 variant by Pasqual Ferry & Jay David Ramos

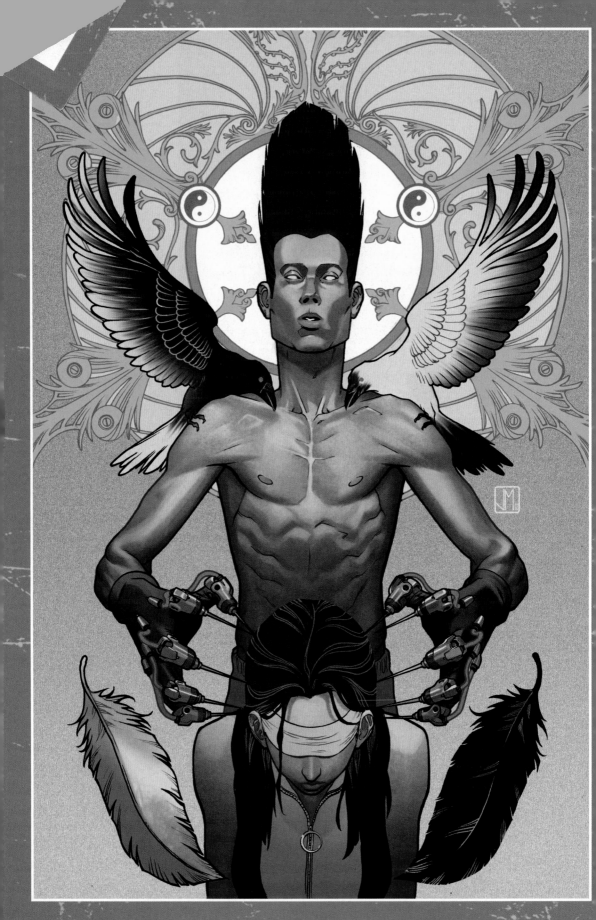

#5 variant by Jorge Molina

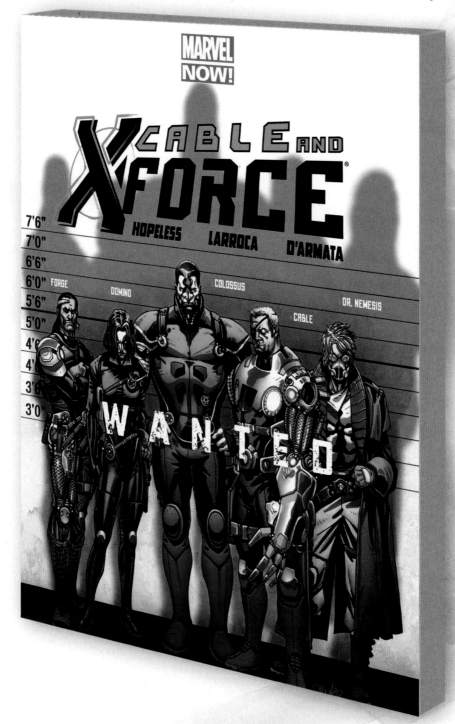

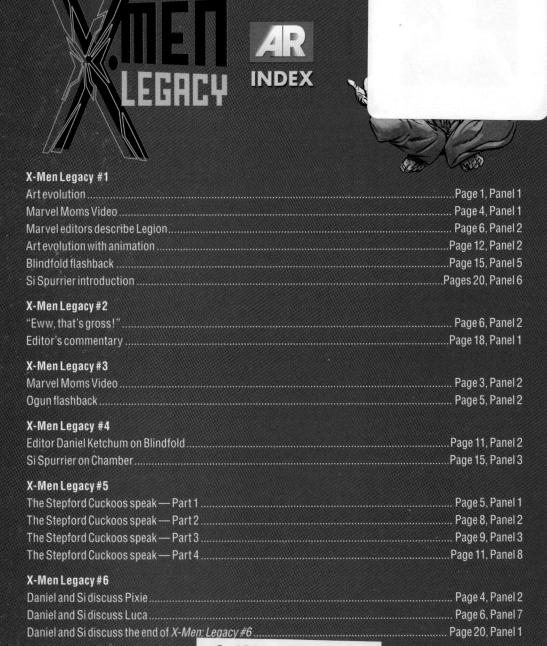

X-MEN LEGACY
AR INDEX